Collins

Cambridge Lower Secondary

Science

STAGE 7: TEACHER'S GUIDE

Aidan Gill, Beverly Rickwood, Amanda Graham, Gemma Young, Mark Levesley, Chris Meunier, Sheila Tarpey, Nigel Saunders

William Collins' dream of knowledge for all began with the publication of his first book in 1819.

A self-educated mill worker, he not only enriched millions of lives, but also founded a flourishing publishing house. Today, staying true to this spirit, Collins books are packed with inspiration, innovation and practical expertise. They place you at the centre of a world of possibility and give you exactly what you need to explore it.

Collins. Freedom to teach.

Published by Collins
An imprint of HarperCollins*Publishers*
The News Building
1 London Bridge Street
London
SE1 9GF

HarperCollins*Publishers*
1st Floor
Watermarque Building
Ringsend Road
Dublin 4
Ireland

Browse the complete Collins catalogue at
www.collins.co.uk

© HarperCollins*Publishers* Limited 2021

10 9 8 7 6 5 4 3

ISBN 978-0-00-836434-2

British Library Cataloguing-in-Publication Data. A catalogue record for this publication is available from the British Library.

Updating authors: Aidan Gill, Beverly Rickwood, Amanda Graham, Gemma Young, Mark Levesley, Chris Meunier, Sheila Tarpey, Nigel Saunders
Contributing authors: Fran Eardley
Development editors: Amanda Harman, Lynette Woodward, Gillian Lindsey, Tony Wayte, Fiona McDonald, Sarah Binns
Product manager: Joanna Ramsay
Content editor: Tina Pietron
Project manager: Amanda Harman
Copyeditor: Debbie Oliver
Proofreader: Heather Addison
Safety checker: Joe Jefferies
Illustrator: Jouve India Private Limited
Cover designer: Gordon Macgilp
Cover artwork: Maria Herbert-Liew
Internal designer: Jouve India Private Limited
Typesetter: Jouve India Private Limited
Production controller: Lyndsey Rogers
Printed and bound in the UK using 100% Renewable Electricity at CPI Group (UK)

Acknowledgements

(t = top, c = centre, b = bottom, r = right, l = left)

Student's Book answers:

p 22, p 23t, ct, b Designua/Shutterstock,
p 25 vectortatu/Shutterstock,
p 28 vectortatu/Shutterstock.

Workbook answers:

p 14 Windows Original after Northcott

Worksheets:

Worksheet 3.2b tl, tc, tr, br Eric Isselee/Shutterstock, Worksheet 3.2b bl sevenke/Shutterstock, Worksheet 3.2b bc jaroslava V/Shutterstock, Worksheet 9.2b(1) t joingate/Shutterstock, Worksheet 9.2b(1) tc ekipaj/Shutterstock, Worksheet 9.2b(1) bc Stuarts Photography/Shutterstock, Worksheet 9.2b(1) b pokchu/Shutterstock.

MIX
Paper from
responsible sources
FSC
www.fsc.org
FSC™ **C007454**

This book is produced from independently certified FSC paper to ensure responsible forest management.

For more information visit: **www.harpercollins.co.uk/green**

Contents

Downloads of editable learning episodes, worksheets, practical notes and answers are available at www.collins.co.uk/CambridgeInternationalDownloads. These are all supplied in Word format as well as pdf, so that teachers are able to edit the resources to suit their own teaching methods and lesson plans.

Chapter 8 • Sound

Chapter 9 • Electricity and circuits

Chapter 10 • The Earth and its atmosphere

Chapter 11 • The Earth in space

Introduction

Welcome to the Collins Cambridge Stage 7 Lower Secondary Science course, which has been written by a team of highly experienced authors and teachers to help you deliver an effective and successful Stage 7 Lower Secondary Science curriculum framework.

Student's Book

The Student's Book provides full coverage of the Cambridge Lower Secondary Science curriculum framework and includes the following features:

'You will learn', a list of key concepts that will be covered in each topic.

Starting points that can be used as part of a quick baseline assessment. Previous ideas, terminology and skills are outlined to aid recall and help students to build links between topics.

Questions throughout, including **challenge questions**, for formative assessment (aiding continuous feedback and monitoring of progress).

Key terms and **glossary** that provide language support for students and help them to develop their use of scientific vocabulary.

Activities that encourage students to apply their knowledge to practical and research-based contexts. These can then be used as a basis for formatively assessing depth of knowledge and understanding of both topic material and of scientific enquiry skills.

Global dimensions features that provide international context and relevance for students of the course around the world.

Key facts and **Check your skills progress** that enable students to take ownership of their own learning (and identify specific areas of knowledge and understanding that still need attention).

End of chapter and End of stage reviews

These can be used for summative assessment and may also be used formatively.

The End of chapter reviews start with quick questions on knowledge, and then move on to questions that test deeper understanding. These are designed to be used after a chapter has been completed, and can be used for formative assessment.

The End of stage review is designed to be used after all chapters in a stage have been completed and can be used in a number of ways:

- Ask students to answer the questions under test conditions. You could give students the End of stage review to complete as a practice for a mock test.
- Alternatively, ask students to go through the questions, or a selection of them, and prepare mark schemes. Students then work together and amend their mark schemes as necessary. Ask students which part of their mark schemes was most difficult to write, and use those topics for focused revision.
- Check the subject matter for one or two of the questions, and ask students to revise these topics for homework. In class, ask students to complete the questions. Checking how well students have done will provide feedback on lingering misconceptions and the quality of students' revision.

Teacher's Guide

This Teacher's Guide comprises two components – this printed book and downloadable material.

Printed book

The printed book mirrors the Student's Book topics and contains:

- **Chapter overviews** summarising all learning episodes, learning objectives and outcomes, and the match to the Cambridge Lower Secondary curriculum framework, along with notes on common misconceptions, glossary words and starting point activities as an informal baseline assessment to find out what students already know and to get students thinking in the right direction for what they are about to learn.
- **Activity plans** with resource lists, learning outcomes, and detailed guidance including ideas for differentiation and extension.
- Teaching notes on **checking students' progress** for each chapter.

Downloadable material

Printable, editable resources in MS Word format are available as digital downloads at www.collins.co.uk/CambridgeInternationalDownloads so that you can tailor your lessons and activities. The content has been arranged in folders by section and then by topic, with all the materials you need so that you can quickly and easily prepare for your lessons:

- **Worksheets** for students – some are designed to support teaching and learning, others contain guidance for practical work.
- **Practical activities** including teacher demonstrations and student experiments.
- **Practical notes** – technician's or teacher's notes with lists of equipment, resources and set-up information are included with the relevant lesson topic. All the notes for each section are also collated in one handy document.
- A **planning guide** that maps out all the learning episodes, learning outcomes and lesson resources in a convenient chart.
- **Answers** to all the questions in the Stage 7 Student's Book, Workbook and worksheets.

Learning episodes

The Teacher's Guide has been matched topic by topic to the Student's Book to allow easy cross-referencing between the books. Each topic has a brief introduction and an overview of the activities in an easy-to-navigate table. Activity plans give guidance on delivering learning episodes that can be combined for longer lessons to give you complete flexibility and control.

Activity plans cover the following:

- Lesson outcomes aligned with the 'You will learn' lists given for each topic in the Student's Book
- **Common misconceptions** that students hold, which may need addressing
- **Resources** you will need for activities
- A detailed pick-up-and-teach **approach** for varied tasks
- Suggestions for **differentiation** and **extension** tasks
- **Homework suggestions**, including those from the associated Workbook

Activity plans are supported by **worksheets, practical notes** and all **answers**.

Worksheets

Worksheets provide engaging activities for students. Most of the worksheets contain standalone activities, but there are some that give step-by-step guidance for students to ensure that they carry out their investigations safely and successfully:

- Worksheet 1.1c(1) is linked to Activity 1.1 in the Student's Book
- Worksheet 1.1c(2) is linked to Activity 1.2 n the Student's Book
- Worksheet 1.1c(3) is linked to Activity 1.4 in the Student's Book
- Worksheet 1.4b is linked to Activity 1.8 in the Student's Book
- Worksheet 3.2c is linked to Activity 3.4 in the Student's Book
- Worksheet 4.2b is linked to Activity 4.2 in the Student's Book
- Worksheet 4.2e(2) is linked to Activity 4.3 in the Student's Book
- Worksheet 4.6c is linked to Activity 4.8 in the Student's Book
- Worksheet 4.6d is linked to Activity 4.9 in the Student's Book
- Worksheet 5.3a is linked to Activity 5.3 in the Student's Book
- Worksheet 6.2c is linked to Activity 6.2 in the Student's Book
- Worksheet 6.2d is linked to Activity 6.4 in the Student's Book
- Worksheet 7.1b(1)/(2) is linked to Activity 7.1 in the Student's Book
- Worksheet 7.2b is linked to Activity 7.3 in the Student's Book
- Worksheet 8.2c is linked to Activity 8.5 in the Student's Book
- Worksheet 9.2c is linked to Activity 9.3 in the Student's Book
- Worksheet 10.2c(1) is linked to Activity 10.3 in the Student's Book
- Worksheet 10.2d(1) is linked to Activity 10.4 in the Student's Book
- Worksheet 10.2d(2) is linked to Activity 10.5 in the Student's Book
- Worksheet 10.4c is linked to Activity 10.9 in the Student's Book
- Worksheet 11.1b is linked to Activity 11.1 in the Student's Book
- Worksheet 11.3b is linked to Activity 11.3 in the Student's Book
- Worksheet 11.3c is linked to Activity 11.4 in the Student's Book

All worksheets are available in editable MS Word format as well as in PDF format.

Practical notes

Detailed **teacher's** or **technician's notes** are provided for lessons with lists of resources needed for practical activities and/or demonstrations, set-up instructions and safety notes.

For Today's Safety Information, which you will need to check before setting up any practical activity or demonstration, please refer to your employer's guidelines or visit: science.cleapss.org.uk (subscription is necessary to access all CLEAPSS resources).

Practical notes for technicians or teachers appear as separate printable files.

It is always best for the technician or teacher to try out a practical first and determine the best concentrations to use; it is always a good idea to get a set of specimen results.

Answers

Answers to all questions in the Student's Book, Workbook and worksheets are available in MS Word and PDF format and are arranged by chapter.

Planning guide

The detailed **planning guide** provides a comprehensive overview of the Cambridge Lower Secondary Science curriculum framework, matching each lesson plan to the lesson outcomes and showing at a glance where the practical activities and demonstrations occur so that you can plan ahead.

Cambridge Global Perspectives™

Cambridge Global Perspectives is a unique programme that helps learners develop outstanding transferable skills, including critical thinking, research and collaboration. The programme is available for learners aged 5–19, from Cambridge Primary through to Cambridge Advanced. For Cambridge Primary and Lower Secondary learners, the programme is made up of a series of Challenges covering a wide range of topics, using a personal, local and global perspective. The programme is available to Cambridge schools but participation in the programme is voluntary. However, whether or not your school is involved with the programme, the six skills it focuses on are relevant to **all** students in the modern world. These skills are: research, evaluation, analysis, communication, collaboration and reflection.

Collins supports Cambridge Global Perspectives by including activities, tasks and projects in our Cambridge Primary and Lower Secondary courses, in order to develop and apply these skills. Activities that link to the skills are listed at the back of this book on page 204.

Deeper learning at the heart of the course

This course has been designed with the idea of deep learning in mind. Deeper learning is best enhanced through a student's own engagement and exploration of a topic, reinforced with strong practice, consolidation and reflection. Deep learning is encouraged through our features and activities, Workbook practice and assessment features. The Student's Book identifies prior knowledge; indicating to students where content has been covered previously. To further this, the Teacher's Guide includes questions for discussion, encouraging students to make links between topics.

Activities throughout all the resources in this course encourage students to work in different ways; individually, in pairs and in groups, all of which contribute to the development of skills such as communication, teamwork, analysis and evaluation. The importance of science in a global context, and its importance in encouraging students to gain a deeper understanding of the subject, is highlighted throughout this course.

Registered Cambridge International Schools benefit from high-quality programmes, assessments and a wide range of support so that teachers can effectively deliver Cambridge Lower Secondary.

Visit www.cambridgeinternational.org/lowersecondary to find out more.

Mapping document

These learning objectives are reproduced from the Cambridge Lower Secondary Science curriculum framework (0893) from 2020. This Cambridge International copyright material is reproduced under licence and remains the intellectual property of Cambridge Assessment International Education.

	Student's Book topic	Teacher's Guide topic	Workbook topic
Thinking and Working Scientifically			
Models and representations			
7TWSm.01 Describe the strengths and limitations of a model.	1.3 4.3 5.1, 5.2 8.1 9.1 10.2, 10.4 11.3	1.3 4.3 5.1, 5.2 6.1, 6.2 8.1, 8.2 10.2, 10.4 11.2, 11.3	1.3 4.3, 4.5 5.1, 5.2 8.1 10.2, 10.4 11.3
7TWSm.02 Use symbols and formulae to represent scientific ideas.	4.4, 4.5	4.4 7.1	4.4, 4.5 5.1, 5.2
Scientific enquiry: purpose and planning			
7TWSp.01 Identify whether a given hypothesis is testable.	2.2	2.2	2.2
7TWSp.02 Describe how scientific hypotheses can be supported or contradicted by evidence from an enquiry.	1.1, 2.2 10.1 11.1	1.1 2.2 8.1 10.1 11.1	1.1 2.2

	Student's Book topic	Teacher's Guide topic	Workbook topic
7TWSp.03 Make predictions of likely outcomes for a scientific enquiry based on scientific knowledge and understanding.	1.1 2.2 4.2 5.2 6.2 9.1 11.1	1.1 2.2 4.6 6.2 7.2 11.1	1.1 2.2 4.2 5.2
7TWSp.04 Plan a range of investigations of different types, while considering variables appropriately, and recognise that not all investigations can be fair tests.	5.3 6.2 9.3	6.2 7.2 8.2	2.1 4.1 5.3
7TWSp.05 Know the meaning of hazard symbols, and consider them when planning practical work.	4.2 5.1	4.2	4.2 5.1
Carrying out scientific enquiry			
7TWSc.01 Sort, group and classify phenomena, objects, materials and organisms through testing, observation, using secondary information, and making and using keys.	3.1, 3.2 4.3, 4.4, 4.5, 4.6 9.1	3.1, 3.2 4.2, 4.6	3.1, 3.2 4.3, 4.4, 4.5, 4.6
7TWSc.02 Decide what equipment is required to carry out an investigation or experiment and use it appropriately.	4.2 5.3 6.2 8.2	1.3 8.2 10.4	4.1, 4.2, 4.6 5.3

	Student's Book topic	Teacher's Guide topic	Workbook topic
7TWSc.03 Evaluate whether measurements and observations have been repeated sufficiently to be reliable.	5.3 8.1, 8.2 10.3	8.2 10.3	5.3 8.2
7TWSc.04 Take appropriately accurate and precise measurements, explaining why accuracy and precision are important.	8.1, 8.2 10.3	7.2 8.1 10.3	
7TWSc.05 Carry out practical work safely.	1.3 5.1 10.4	1.3 5.3 7.1 10.4	1.3 4.2, 4.6 5.1
7TWSc.06 Evaluate a range of secondary information sources for their relevance and know that some sources may be biased.	2.1	2.1	2.1
7TWSc.07 Collect and record sufficient observations and/or measurements in an appropriate form.	8.1	4.1, 4.2 5.3 7.1 8.1	4.1, 4.5
Scientific enquiry: analysis, evaluation and conclusions			
7TWSa.01 Describe the accuracy of predictions, based on results, and suggest why they were or were not accurate.	11.1	6.2 11.1	4.5
7TWSa.02 Describe trends and patterns in results, including identifying any anomalous results.	4.1 11.1	6.2 7.1, 7.2 8.1 11.1	4.1

	Student's Book topic	Teacher's Guide topic	Workbook topic
7TWSa.03 Make conclusions by interpreting results and explain the limitations of the conclusions.	1.1, 1.4 4.6 11.2	1.1, 1.4 4.6 6.2 7.1, 7.2 8.1 11.2	1.1, 1.4 4.1, 4.2, 4.6 11.2
7TWSa.04 Evaluate experiments and investigations, and suggest improvements, explaining any proposed changes.	3.1, 3.2 4.6 8.2 10.3	8.2 10.3	3.1, 3.2 4.2, 4.6
7TWSa.05 Present and interpret observations and measurements appropriately.	1.1 4.1 6.2 8.1 9.3 10.3 11.2	1.1 6.1 8.1 10.3 11.2	1.1 4.1, 4.5

Mapping document

	Student's Book topic	Teacher's Guide topic	Workbook topic
Biology			
Structure and function			
7Bs.01 Understand that all organisms are made of cells and microorganisms are typically single celled.	1.2 2.1	1.2, 1.3 2.1	1.2 2.1
7Bs.02 Identify and describe the functions of cell structures (limited to cell membrane, cytoplasm, nucleus, cell wall, chloroplasts, mitochondria and sap vacuole).	1.3	1.3	1.3
7Bs.03 Explain how the structures of some specialised cells are related to their functions (including red blood cells, neurones, ciliated cells, root hair cells and palisade cells).	1.4	1.4	1.4
7Bs.04 Describe the similarities and differences between the structures of plant and animal cells.	1.3	1.3	1.3
7Bs.05 Understand that cells can be grouped together to form tissues, organs and organ systems.	1.2	1.2, 1.3	1.3
Life processes			
7Bp.01 Describe the seven characteristics of living organisms.	1.1 3.1	1.1 3.1	1.1, 1.2 3.1
7Bp.02 Discuss reasons for classifying viruses as living or non-living.	3.1	3.1	3.1
7Bp.03 Describe a species as a group of organisms that can reproduce to produce fertile offspring.	3.1	3.1	3.1

	Student's Book topic	Teacher's Guide topic	Workbook topic
7Bp.04 Use and construct dichotomous keys to classify species and groups of related organisms.	3.2	3.2	3.2
Ecosystems			
7Be.01 Know and describe the ecological role some microorganisms have as decomposers.	2.2	2.2	2.2
7Be.02 Construct and interpret food chains and webs which include microorganisms as decomposers.	2.2	2.2	2.2

	Student's Book topic	Teacher's Guide topic	Workbook topic
Chemistry			
Materials and their structure			
7Cm.01 Understand that all matter is made of atoms, with each different type of atom being a different element.	4.3, 4.4	4.3, 4.4	4.3, 4.4
7Cm.02 Know that the Periodic Table presents the known elements in an order.	4.4	4.4	4.4
7Cm.03 Know metals and non-metals as the two main groupings of elements.	4.6	4.4, 4.6	4.6
7Cm.04 Describe the differences between elements, compounds and mixtures, including alloys as an example of a mixture.	4.5	4.5	4.5
7Cm.05 Describe a vacuum as a space devoid of matter.	4.3	4.3	4.3
7Cm.06 Describe the three states of matter as solid, liquid and gas in terms of the arrangement, separation and motion of particles.	4.3	4.3	4.3
7Cm.07 Use the particle model to represent elements, compounds and mixtures.	4.4, 4.5	4.5	4.4, 4.5
Properties of materials			
7Cp.01 Understand that all substances have chemical properties and physical properties.	4.1	4.1	4.1
7Cp.02 Understand that the acidity or alkalinity of a substance is a chemical property and is measured by pH.	4.2	4.2	4.2
7Cp.03 Use indicators (including Universal Indicator and litmus) to distinguish between acidic, alkaline and neutral solutions.	4.2	4.2	4.2

	Student's Book topic	Teacher's Guide topic	Workbook topic
7Cp.04 Use tests to identify hydrogen, carbon dioxide and oxygen gases.	5.1	5.1	5.1
7Cp.05 Describe common differences between metals and non-metals, referring to their physical properties.	4.6	4.6	4.6
7Cp.06 Understand that alloys are mixtures that have different chemical and physical properties from the constituent substances.	4.6	4.5, 4.6	4.6
7Cp.07 Use the particle model to explain the difference in hardness between pure metals and their alloys.	4.6	4.6	4.6
Changes to materials			
7Cc.01 Identify whether a chemical reaction has taken place through observations of the loss of reactants and/or the formation of products which have different properties to the reactants (including evolving a gas, formation of a precipitate or change of colour).	5.1	5.1	5.1
7Cc.02 Explain why a precipitate forms, in terms of a chemical reaction between soluble reactants forming at least one insoluble product.	5.2	5.2	5.2
7Cc.03 Use the particle model to describe chemical reactions.	5.1, 5.2	5.1, 5.2, 5.3	5.1, 5.2
7Cc.04 Describe neutralisation reactions in terms of change of pH.	5.3	5.3	5.3

Physics

Forces and energy

	Student's Book topic	Teacher's Guide topic	Workbook topic
7Pf.01 Describe changes in energy that are a result of an event or process.	6.1	6.1	6.1
7Pf.02 Know that energy tends to dissipate and in doing so it becomes less useful.	6.2	6.2	6.2
7Pf.03 Describe gravity as a force of attraction between any two objects and describe how the size of the force is related to the masses of the objects.	7.1	7.1	7.1
7Pf.04 Understand that there is no air resistance to oppose movement in a vacuum.	7.2	7.2	7.2

Light and sound

	Student's Book topic	Teacher's Guide topic	Workbook topic
7Ps.01 Describe the vibration of particles in a sound wave and explain why sound does not travel in a vacuum.	8.1	8.1	8.1
7Ps.02 Explain echoes in terms of the reflection of sound waves.	8.2	8.2	8.2

Electricity and magnetism

	Student's Book topic	Teacher's Guide topic	Workbook topic
7Pe.01 Use a simple model to describe electricity as a flow of electrons around a circuit.	9.1	9.1	9.1
7Pe.02 Describe electrical conductors as substances that allow electron flow and electrical insulators as substances that inhibit electron flow.	9.1	9.1	9.1
7Pe.03 Know how to measure the current in series circuits.	9.3	9.3	9.3
7Pe.04 Describe how adding components into a series circuit can affect the current (limited to addition of cells and lamps).	9.2, 9.3	9.2, 9.3	9.3
7Pe.05 Use diagrams and conventional symbols to represent, make and compare circuits that include cells, switches, lamps, buzzers and ammeters.	9.2	9.2	9.2

	Student's Book topic	Teacher's Guide topic	Workbook topic
Earth and Space			
Planet Earth			
7ESp.01 Describe the model of plate tectonics, in which a solid outer layer (made up of the crust and uppermost mantle) moves because of flow lower in the mantle.	10.1	10.1	10.1
7ESp.02 Describe how earthquakes, volcanoes and fold mountains occur near the boundaries of tectonic plates.	10.2	10.2	10.2
7ESp.03 Know that clean, dry air contains 78% nitrogen, 21% oxygen and small amounts of carbon dioxide and other gases, and this composition can change because of pollution and natural emissions.	10.3	10.3	10.3
Cycles on Earth			
7ESc.01 Describe the water cycle (limited to evaporation, condensation, precipitation, water run-off, open water and groundwater).	10.4	10.4	10.4
Earth in space			
7ESs.01 Describe how planets form from dust and gas, which are pulled together by gravity.	11.1	11.1	11.1
7ESs.02 Know that gravity is the force that holds components of the Solar System in orbit around the Sun.	11.1	11.1	11.1
7ESs.03 Describe tidal forces on Earth as a consequence of the gravitational attraction between the Earth, Moon and Sun.	11.2	11.2	11.2
7ESs.04 Explain how solar and lunar eclipses happen.	11.3	11.3	11.3

Mapping document

Science in Context	Student's Book topic	Teacher's Guide topic	Workbook topic
7SIC.01 Discuss how scientific knowledge is developed through collective understanding and scrutiny over time.	10.1	7.1 10.1, 10.4 11.1	10.1
7SIC.02 Describe how science is applied across societies and industries, and in research.	5.1 6.1 8.2 10.3	6.1 7.2 10.3	10.2
7SIC.03 Evaluate issues which involve and/or require scientific understanding.	3.1	6.2	
7SIC.04 Describe how people develop and use scientific understanding, as individuals and through collaboration, e.g. through peer-review.	3.2 4.5 10.1 11.1	10.1 11.1	
7SIC.05 Discuss how the uses of science can have a global environmental impact.	3.2 4.2, 4.4 5.2 6.1 10.2, 10.3	6.1 10.2, 10.3	10.3

Chapter 1 — Organisms and cells

Chapter overview

In this chapter students will learn about how scientists define living things, and how plants and animals are made up of cells, tissues, organs and organ systems. This chapter builds on ideas about human organs and their functions, met in work at earlier stages of their education.

Topic title	Number of 40-minute periods	Learning Objectives	Thinking and Working Scientifically Learning Objectives
1.1 Characteristics of living things	3	7Bp.01 Describe the seven characteristics of living organisms.	7TWSp.02 Describe how scientific hypotheses can be supported or contradicted by evidence from an enquiry. 7TWSp.03 Make predictions of likely outcomes for a scientific enquiry based on scientific knowledge and understanding. 7TWSa.03 Make conclusions by interpreting results and explain the limitations of the conclusions. 7TWSa.05 Present and interpret observations and measurements appropriately.
1.2 Cells, tissues, organs and organ systems	1	7Bs.01 Understand that all organisms are made of cells and microorganisms are typically single celled. 7Bs.05 Understand that cells can be grouped together to form tissues, organs and organ systems.	
1.3 Comparing plant and animal cells	3	7Bs.01 Understand that all organisms are made of cells and microorganisms are typically single celled. 7Bs.02 Identify and describe the functions of cell structures (limited to cell membrane, cytoplasm, nucleus, cell wall, chloroplasts, mitochondria and sap vacuole). 7Bs.04 Describe the similarities and differences between the structures of plant and animal cells. 7Bs.05 Understand that cells can be grouped together to form tissues, organs and organ systems.	7TWSm.01 Describe the strengths and limitations of a model. 7TWSc.02 Decide what equipment is required to carry out an investigation or experiment and use it appropriately. 7TWSc.05 Carry out practical work safely.
1.4 Specialised cells	2	7Bs.03 Explain how the structures of some specialised cells are related to their functions (including red blood cells, neurones, ciliated cells, root hair cells and palisade cells).	7TWSa.03 Make conclusions by interpreting results and explain the limitations of the conclusions
End of chapter questions	1	Check students' progress	

© HarperCollins*Publishers* 2021

Cambridge Lower Secondary Biology
Stage 7

Background science

Please note: the background science notes are designed to provide teachers with an overview of the science concepts students may have already been taught earlier in their education, are likely to be taught in this unit and are likely to be taught in later stages. They are not a checklist of the content to be covered by the teacher in each unit.

The background science notes also serve to provide the teacher with some understanding of the background science needed in order to deliver the content of each chapter.

The 'scientific method' is any sequence of events in which a question is asked, and ideas on answering that question are generated and tested by experiments or observations. The evidence from the experiments or observations is then used to say whether an idea is likely to be correct or whether an idea is likely to be incorrect. We say that the evidence 'supports' or 'contradicts' an idea. Evidence does not *prove* that an idea is correct.

The first part of this chapter introduces the idea of living organisms. If something moves all or part of its body, reproduces, senses things around it, grows, respires, excretes wastes and needs nutrition then it is living. We call these seven things 'life processes'. Some students may be confused by the idea that plants move, but they can move parts of themselves.

Plants and animals are made of many cells. Cells of the same type are grouped together in tissues. Groups of different tissues form organs, and organs work together in organ systems. Anything in the body that contains different tissues is an organ.

The group of plants that have flowers are 'flowering plants' and the flowers themselves are actually containers for the sexual organs of a plant (some contain just male organs, some contain female organs and some contain both). So, flowers are technically collections of organs rather than single organs. In this chapter we are only considering roots, stems and leaves and so the distinction of how to classify a flower is not an issue.

An organ is classified as a group of different tissues working together. A tissue is described as a group of cells of the same type working together.

A group of organs that work together for a common purpose is called an organ system. Examples include the water transport system in plants, and the digestive, respiratory and circulatory systems in humans.

1.1 Characteristics of living things

Topic overview

		Student's Book	Workbook	Downloadable material
1.1a	**Starting point** This short activity provides an opportunity for students to demonstrate their understanding of how we can tell that something is living	Starting point table		
1.1b	**Working as a scientist** This activity illustrates the sequence of stages that scientists use to develop and investigate ideas	Question 1		Worksheets 1.1b(1), 1.1b(2)
1.1c	**Life processes** This activity introduces students to the seven life processes	Questions 2–18 Activity 1.1 Activity 1.2 Activity 1.3 Activity 1.4	Questions 1–9	Practical notes 1.1c(1), 1.1c(2), 1.1c(3) Worksheets 1.1c(1), 1.1c(2), 1.1c(3)

Learning Objectives

- 7Bp.01: Describe the seven characteristics of living organisms
- 7TWSp.02: Describe how scientific hypotheses can be supported or contradicted by evidence from an enquiry
- 7TWSp.03: Make predictions of likely outcomes for a scientific enquiry based on scientific knowledge and understanding
- 7TWSa.03: Make conclusions by interpreting results and explain the limitations of the conclusions
- 7TWSa.05: Present and interpret observations and measurements appropriately
- 7SIC.02: Describe how science is applied across societies and industries, and in research.
- 7SIC.04: Describe how people develop and use scientific understanding as individuals and through collaboration, e.g. through peer review
- 7SIC.05: Discuss how the uses of science can have a global environmental impact.

Links to other topics

- The 'scientific method' is introduced in this topic, and will be further expanded on in the rest of the course. Ensure that students develop a familiarity with the key words (hypothesis, prediction, data, evidence, conclusion).
- Students will be able to apply learning about life processes from this topic to Chapter 3 Topic 1, in which the problem of classifying viruses is looked at.

Using models

- Students often find constructing hypotheses and predictions quite difficult. A useful model to help students structure hypotheses is to ask them to use the words 'depends on'. In general terms, a hypothesis can be presented as: (dependent variable) depends on (independent variable). Note that, at this stage, students may know about the different types of variables from previous studies but this content may need to be revisited. Equally, a useful model to construct a prediction is to use 'If ... then ...'. In general terms: If I change the independent variable in a certain way, then the dependent variable will change in a certain way. Obviously, these methods of scaffolding hypotheses and predictions will not suit every example that you meet.

Cambridge Lower Secondary Biology
Stage 7

Science in context

- The Science in context: Uses of urine box in Topic 1.1 of the Student's Book covers the following learning objectives:
  - 7SIC.02 Describe how science is applied across societies and industries, and in research.
  - 7SIC.04 Describe how people develop and use scientific understanding as individuals and through collaboration, e.g. through peer review
  - 7SIC.05 Discuss how the uses of science can have a global environmental impact.
- Use local examples of plants and animals while looking at life processes, and encourage students to describe how they can tell that life processes are occurring in these organisms.
- If you have access to data about some local plants and/or animals, show students how this data is presented using tables, bar charts and line graphs.

Common misunderstandings

- Many students don't think that plants can move or sense things. If you search the internet for a video, using search terms such as 'time lapse plants moving' you will find many videos that demonstrate plant movement. Students should realise that plants only move parts of themselves and that this movement happens more slowly than with many familiar animals.

1.1a Starting point

Point out various things that students are familiar with; for example, living and dead plants and animals (or parts of them), building materials, rocks. Ask students which of the things are alive, which are now dead but were once alive, and which have never been alive.

Then challenge students to explain how they can tell that something is alive. You could write their ideas up on the board. Tell students that in this topic they are going to find out how scientists work out if something is alive or not.

1.1b Working as a scientist

Students will learn:

- To be able to talk about the importance of asking questions, inventing hypotheses, designing experiments to test hypotheses, making predictions, using data as evidence to draw conclusions
- To make careful observations
- To present results in the form of tables, bar charts and line graphs

Glossary words

bar chart, conclusion, data, evidence, hypothesis (plural hypotheses), line graph, prediction

Resource preparation

Worksheets 1.1b(1), 1.1b(2)

Teaching and learning ideas

- Explain to students that all scientists work in a similar way: they ask questions and then try to answer them using evidence from experiments and observations.
- Together with students, look at the first section in the Student's Book 'Working as a scientist'. Summarise the way in which scientists work as a flow chart on the board:

    question → hypothesis that answers the question → prediction → experiment →
    data used as evidence → conclusion

- Go through an example to illustrate:
  - Question: Why do maggots appear in dead animals?
  - Hypothesis: Flies lay eggs on dead animals (or the appearance of maggots in dead animals depends on flies laying their eggs there).
  - Prediction: If flies are stopped from getting to the meat then it will not get maggots in it.

Chapter 1: Organisms and cells

- Experiment: Take two pieces of meat and leave them outside. Put a screen around one piece so that flies cannot get to it. Leave the other piece without a screen.
    - Data: The unscreened meat got maggots in it. The screened meat did not.
    - Conclusion: The data is supporting evidence that the hypothesis is correct.
- Challenge some students to come up with their own examples, based on experiments that they may have done at an earlier stage of their formal education. Note that evidence does not *prove* that an idea is correct; it only supports the idea. This sequence of steps is often referred to as the 'scientific method'.
- Students should be familiar with tables, bar charts and line graphs from work completed at an earlier stage of their formal education. These ideas will be met and used in the next activity, and so it is useful to have a reminder at this stage to ensure that all students have the necessary foundation understanding. Explain to students that scientists present their data in tables, charts and graphs. Look at the examples in the Student's Book. Ask students questions such as 'How old was Mark when he was 108 cm tall?' (answer: 4) to ensure that students can read values off bar charts and line graphs.
- Students can use Worksheets 1.1b(1) and 1.1b(2) to practise their chart and graph drawing skills (or these could be used for homework).
- Finish by removing your flow chart from the board and asking students to answer question 1 in the Student's Book. Ask students to work together to check their ideas and make corrections/additions to their own work as necessary. Then write up your flow chart on the board again, as a final check for students.

Differentiation

Some students will need help drawing charts and graphs. Go through plotting charts and graphs one stage at a time (e.g. choosing axes, drawing the axes, numbering the scale, plotting the points). Ask students to copy each stage after you have demonstrated it.

Some students could be challenged to do a survey in the school to find out the most popular colours or foods or music. They should then present their work on an appropriate chart or graph.

Homework suggestions

Students complete Worksheets 1.1b(1) and 1.1b(2).

Or give students some data to plot as either a bar chart and/or a line graph. There are plenty of examples that can be found on the internet; for example, numbers of people living in the major cities in your country (bar chart); population of your country in the last 20 years (line graph).

Alternatively, ask students to draw a flow chart to show how scientists work, and to illustrate the steps using an example from an experiment that they have done in the past. It might be wise to check that all students can think of an experiment before setting them this activity as a homework.

1.1c Life processes

Students will learn:

- To describe the seven characteristics of living organisms
- To make predictions and review them against evidence
- To use hypotheses to make predictions, referring to previous scientific knowledge and understanding
- To make careful observations
- To make conclusions from collected data

Glossary words

excrete, life process, calcium hydroxide (limewater), nutrient, nutrition, offspring, organism, reproduce, respiration, sensitivity, urine

Resource preparation

For Activity 1.1: U-shaped piece of wire, ruler. Optional: blindfold.

For Activity 1.2: eye protection, straws, tubes/beakers of calcium hydroxide (limewater).

For Activity 1.4: small, easy-to-grow seeds (e.g. cress), paper towel, dishes in which to grow seeds, sticky tape, card, scissors.

Graph paper (for Student's Book questions 5 and 13).

Worksheets 1.1c(1), 1.1c(2), 1.1c(3)

Practical notes 1.1c(1), 1.1c(2), 1.1c(3)

Teaching and learning ideas

- Tell students that for something to be living it must move, reproduce, sense things around it, grow, respire, excrete wastes and need nutrition. Write these as a list on the board, and then go through each one in turn referring to the appropriate section in the Student's Book and answering the questions.

- When you get to 'Sensitivity' there is an option to carry out an activity in which students find out which part of the hand is most sensitive to touch/light pressure. Instructions for students are on Worksheet 1.1c(1) and further details are given in the Practical notes 1.1c(1). Finish by writing the following headings on the board and asking students to identify the parts of their investigations that correspond to each title: scientific question, hypothesis, prediction, data, evidence, conclusion. Note that this activity may involve touching, and so may not be suitable for use in your classroom. Note also that this activity is also suitable for use in topic 1.2, when students have looked at organ systems.

- When you get to 'Respiration', demonstrate the limewater test (using calcium hydroxide) for carbon dioxide, or ask students to do it. Refer to Activity 1.2 *Investigating excretion of carbon dioxide*. Practical notes 1.1c(2) provides full details. Ask students to answer the questions in the activity box (Student's Book) or to complete the questions on Worksheet 1.1c(2) (which provides more structured help).

- Activity 1.3 *Investigating living things on Mars*. This is a simple comprehension exercise, asking students to use ideas about how scientists work (revising previous work from this topic).

- Activity 1.4 *Investigating how plants respond to light*. Practical notes 1.1c(3) provides full details. Ask students to answer the questions in the activity box (Student's Book) or to complete the questions on Worksheet 1.1c(3) (which provides more structured help). This activity will take several days to provide evidence for students to use. A suitable method may be placing the plant on a central spot from which it is not moved. A circle could then be drawn around the plant and the light source could then be placed at different positions on that circle. The student can then use their observations of whether the plant is growing towards or away from the light in each position.

- Finish by asking students to summarise the seven life processes as a table. The first column should name the life processes and the second column should describe each one. Students could use the mnemonic MRS GREN to remember the life processes, or make up a mnemonic of their own.

Differentiation

Some students may need help drawing charts and graphs for questions 5 and 13. Go through plotting charts and graphs one stage at a time (e.g. choosing axes, drawing the axes, numbering the scale, plotting the points). Ask students to copy each stage after you have demonstrated it.

In Activity 1.1, it may help less confident students to use a volunteer to show students what to do. For more confident students, give them the question only and ask them to plan their own investigations using the U-shaped piece of wire (and without access to the Student's Book). They must show you their plans before being allowed to carry them out.

Homework suggestions

Students answer the questions in topic 1.1: Characteristics of living things in the Workbook.

Alternatively, ask students to state the life processes and describe the ways that we can see these in humans (or another animal).

Topic overview

		Student's Book	Workbook	Downloadable material
1.2a	**Starting point** This short activity allows students to demonstrate their understanding of human organs	Starting point table		
1.2b	**Human organs** This activity introduces some of the main organs in the human body – their names, positions and functions	Questions 1–5		Worksheet 1.2b
1.2c	**Human organ systems** This activity introduces organ systems, in the context of the human body	Questions 6–7	Questions 1–2, 4–9 and 12	
1.2d	**Organs and tissues** In this activity, students explore the different tissues in a chicken wing	Activity 1.5 Questions 8–10		Practical notes 1.2d

Learning Objectives

- 7Bs.01: Understand that all organisms are made of cells (and microorganisms are typically single celled)
- 7Bs.05: Understand that cells can be grouped together to form tissues, organs and organ systems
- 7SIC.02: Describe how science is applied across societies and industries, and in research.

Links to other topics

- Ideas about organs and organ systems will be required again in Stage 8, in which the circulatory system, respiratory system, digestive system and skeletal system are all covered in more detail.
- 7Bs.01 is only partially covered here. The 'microorganisms are typically single celled' part of this learning objective is covered in Topic 2.1.

Using models

- A three-dimensional model of the human body can be useful to show how the different organs in the torso fit together. This is very difficult to show on a two-dimensional drawing, and if you have such a model available encourage students to highlight some of the advantages of the three-dimensional model. Equally, you can use such a model to illustrate the components of one particular organ system (by removing organs from other organ systems). A model skeleton is also useful to illustrate the skeletal system.
- There is an opportunity here to address learning objective 7TWSm.01, where the students are asked to discuss the strengths and limitations of the models shown.

Cambridge Lower Secondary Biology
Stage 7

Science in context

- The Science in context: Organ transplants box in Topic 1.2 of the Student's Book covers the following learning objectives:
  - 7SIC.02 Describe how science is applied across societies and industries, and in research.
- Look for examples in your country of organ transplants or skin grafting to illustrate how a knowledge of organs and what they do is used to help people with certain conditions.

Common misunderstandings

- Many students will not think of the skin as an organ. Point out to students that it is the largest organ in the human body and has more than one important function (e.g. protection and sensing hot/cold/pressure).
- The word 'tissue' can cause problems if students muddle it with paper tissues. Referring to 'living tissue' may help.

1.2a Starting point

Remind students that bones and muscles are organs, and that organs are parts of an organism that carry out important jobs.

Ask students to name some organs in the human body and suggest what they do. Write the ideas up on the board. Draw an outline of a human on the board and ask students to suggest where each of the organs should go. Then ask students to look at the diagram of the human organs in the Student's Book. They should point out any errors in the information on the board and suggest corrections.

1.2b Human organs

Students will learn:

- To describe some organ systems and their functions
- To research the work of scientists studying the human body
- To use information from secondary sources

Glossary words

bladder, blood, blood vessels, diaphragm, function, heart, kidneys, large intestine, liver, lungs, organ, skin, small intestine, stomach, wilt

Resource preparation

Access to secondary sources of information about organs and organ transplants (e.g. internet, books).

For Worksheet 1.2b: scissors, glue.

Worksheet 1.2b

Teaching and learning ideas

- Remind students that the main parts of an organism that have important jobs to do are called organs.
- The diagram in the Student's Book gives the names and functions of some of the major human organs. Encourage students to answer questions 1–4 as they meet them.
- Worksheet 1.2b asks students to identify some organs and describe their functions. Students should complete the labelling without access to secondary sources. They can either copy the information from the bottom of the sheet, or cut out the boxes and stick them onto the diagram. Students could then work together in groups to share their thoughts and add to or correct their work as necessary. They could then have access to secondary sources as a final check.
- The Organ transplants box in the Student's Book gives a short history of organ transplants. Discuss with students why people may need organ transplants (concentrating on the important functions performed by organs). Encourage students to answer question 5, which will require access to secondary sources.
- Finish by drawing a table on the board showing the names of these organs: lungs, skin, small intestine, kidney. Ask students to give the function of each organ and to say which life process(es) each one helps with.

Differentiation

For less confident students, go through the words on Worksheet 1.2b one at a time and discuss where each label should go. Then ask the students to complete their own sheets.

For more confident students, remove the list of organ names at the bottom of Worksheet 1.2b. You could also remove the list of organ functions.

Extension ideas

You could extend the scope of Worksheet 1.2b by adding other organs for students to identify or by asking students to add their own labels to additional organs. They may be encouraged to do some independent research using secondary sources.

Homework suggestions

Ask students to prepare a table to show six important human organs and their functions.

1.2c Human organ systems

Students will learn:

- To describe some organs systems and their functions

Glossary words

circulatory system, digestive system, nervous system, respiratory system, skeletal system

Resource preparation

Small pieces of paper, chalk.

Teaching and learning ideas

- Ask students what organs are working together in the skeletal system. Remind them that all the bones in the body need to work together, and that bones are organs. Remind them that a group of organs that are working together form an organ system.
- Tell students that the circulatory system carries blood all around the body. Ask for suggestions about the organs that it contains. Most students should be able to name the heart. Establish that it also contains the blood vessels and blood.
- Activity 1.1 (from topic 1.1, on the sensitivity of skin) is also suitable for use here. If it is to be used here, ensure that students know that the skin is an organ that contains 'touch detectors' (or more properly 'pressure receptors'). Information from the touch detectors in the hand is transmitted to the brain through nerves and the spinal cord, which form the nervous system. Refer to 1.1c in topic 1.1 for full details.
- Read through the section on Human organ systems in the Student's Book, which gives the names and functions of some of the major human organ systems.
- Activity – Ask students to write the names of some organs on small pieces of paper. There should only be one name on each piece. Put students together in groups of three or four and ask them to pool their pieces of paper, and then to decide which organ system each belongs to. Once students have finished matching up their cards, ask them to identify any organs that are missing from their organ systems. Some students may have included bones and the skeletal system. Some students may have included muscles (which form part of the muscular system).
- Activity – If there is time, you could ask students to draw outlines of themselves in the playground/yard (e.g. using chalk) and then draw in the organs belonging to one organ system.
- Finish by asking students to answer question 6 in the Student's Book, which could be done as group work. Challenge some students to answer question 7 in the Student's Book.

Differentiation

For less confident students, give them the names of the organ systems to use in the first activity (circulatory system, nervous system, respiratory system, digestive system).

For more confident students, ask them to prepare a large table for question 6, which includes the functions of each of the organs in each organ system.

Extension ideas

You could extend the scope of this topic by asking students to describe the water transport system of plants.

© HarperCollins*Publishers* 2021

Homework suggestions

Students answer the questions in topic 1.2: Cells, tissues, organs and organ systems in the Workbook.

Ask students to write a paragraph about an organ system of their choice. They should explain what an organ system is, what their chosen organ system does and what organs it contains. Some students could go further and describe the functions of the individual organs in the system.

1.2d Organs and tissues

Students will learn:

- To state that all organisms are made of cells
- To describe the relationship between cells, tissues, organs and organ systems

Glossary words

tissue

Resource preparation

For Activity 1.5: raw chicken wing, sharp scissors, sharp knife, cutting board.

Practical notes 1.2d

Teaching and learning ideas

- Remind students that skin, bones and muscles are different types of organ.
- Activity 1.5 (demonstration) – Point out the skin on the chicken wing, and then remove it by following the instructions given in Practical notes 1.2d. You may find yellowish tissue under the skin, which is fat tissue. Explain to students that skin is an organ and contains different types of tissues, including fat tissue. You should then be able to see the muscles. Point out the biceps and the triceps to students, and remind them of the function of these muscles in humans. Pull gently on each of these muscles to show students what happens to the wing bones when these muscles contract. Point out the white-coloured tendons at the ends of the muscles. Note: tendons are beyond Stage 7 and are much more appropriate for Stage 8, when bones and muscles are considered in detail. Explain to students that muscles are organs and so contain different types of tissue, including muscle tissue and tendon tissue. Then remove the muscles with the knife, and show students the white cartilage at ends of one or more of the bones. Explain that bones contain bone tissue and cartilage (a slippery substance that allows bones to slide against one another).
- Finish by asking students to copy and complete this table.

	Example in a chicken wing	Tissues it contains	Organ system it is part of
Bone			
Muscle			muscular system

Differentiation

For less confident students, go through the table part by part asking students for suggestions and writing correct suggestions on the board. Then ask students to copy down the correct version of the table.

For more confident students, ask them to make labelled drawings of the parts of a chicken wing as you go through the dissection. They should label their drawings with the names and functions of the different parts.

Homework suggestions

Students answer the questions in topic 1.2: Cells, tissues, organs and organ systems in the Workbook.

Ask students to write two short paragraphs about muscles and bones and the tissues that they contain.

Topic overview

		Student's Book	Workbook	Downloadable material
1.3a	**Starting point** This short activity reminds students of the idea of a cell and allows them to demonstrate their understanding of magnification	Starting point table		
1.3b	**Cells, tissues, organs and systems** This activity introduces the idea of a cell as the basic building block for all life on Earth	Questions 1–2		
1.3c	**Plant and animal cells** This activity introduces the differences between plant and animal cells	Questions 3–4 Activity 1.6	Questions 1–4 and 7	Practical notes 1.3c Worksheet 1.3c
1.3d	**Using a microscope** In this activity, students have the opportunity to learn how to use microscopes	Questions 5–11 Activity 1.7	Question 6	Practical notes 1.3d(1), 1.3d(2) Worksheet 1.3d
1.3e	**Unicellular and multicellular organisms** In this activity, students use plastic building bricks to model tissues in a multicellular organism and cells in a unicellular organism	Questions 12–13	Question 5	

Learning Objectives

- 7Bs.01: Understand that all organisms are made of cells and microorganisms are typically single celled
- 7Bs.02: Identify and describe the functions of cell structures (limited to cell membrane, cytoplasm, nucleus, cell wall, chloroplasts, mitochondria and sap vacuole)
- 7Bs.04: Describe the similarities and differences between the structures of plant and animal cells
- 7Bs.05: Understand that cells can be grouped together to form tissues, organs and organ systems
- 7TWSm.01: Describe the strengths and limitations of a model
- 7TWSc.02: Decide what equipment is required to carry out an investigation or experiment and use it appropriately

- 7TWSc.05: Carry out practical work safely
- 7SIC.01: Discuss how scientific knowledge is developed through collective understanding and scrutiny over time.
- 7SIC.02: Describe how science is applied across societies and industries, and in research.
- 7SIC.04: Describe how people develop and use scientific understanding as individuals and through collaboration, e.g. through peer review

Links to other topics

- Students will be able to apply learning here to Chapter 2 and Chapter 3 Topic 1, in which microorganisms will be met again but in more detail to fulfil the second half of 7Bs.01.

Using models

- There is an opportunity here to address learning objective 7TWSm.02. Students could be asked to discuss the strengths and limitations of the models presented.
- They could also be asked to design their own models of plant and animal cells which they could then describe and discuss their strengths and limitations.
- The use of model plastic building bricks helps students to reinforce the idea of a cell and of a tissue. It is hoped that students themselves will be able to design this model.

Cambridge Lower Secondary Biology
Stage 7

- The building of physical models to represent cells is useful to get students to understand the three-dimensional nature of cells. Using these models will also help students to understand why certain sub-cellular parts are not seen in every cell (because the plane of focus on the microscope is so narrow). Encourage students to think about these advantages of these models but also to consider ways in which these models are not so good at representing real cells.

Science in context

- The Science in context boxes 'Discovering microorganisms' and 'Inventing the modern microsope' in Topic 1.3 of the Student's Book cover the following learning objectives:
    - 7SIC.01 Discuss how scientific knowledge is developed through collective understanding and scrutiny over time.
    - 7SIC.02 Describe how science is applied across societies and industries, and in research.
    - 7SIC.04 Describe how people develop and use scientific understanding as individuals and through collaboration, e.g. through peer review
- Look out for uses of lenses and microscopes outside science (e.g. in examining documents or bank notes to look out for fakes, in examining fabrics to look for flaws in the weave, in jewellery making). If there is a local industry that makes use of instruments for magnification, consider using this as a context through which to introduce the use of microscopes.

Common misunderstandings

- Cells are quite an abstract concept for students, because they need special equipment in order to see them. Chief among the misconceptions that students develop about cells is that they are flat. This is because microscope images and the drawings in books are all two-dimensional. Stress to students that cells are three-dimensional objects. The model building activity, suggested in Practical notes 1.3b, will also help.
- 'Cell' is one of those English words that can cause confusion. Here, a cell is the smallest living unit of an organism. However, in physics a 'cell' can refer to what is commonly called a 'battery', it is also the word used to describe a very small room in a building such as a prison or monastery, and in some countries people refer to their mobile telephones as 'cells'. To add to this, the word is pronounced the same way as 'sell'. Be sure that students are clear what sort of 'cell' you are talking about and it is often a good idea to refer to 'living cells' rather than just 'cells' to help understanding.

1.3a Starting point

Ask students to say what they understand by the term 'cell' in Biology. Establish that this is the smallest living part of any organism. Ask students why we can't see individual cells, and ensure that students understand that they are too small to see with your eyes and so we need something to magnify them. Remind students about the use of hand lenses/magnifying glasses to magnify nearby things that are very small.

1.3b Cells, tissues, organs and systems

Students will learn:

- To state that all organisms are made of cells
- To describe the relationship between cells, tissues, organs and organ systems

Glossary words

cell, tissue

Resource preparation

Microscope images of tissues, downloaded from the internet.

Teaching and learning ideas

- Remind students that skin, bones and muscles are different types of organ and that an organ is part of an organism that has a very important function. Remind students that organs are made of different tissues, which are sometimes easy to see because different tissues may look different.
- Read through the first two paragraphs in topic 1.3: Comparing plant and animal cells.

- Show students some microscope images of tissues, showing cells. Choose examples (from both animals and plants) that clearly show the compartmentalised nature of cells. Good examples include human dermis and fat tissues, and the tissues in a plant root. Tell students that they will find out more about microscopes and cells in the next topic. For now, they just need to appreciate that tissues contain many thousands of similar units called cells. Explain to students that a cell is the smallest living part of an organism that you can have, and that some organisms have only one cell.
- Finish by asking students to write definitions of the terms: cell, tissue, organ, organ system.

Differentiation

For less confident students, write up the definitions of cell, tissue, organ and organ system on the board, without the words that are being defined. Ask students to say which definition belongs to which word.

For more confident students, ask them to design a diagram to show the relationship between cells, tissues and organs in a multicellular organism (one with many cells). Their diagrams should convey the idea that organs contain different tissues, each of which is made of many similar cells.

Homework suggestions

Ask students to describe themselves in terms of cells, tissues, organs and organ systems. This could be in the form of drawings or text, or a mixture of both.

1.3c Plant and animal cells

Students will learn:

- To identify the main parts of cells and describe their functions
- To compare and contrast animal and plant cells

Glossary words

cell membrane, cell wall, chloroplasts, cytoplasm, mitochondria, model, nucleus, sap vacuole

Resource preparation

Access to secondary sources of information about cells (e.g. internet, books).

For Worksheet 1.3c: scissors, glue.

For Activity 1.6: a selection of locally available items to use to build cell models.

Worksheet 1.3c

Practical notes 1.3c

Teaching and learning ideas

- Remind students that a tissue is made of many cells of the same type and that cells are the smallest living units of an organism.
- Read through the section on plant and animal cells in the Student's Book (down to where microscopes are introduced). Encourage students to answer the questions as they come to them.
- Worksheet 1.3c asks students to identify the parts of plant and animal cells, and to recall the functions of those parts. Students should complete the labelling without access to secondary sources. They can either copy the information from the bottom of the sheet, or cut out the boxes and stick them onto the diagrams. Students could then work together in groups to share their thoughts and add to or correct their work as necessary. They could then have access to secondary sources as a final check.
- Activity 1.6 *Investigating cells 1*. This can be done as a demonstration or by students. The idea is that you use common objects to represent the different parts of plant and animal cells. Full details are given in Practical notes 1.3b. Ask students how they could use their models to make a model of some plant tissue from a leaf, and reinforce the idea of a tissue as a collection of the same type of cells by stacking some of the plant cell models together.
- Finish by asking students to make labelled sketches of plant and animal cells to show their parts.

Differentiation

For less confident students, go through the words on Worksheet 1.3c one at a time and discuss where each label should go. Then ask the students to complete their own sheets.

For more confident students, remove the list of cell parts at the bottom of Worksheet 1.3c. You could also remove the list of functions.

Extension ideas

You could extend the scope of Worksheet 1.3c by encouraging students to do some independent research using secondary sources to find out the names of two other parts found in both animal and plant cells, and what those parts do. Examples might include lysosomes and ribosomes.

Ask students to evaluate the models of the animal and plant cells, pointing out ways in which the models are good and ways in which they are poor.

Homework suggestions

Ask students to prepare a table to show the parts of plant and animal cells, what the parts do and which parts are found in which type of cell.

1.3d Using a microscope

Students will learn:

- To describe how and why we use a microscope to observe very small things
- To make careful observations including measurements
- To choose appropriate apparatus and use it correctly
- To carry out practical work safely

Glossary words

eyepiece lens, focusing wheel, magnification/magnify, microscope, objective lens, slide, specimen, stage

Resource preparation

For demonstration: slides, coverslips, mounted needles/cocktail sticks, onion *(Allium cepa)* (or other suitable source of cells), stain (e.g. methylene blue), dropper, forceps/tweezers. Optional: clean small wooden scraper (e.g. tongue depressor, ice lolly stick).

For Activity 1.7: microscope, pre-prepared slides of animal and plant cells, light source.

Worksheet 1.3d

Practical notes 1.3d(1), 1.3d(2)

Teaching and learning ideas

- Remind students that cells are the smallest living units of organisms. Some organisms have many cells, which then form tissues, organs and organ systems. Other organisms have only one cell. Explain to students that in order to see cells we need to magnify them using a microscope.
- Read through the section on microscopes and using microscopes shown in the Student's Book. If possible, have a microscope to show students the parts as they are met in the Student's Book and demonstrate the use of a microscope. Note that some microscopes have a mirror instead of a lamp as a light source. Encourage students to answer the questions as they come to them.
- Demonstrate how slides are prepared. Full instructions for this are given in Practical notes 1.3d(1). If there is time, and enough available equipment, students could also prepare slides.
- Activity 1.7 *Investigating cells 2*. In this activity, students get to use microscopes to look at slides. Full instructions on the use of a microscope are given on Worksheet 1.3d(1) Practical details are given in Practical notes 1.3d(2).
- Finish by asking students to make labelled sketches of the cells that they have seen.

Differentiation

For less confident students, go through the words on Worksheet 1.3d(1) one step at a time, with students copying what you have done after each step.

Challenge more confident students to look at more than one type of cell. Alternatively, give them pre-prepared slides containing either plant or animal cells and ask them to decide whether the cells are from a plant or from an animal, giving reasons for their choice.

Extension ideas

The total magnification of a microscope is worked out by multiplying the magnification of the objective lens by the magnification of the eyepiece lens. For example, a ×5 eyepiece lens and a ×10 objective lens will give an overall magnification of ×50. Challenge students to work out the magnifications that they are using on the microscopes.

Cambridge Lower Secondary Biology
Stage 7

Ask students to sketch a microscope, and label its parts.

1.3e Unicellular and multicellular organisms

Students will learn:

- To describe the difference between unicellular and multicellular organisms
- To make careful observations
- To describe the strengths and limitations of a model

Glossary words

microorganism, multicellular, unicellular

Resource preparation

For demonstration: light microscope pictures (micrographs) of animal or plant tissue, light microscope pictures of microorganisms, electron microscope pictures of animal/plant/microorganism cells (e.g. downloaded from the internet).

For modelling: plastic building bricks (of the type that can be attached to one another)

Teaching and learning ideas

- Ask students what a tissue is, and ensure that all students are able to say that it is a collection of (the same type of) cells working together. Explain to students that any organism with tissues is said to be multicellular because it has many cells.
- Read through the section on unicellular and multicellular organisms in the Student's Book and answer the questions.
- Activity: Show students some plastic building bricks and challenge students to work in groups to come up with a way of using these bricks to illustrate a tissue in a multicellular organism and cells of a unicellular organism. For the former, students should choose bricks that are similar in shape and colour, and attach them to one another. For the latter, students should choose bricks that are similar in shape and colour but leave them unattached. Challenge students who complete this task quickly, to go on and extend the model to cover organs.
- Finish by showing students some light micrographs of unicellular organisms and of tissues from multicellular organisms and asking them whether each micrograph shows the former or the latter and to give their reasoning.

Differentiation

For less confident students, demonstrate the use of the model building bricks to create models of unicellular and multicellular organisms.

Show more confident students some electron micrographs. Explain that these images are obtained by using very powerful electron microscopes, which can see cells in much more detail, allowing many more sub-cellular structures (such as mitochondria) to be visible. These microscopes also allow scientists to study the internal structure of microorganisms in detail.

Extension ideas

Challenge more confident students to research some of the cellular features of *Euglena* and bacteria, and to develop a table that compares the sub-cellular structures in plant cells, animal cells, bacterial cells and algae (such as *Euglena*).

Homework suggestions

Ask students to write a short section for a new science textbook about microorganisms and how they different from plants and animals.

Students answer the questions in topic 1.3: Comparing plant and animal cells in the Workbook.

1.4 Specialised cells

Topic overview

		Student's Book	Workbook	Downloadable material
1.4a	**Starting point** This short activity tests students' understanding of plant and animal cells, and introduces the idea of cell specialisation	Starting point table		
1.4b	**Specialised plant cells** This activity introduces some specialised plant cells	Questions 1–4 Activity 1.8	Questions 4–5	Practical notes 1.4b Worksheet 1.4b
1.4c	**Specialised animal cells** This activity introduces some specialised animal cells	Questions 5–7	Questions 1–3, 6–8	Worksheet 1.4c

Learning Objectives

- 7Bs.03: Explain how the structures of some specialised cells are related to their functions (including red blood cells, neurones, ciliated cells, root hair cells and palisade cells)
- 7TWSa.03: Make conclusions by interpreting results and explain the limitations of the conclusions
- 7SIC.01: Discuss how scientific knowledge is developed through collective understanding and scrutiny over time.

- 7SIC.02: Describe how science is applied across societies and industries, and in research.
- 7SIC.03: Evaluate issues which involve and/or require scientific understanding.

Links to other topics

- Students will be able to apply learning about specialised cells to various tissues in the skeletal, digestive, circulatory and respiratory systems in Stage 8. In particular, the functions of blood cells will be looked at in more detail in Stage 8 Chapter 1 Topic 1.

Using models

- Compare the diagrams of the specialised cells in the Student's Book with some microscope images. Point out to students that modelling these cells by using diagrams allows their structure to be more easily understood, whereas some images are difficult to interpret.
- There is an opportunity here to address learning objective 7TWSm.01, where the students are asked to discuss the strengths and limitations of the textbook models

Science in context

- The Science in context: Stem cells box in Topic 1.4 of the Student's Book covers the following learning objectives:
  - 7SIC.01 Discuss how scientific knowledge is developed through collective understanding and scrutiny over time.
  - 7SIC.02 Describe how science is applied across societies and industries, and in research.
  - 7SIC.03 Evaluate issues which involve and/or require scientific understanding.
- Use local examples of plants and animals while looking at tissues and specialised cells. If possible, use microscope pictures of the cells of familiar local organisms.

1.4a Starting point

Write two headings up on the board: 'plant cells', 'animal cells'. Ask students to give the names of the parts that we would expect to find in each type of cell. Remind students of the functions of each part.

Introduce the idea that not all cells are the same shape or size, because they have certain special functions. Show students some microscope images of specialised cells (e.g. from the internet) and point out that some cells have features that are not found in other cells in the same organism.

Resource preparation

Microscope pictures (micrographs) of plant and animal cells to display (e.g. downloaded from the internet).

1.4b Specialised plant cells

Students will learn:

- To identify some specialised cells
- To explain how some cells are adapted for certain functions
- To make careful observations including measurements
- To make conclusions from collected data

Glossary words

adaptation, palisade cell, root hair cell, surface area, volume

Resource preparation

For Activity 1.8: cuboid-shaped sponge, ruler, stopwatch/stopclock, cup/beaker/measuring cylinder, flat dish/tray, water (refer to Practical notes 1.4b).

Access to secondary sources of information about specialised plant cells (e.g. internet, books).

Worksheet 1.4b

Practical notes 1.4b

Teaching and learning ideas

- Remind students of the parts of plant cells and what the parts do.
- Read through the section on plant cells in the Student's Book. Encourage students to answer the questions as they come to them.
- Explain to students that the 'root hair' is not an actual hair, and point this out on the diagram in the Student's Book (figure 1.23).
- Activity 1.8 *Investigating root hair cells*. This can be done as a demonstration or by students. The activity demonstrates that the greater the surface area, the faster substances can be absorbed. A cuboid-shaped sponge is used to represent a cell. Instructions are given for students to follow in Worksheet 1.4b and further details are given in Practical notes 1.4b. Discuss the results of the activity with students, reinforcing the idea that the 'root hair' on a root hair cell increases the surface area of the cell and so allows it to absorb water more quickly.
- Finish by asking students to make a labelled diagram of a root hair cell, pointing out its features and how it differs from a palisade cell.

Differentiation

For less confident students, demonstrate how the readings should be obtained in the activity before students do the activity for themselves. Help students with the calculations of the surface areas of the different sides of the sponge.

Ask more confident students to work without access to the Student's Book or Worksheet 1.4b. They should plan and carry out their own investigations to discover how the surface area affects the speed with which a sponge can soak up water.

Extension ideas

Ask students to use secondary sources to find out the names of one or two other specialised plant cells, and how they are adapted for their functions.

Homework suggestions

Students answer questions 4–5 in topic 1.4: Specialised cells in the Workbook.

Ask students to write two short descriptions of how palisade cells and root hair cells are adapted for their functions.

1.4c Specialised animal cells

Students will learn:

- To identify some specialised cells
- To explain how some cells are adapted for certain functions

Glossary words

haemoglobin, specialised cell

Resource preparation

Access to secondary sources of information about specialised animal cells (e.g. internet, books).

For Worksheet 1.4c: scissors, glue.

Worksheet 1.4c

Teaching and learning ideas

- Ask students to explain how a palisade cell is adapted for its function and reinforce the idea that it contains a lot of chloroplasts to help it make its food. Remind students of the parts of animal cells and what the parts do.
- Read through the section on specialised animal cells in the Student's Book. Encourage students to answer the questions as they come to them.
- Ask students to spot the difference in the way that the neurone and the ciliated epithelial cells have been drawn and the two blood cells (in figure 1.24). Point out that the latter two show the outsides of the cells but the neurone and ciliated epithelial cell have been drawn in cross-section to show some of the internal features of the cells. Then ask students to spot the parts of the cell that they would expect to find in neurones and ciliated epithelial cells but which are not shown. Elicit the idea that the mitochondria have not been shown (which is often the case in simplified drawings of cells). Point out to students that these drawings are models; they are useful for explanations but are simplifications of what real cells are like.
- Worksheet 1.4c contains drawings of specialised plant and animal cells for students to name and explain how they are adapted for their functions.
- Finish by asking students to make a labelled diagram of a ciliated epithelial cell, pointing out its features and how these are adaptations for its function.

Differentiation

For less confident students, go through the words and phrases on Worksheet 1.4c one at a time and discuss where each label should go. Then ask the students to complete their own sheets.

For more confident students, remove the list of functions in the bottom two rows of the grid at the bottom of Worksheet 1.4c.

Extension ideas

Ask students to use secondary sources to find out the names of one or two other specialised animal cells, and how they are adapted for their functions.

Homework suggestions

Students answer questions 6–8 in topic 1.4: Specialised cells in the Workbook.

Ask students to write two short descriptions of how red blood cells and ciliated epithelial cells are adapted for their functions.

Chapter 1 Checking students' progress

End of chapter reflection
- To review the learning points of the topic
- To test understanding through answering questions

Resources
- Student's Book [End of chapter review questions]
- Workbook [Self-assessment grid, Test-style questions]
- Worksheets 1.1c(1), 1.1c(2), 1.1c(3), 1.2b, 1.3c, 1.4b, 1.4c [all of which may have already been used]

Approach

Ask students to complete the self-assessment section at the end of Chapter 1 in the Workbook. Encourage students to work together in small groups to discuss which aspects of the material are the most difficult to understand, and then have a class vote.

Use the Student's Book pages to go through aspects of the work that students have identified as difficult, using the worksheets listed above as necessary.

Ask students to complete some or all of the end of chapter review questions in the Student's Book. These can be gone through orally in class, or students could be given specific questions to answer in their books.

Ask students to work together in groups to develop a concept map for the learning in this chapter. Use the word 'organism' at the centre of the map and then ask students to build links to other words and phrases from that. Details and ideas for how to construct concept maps are easily found on the internet.

Use the Context worksheet (Worksheet 1.5) as a framework for students to conduct their own research enquiries about cells and/or microscope development. This activity provides the opportunity to cover the following learning objectives: 7SIC.01 and 7SIC.02. For example, students could focus on how the development of lenses and microscopes (from the 16th century until today) has led to our increased knowledge about the structure of cells and the differences between plants, animals, bacteria and other microorganisms.

Finish by asking students to complete the test-style questions at the end of Chapter 1 in the Workbook. Provide feedback on students' answers, and work with students to identify areas that still need more work.

Chapter 2   Microorganisms

Chapter overview

In this chapter students will learn about microorganisms, how they decay matter and the diseases that they cause. This includes study of the work of Louis Pasteur. Students will also identify some uses of microorganisms. This chapter builds on ideas about diseases and keeping healthy, met earlier stages of their education, with the focus now being more on how some diseases are caused.

Topic title	Number of 40-minute periods	Learning Objectives	Thinking and Working Scientifically Learning Objectives
2.1 Types of microorganisms	2	7Bs.01 Understand that all organisms are made of cells and microorganisms are typically single celled.	7TWSc.06 Evaluate a range of secondary information sources for their relevance and know that some sources may be biased. 7TWSc.02 Decide what equipment is required to carry out an investigation or experiment and use it appropriately. 7TWSc.05 Carry out practical work safely 7TWSc.07 Collect and record sufficient observations and/or measurements in an appropriate form 7TWSp.04 Plan a range of investigations of different types, while considering variables appropriately, and recognise that not all investigations can be fair tests.
2.2 Microorganisms and decay	2	7Be.01 Know and describe the ecological role some microorganisms have as decomposers. 7Be.02 Construct and interpret food chains and webs which include microorganisms as decomposers.	7TWSp.01 Identify whether a given hypothesis is testable. 7TWSp.02 Describe how scientific hypotheses can be supported or contradicted by evidence from an enquiry. 7TWSp.03 Make predictions of likely outcomes for a scientific enquiry based on scientific knowledge and understanding.
End of chapter questions	1	Check students' progress	

Background science

Please note: the background science notes are designed to provide teachers with an overview of the science concepts students may have already been taught earlier in their education, are likely to be taught in this unit and are likely to be taught in later stages. They are not a checklist of the content to be covered by the teacher in each unit.

The background science notes also serve to provide the teacher with some understanding of the background science needed in order to deliver the content of each chapter.

In this chapter, students look at the 'scientific method' in a little more depth, by studying the work of Louis Pasteur who used experimental evidence to show that foods spoiled due to microorganisms from the air. This went against the prevailing belief at the time that foods created any organisms that were found within them (the idea of 'spontaneous generation'). Students can use secondary sources of information to discover how Joseph Lister used Pasteur's experiments to develop modern surgery. Activity 2.3 reinforces the four stages of the scientific method.

Microorganisms are a more abstract concept for students because they can only be seen using microscopes. While mould fungi and yeast can be seen using a school microscope, these microscopes are not generally powerful enough to observe bacteria in any meaningful way, and are nowhere near powerful enough to see viruses.

In this chapter, we classify viruses, bacteria and some types of fungi as 'microorganisms' and can only be seen with a microscope. It is important for students to remember that not all fungi are microorganisms. However, all bacteria are. Viruses are also too small to be seen without the aid of a very powerful microscope, and technically they are not living because they cannot replicate unless they are inside another living cell. This means that scientists do not like the term 'microorganism' being used to describe them. They often prefer the term 'microbe' to be used for viruses, bacteria and some fungi, and the term 'microorganism' to refer to those microbes that show all seven life processes (i.e. bacteria and some fungi). Students are not expected to know about any of these distinctions, and often the terms 'microbe' and 'microorganism' are used interchangeably. However, students may come across the term 'microbe' if they are doing research using secondary sources. Students will have covered microorganisms as causes of disease at earlier stages of their education. In this chapter, students are reminded that microorganisms cause food spoilage. They then build upon their knowledge, in part 2.2c, by thinking about decay as a use of microorganisms.

There are other microorganisms that are not described in this chapter, notably those that belong to the protoctist or protist kingdom. These include algae and *Plasmodium* (the microorganism responsible for malaria). Students do not need to know this at Stage 7.

Topic overview

		Student's Book	Workbook	Downloadable material
2.1a	**Starting point** This short activity reminds students of life processes and the concept of an organism, and extends this to introduce microorganisms	Starting point table Activity 2.1 Questions 1–3	Questions 1–3	
2.1b	**Fungi** This activity introduces the fungus kingdom and gives students the opportunity to examine fungal cells using a microscope	Questions 4–6 Activity 2.2	Questions 5, 6 and 9	Practical notes 2.1b(1), 2.1b(2) Worksheet 2.1b
2.1c	**Bacteria** This activity introduces bacteria, and students look at some differences between bacterial and fungal cells	Questions 7–9	Questions 4, 7 and 8	Practical notes 2.1c
2.1d	**Viruses** This activity introduces viruses, and students examine the reasons why viruses are not usually considered to be organisms	Questions 10–12	Questions 3 and 8	

Learning Objectives

- 7Bs.01: (Understand that all organisms are made of cells and) microorganisms are typically single celled
- 7TWSc.06: Evaluate a range of secondary information sources for their relevance and know that some sources may be biased
- 7SIC.01: Discuss how scientific knowledge is developed through collective understanding and scrutiny over time.

- 7SIC.02: Describe how science is applied across societies and industries, and in research.
- 7SIC.04: Describe how people develop and use scientific understanding as individuals and through collaboration, e.g. through peer review
- 7SIC.05: Discuss how the uses of science can have a global environmental impact.

Links to other topics

- Biology 1.1 Characteristics of living things is essential prior understanding.
- Biology 1.3d Using a microscope needs to have been covered in Chapter 1. Worksheet 2b can be used as a reminder of how to use a microscope.
- Biology 1.3e 'Unicellular and multicellular organisms' is essential prior understanding.

Science in context

- The Science in context boxes 'Inventing antibiotics' and 'Using chlorine' in Topic 2.1 in the Student's Book cover the following learning objectives:
  - 7SIC.01 Discuss how scientific knowledge is developed through collective understanding and scrutiny over time.
  - 7SIC.02 Describe how science is applied across societies and industries, and in research.
  - 7SIC.04 Describe how people develop and use scientific understanding as individuals and through collaboration, e.g. through peer review
  - 7SIC.05 Discuss how the uses of science can have a global environmental impact.

- Look out for opportunities to describe how chemicals produced by some microorganisms can be used to kill harmful insect infestations, moulds and fungi on food crops. The microorganisms that produce these chemicals are called 'biocontrols'. Two examples of using microorganisms as biocontrols are using yeasts to stop mould disease on grapes and bacteria to stop white mould growth which can destroy more than 400 types of plant. Supporting resources are available from the American Phytopathical Society at: https://www.apsnet.org, using the keyword 'biocontrol'.

Common misunderstandings

- Many students think that fungi are plants. Ensure that students realise that fungi are in a different group of organisms from plants and animals. Although some of them may look like plants (and many moulds are green), ensure students realise that fungi do not make their own food (like plants do) and that the green colour of some moulds is nothing to do with chloroplasts.

2.1a Starting point

Resource preparation

Access to secondary sources of information about microorganisms (e.g. internet, books).

Ask students to list the seven life processes. Introduce the prefix 'micro' meaning 'very small'. Remind students of the 'microscope' and that it is a piece of equipment that enables us to see very small things. Then ask students to invent definitions for the word 'microorganism'. Ask students for their suggestions and establish the idea that a microorganism is a living thing, which carries out all seven life processes but which needs a microscope to be seen.

For more confident students, introduce the micrometre (symbol μm). There are 1000 μm in 1 mm (millimetre).

Activity 2.1 *Investigating microorganisms* in the Student's Book. Ask students to use the Student's Book and/or secondary sources to find out about microorganisms and prepare a table. Some students may need help with the table headings:

Type of microorganism	Example of microorganism	How this microorganism is useful or harmful	Where I got this information

2.1b Fungi

Students will learn:

- To describe what microorganisms are like
- To describe different types of microorganism
- To outline plans to carry out investigations
- To choose appropriate apparatus and use it correctly
- To make careful observations
- To carry out practical work safely

Glossary words

cell, evaluate, fungus/fungi, life process, magnify, microbe, microorganism, microscope, mould, organism, spore, yeast

Resource preparation

For Activity 2.2: microscope, pre-prepared slides of fungal cells (mould, yeast cells), light source, slides, coverslips, mounted needles/toothpicks, stain (e.g. methylene blue), dropper, forceps/tweezers, mouldy food (e.g. bread), disinfectant, face mask, clear nail varnish, transparent ruler (optional).

For demonstration of mould: mouldy food (e.g. bread) sealed in a clear plastic bag. This can easily be prepared by placing some bread in a clear, sealable bag together with a few drops of water. Prick 4–5 holes in the bag using a pin to ensure that some oxygen can get into the bag in order to prevent the growth of potentially harmful anaerobic bacteria. Leave the bag in a warm dark place for a week. Once the mould has grown, do not open the bag and do not allow students to open it.

For activity on investigating yeast cells see Practical notes 2.1b(2). You will need: pre-prepared slides of yeast, microscopes, sources of light. To prepare yeast slides you will need: bread yeast, sugar, flask, slides, droppers, stain, clear nail varnish, mounted needle.

Microscope images (micrographs) of mould and mould spores downloaded from the internet.

Worksheet 2.1b

Practical notes 2.1b(1), 2.1b(2)

Teaching and learning ideas

- Ask students to name or describe a fungus. Some might mention mushrooms or toadstools. Explain that some fungi are large and can be seen but others are very small and are examples of microorganisms.

- Remind students of the seven life processes and explain that microorganisms carry out the life processes but are too small to be seen without a microscope.

- Introduce mould as an example of a microorganism which is a fungus and ask students what mould looks like. Explain that we can see mould only when enough of the fungus has grown in the same place.

- Show students a sample of mouldy food (e.g. bread), which has been sealed in a clear plastic bag. Do not open the bag or allow students to do so.

- Ask students to think about where moulds and other fungi are found. Establish that they are most often found in dark, damp and warm places and these are the best growing conditions for fungi.

- Together with students, look at the first section in the Student's Book and the next section on 'Fungi'. Encourage students to answer the questions (1–6).

- Activity 2.2 *Investigating mould* in the Student's Book. Ask students what piece of apparatus they will need to observe microorganisms in more detail and establish that this is the function of a microscope. Students can use Worksheet 2.1b to remind themselves how to use a microscope. Further details are given in Practical notes 2.1b(1). Students should be able to see long strands (called hyphae). These consist of one or more mould cells, which contain nuclei. Note that students need to be given pre-prepared slides – they should not prepare their own slides. If the students study mould they should make a drawing of its cells if they can see them. A fungus cell has a cell wall, cytoplasm, nucleus and cell membrane. Students may not be able to see all of these, especially the nucleus. If students can see individual cells they may be able to see that they are different from plant cells because they do not have a large vacuole or chloroplasts. Note that many hyphal cells can contain more than one nucleus, which is best not mentioned at this stage.

- Show students microscope images of mould (downloaded from the internet). Use search terms such as 'micrograph mould hyphae' to find appropriate images. Establish the idea that these branches grow into a food source and break it down as the mould feeds.

- Show students microscope images of mould spores. Point out that most of these spores are only about 0.003–0.04 mm in diameter. They are very small and very light and so easily carried in the air.

- Challenge some students to convert these measurements into micrometres (μm). Work with students to calculate the magnifications of the spores in the images.

- Finish by asking each student to prepare a list of key facts about fungi. Then ask them to work together in groups to produce combined lists. Ask random groups to share their lists with the class, and correct any misconceptions as they arise.

Differentiation

For less confident students, go through the words on Worksheet 2.1b one step at a time, with students copying what you have done after each step.

Activity – Investigating yeast cells. Ask more confident students to look at yeast cells using a microscope. Details are given in Practical notes 2.1b(2). Students may be able to see some yeast cells forming 'buds'. These are how yeast cells reproduce – a bud grows out of a cell and then breaks off to form a new cell.

Extension ideas

Challenge students to use a transparent ruler to measure the width of the lit area that they can see when looking through a microscope (the 'field of view'). Ask them to use this to estimate the sizes of some of the things that they observe (e.g. the width of a hypha).

Alternatively, challenge students to work out the magnifications that they are using on the microscopes. The total magnification of a microscope is worked out by multiplying the magnification of the objective lens by the magnification of the eyepiece lens. For example, a ×5 eyepiece lens and a ×10 objective lens will give an overall magnification of ×50.

Homework suggestions

Ask students to write a paragraph to explain why some fungi are microorganisms and some are not.

2.1c Bacteria

Students will learn:

- To describe what microorganisms are like
- To describe different types of microorganism
- To make careful observations

Glossary words

bacteria/bacterium

Resource preparation

For the demonstration: bacterial colony (or live yoghurt), inoculating (wire) loop, meat stock (bouillon) cube/microbiological nutrient extract, Petri dish(es), sticky tape, agar or gelatine powder, saucepan/large beaker, Bunsen burner or other source of heat, thermometer, incubator, autoclave. (An alternative is to buy commercially prepared nutrient agar plates.) For disposal of plates, if an autoclave is not available to sterilise the plates when you have finished with them, they can be submerged in a bucket of disinfectant. Further details are in Practical notes 2.1c.

For demonstration: Step 3 in Practical notes 2.1c suggests the preparation of a nutrient agar plate that has been swiped through before being incubated. This will allow students to see the variety of microorganisms that are found in the air. You may wish to prepare this a week or so before the lesson.

High-power microscope images (micrographs) of bacteria downloaded from the internet, showing different shapes (e.g. *Coccus*, *Bacillus*).

Access to secondary sources of information about bacterial and fungal cells (e.g. internet, books).

Practical notes 2.1c

Teaching and learning ideas

- Ask students to name some different microorganisms. Establish the idea that bacteria are one type of microorganism.
- Together with students, look at the section in the Student's Book on 'Bacteria'. Encourage students to answer the questions (7–9).
- Demonstration – Investigating bacteria. This demonstration will allow students to see first-hand what bacteria look like when billions of them grow together. Details are given in Practical notes 2.1c. Show students the dish prepared by streaking nutrient agar. Students should be able to see round 'colonies' of bacteria growing on the agar in the final set of streaks. Ask students how they would examine the bacteria in more detail and establish that a microscope is used. Tell students, however, that bacteria are so small that they can't be seen very well using a school microscope. (You may also wish to show students the dish of nutrient agar containing fungi and bacteria from the air that is prepared in Step 3 in the Practical notes 2.2b.)
- Show students high-power microscope images of bacteria (e.g. downloaded from the internet). Ask students why bacteria don't have tissues and establish that bacteria (unlike plants and animals) only ever have one cell. Point out the different shapes that bacteria can have and tell students that most are 0.0002–0.002 mm in diameter and the ones that have elongated shapes are rarely longer than about 0.02 mm.
- Challenge some students to convert these measurements into micrometres (μm). Work with students to calculate the magnifications of the images.
- Finish by asking each student to state one way in which bacteria are different from fungi and one way in which they are similar. Ask for suggestions and write the correct ones on the board. Ideas might include:
  - differences, such as: bacteria only ever have one cell and fungi often have more; bacteria and fungi belong to different groups of organisms (kingdoms); bacteria are smaller than fungi.
  - similarities, such as: bacteria and fungi both have cells; bacteria and fungi both need a source of food (they don't make their own).

Differentiation

Remind less confident students of their work on cells in Chapter 1 and what a cell is. Explain that although bacteria may grow together in large clumps, all those cells are not working together and so a large clump of bacteria is not a tissue.

Ask more confident students to explain the processes by which a single bacterium forms a colony when growing on nutrient agar.

Extension ideas

Ask students to find out how the cells of bacteria are different from the cells of fungi (e.g. bacteria don't have a nucleus and have a different type of cell wall).

Cambridge Lower Secondary Biology Stage 7

Homework suggestions

Ask students to describe, in a single sentence, what is meant by the word 'bacterium'.

2.1d Viruses

Students will learn:

- To describe what microorganisms are like
- To describe different types of microorganism

Glossary words

virus

Resource preparation

Very high power (electron) micrographs of viruses downloaded from the internet.

Access to secondary sources of information about microscopes and viruses (e.g. internet, books).

Teaching and learning ideas

- Together with students, look at the section in the Student's Book on 'Viruses'. Encourage students to answer questions 10, 11 and 12. Students may need access to secondary sources in order to answer the last question.
- Discuss with students the idea that viruses can only replicate when they are inside a living cell. For this reason, many scientists do not think that they are organisms. So we refer to 'virus particles' rather than 'virus cells'.
- Show students high-power microscope images of viruses (e.g. downloaded from the internet). Tell students that most virus particles are 0.00002–0.0004 mm in diameter.
- Challenge some students to convert these measurements into micrometres (μm). Work with students to calculate the magnifications of the images.
- Compare the magnifications of the virus images with those of the bacteria and the yeast. Establish that in general terms yeasts are larger than bacteria, which are larger than viruses.
- Finish by asking each student to come up with a key fact about each of the three types of microorganism. Ask students to share their ideas with the class and write them on the board to build up a table of key facts about each of the microorganisms. Correct misconceptions as they arise.

Differentiation

Help less confident students interpret the images of viruses by comparing their size to the width of a human hair, which varies from about 0.04 mm to 0.12 mm in diameter. That makes the largest virus particles 100 times smaller than the thinnest human hair.

Ask more confident students to explain why virus particles cannot be grown by scientists on nutrient agar (in the way that fungi and bacteria can).

Homework suggestions

Students answer the questions in topic 2.1: Types of microorganisms in the Workbook.

Ask students to write a question about microorganisms worth 2 marks. They should supply mark schemes with their questions. If time allows, get students to try out their questions on one another in the next lesson. Ask students to work together to improve their questions, answers and mark schemes.

2.2 Microorganisms and decay

Topic overview

		Student's Book	Workbook	Downloadable material
2.2a	**Starting point** This short activity allows students to demonstrate their understanding of why foods spoil and of the scientific method	Starting point table		
2.2b	**Pasteur and the scientific method** This activity examines how Louis Pasteur used the scientific method in order to develop his ideas about microorganisms causing food to spoil	Questions 1–5 Activity 2.3	Questions 1, 2 and 5–8	Worksheets 2.2b(1), 2.2b(2) Practical notes 2.2b
2.2c	**Decay** This activity looks at the importance of decay and the role of microorganisms as decomposers in food chains	Questions 6–17 Activity 2.4	Questions 3, 4 and 9–19	

Learning Objectives

- 7Be.01: Know and describe the ecological role some microorganisms have as decomposers
- 7Be.02: Construct and interpret food chains and webs which include microorganisms as decomposers
- 7TWSp.01: Identify whether a given hypothesis is testable
- 7TWSp.02: Describe how scientific hypotheses can be supported or contradicted by evidence from an enquiry
- 7TWSp.03: Make predictions of likely outcomes for a scientific enquiry based on scientific knowledge and understanding
- 7SIC.01: Discuss how scientific knowledge is developed through collective understanding and scrutiny over time.
- 7SIC.02: Describe how science is applied across societies and industries, and in research.

Science in context

- The Science in context: Preserving food box in Topic 2.2 of the Student's Book covers the following learning objectives:
  - 7SIC.01 Discuss how scientific knowledge is developed through collective understanding and scrutiny over time.
  - 7SIC.02 Describe how science is applied across societies and industries, and in research.
- Look out for opportunities to discuss how microorganisms acting as decomposers are important in recycling plant-based packaging materials, which include paper, cardboard and some types of plastic. Decomposition of biodegradable materials by microorganisms is beneficial because it reduces environmental damage caused by the creation of landfill sites to dispose of non-biodegradable material, and reduces the harmful effects of plastics in the environment. Resources to support this discussion are available from the Royal Society of Biology via http://www.scibermonkey.org and the Microbiology Society https://microbiologysociety.org.

Links to other topics

- Microorganisms' involvement in decay, that releases nutrients back into the environment, is relevant to Stage 8 Chapter 3, Topic 2 'Bioaccumulation in food chains'.

Cambridge Lower Secondary Biology Stage 7

2.2a Starting point

Ask students to list some foods that 'go off' or 'spoil' quite quickly. Ask them what sort of microorganisms they think cause this. Establish the idea that fungi, such as moulds, often cause foods to spoil and introduce the idea that bacteria can as well. Viruses do not cause food to spoil.

Ask students how scientists work to find out about things. Look back the 'Working as a scientist' section in Chapter 1 of the Student's Book to remind students of previous work, and how scientists ask questions, design experiments, make predictions and then use their evidence to make conclusions.

2.2b Louis Pasteur and the scientific method

Students will learn:

- To describe the role ecological role of microorganisms as decomposers
- To describe the common stages of scientific investigations
- To be able to talk about the importance of questions, evidence and explanations
- To make predictions and review them against evidence
- To suggest hypotheses that may be tested
- To predict likely outcomes for a scientific enquiry
- To identify appropriate evidence to collect and suitable methods of collection
- To make conclusions from collected data
- To consider explanations for predictions using scientific knowledge and understanding and communicate these

Glossary words

conclusion, evidence, hypothesis, Louis Pasteur, prediction, scientific method, scientific question

Resource preparation

For activity: clear liquid broth (could also use stock made up from stock cubes), boiling tubes, bungs, short delivery tubes, S-shaped delivery tubes, autoclave, water bath.

For demonstration: plate containing nutrient agar and growing microorganisms from the air (prepared in 2.1c. See Practical notes 2.1c).

For Activity 2.3: access to secondary sources of information about Joseph Lister (e.g. internet, books).

Worksheets 2.2b(1), 2.2b(2)

Practical notes 2.2b

Teaching and learning ideas

- Remind students that scientists ask questions about the world around them. They then think up ideas to answer their questions and test those ideas using experiments. Point out to students that only questions that can be answered by doing experiments or making observations are scientific. Ask students to invent some scientific questions. Ideas should be simple and based on observations that students make in their daily lives, such as 'Why are plants green?'
- Remind students that foods often go bad when microorganisms feed, reproduce and grow on them. However, some foods are spoiled when larger organisms feed on them. Give students the example of meat being spoiled by maggots.
- Tell students that until about 350 years ago, people thought that meat got maggots in it because the meat made the maggots. Ask students where maggots come from and establish that it is flies that lay their eggs on the meat, and the eggs hatch into maggots.
- Worksheet 2.2b(1) describes the scientific method and provides an opportunity to look at the work of Francesco Redi (who showed that meat did not create maggots). Help less confident students to construct the flow chart for question 2 on the board.

- Tell students that although scientists accepted Redi's ideas about larger organisms, until about 150 years ago many still thought that foods such as soup spoiled because the soup created microorganisms in it.
- Together with students, look at the first section in the Student's Book and the next section on 'Scientific method'. Encourage students to answer the questions (1–5).
- Students may benefit from thinking of predictions being phrased using 'If … then …' For example: If I add fertiliser to my plants, then they will grow faster.
- Activity – Pasteur's experiment. Ask students how they could test Pasteur's ideas. Then give students Worksheet 2.2b(2), which contains instructions on setting up two tubes of clear soup to recreate one of Pasteur's experiments. Further details are given in Practical notes 2.2b. This could just be done as a demonstration. Remind students about spores (from the previous topic) and how they will allow fungi to grow in the broth. Bacteria are single-celled and very light and so will also be carried in the air.
- Demonstration – Investigating bacteria. This demonstration will allow students to appreciate the variety of bacteria and fungal spores in the air. Details are given in Practical notes 2.1c. Show students the dish prepared by sweeping an open dish of nutrient agar through the air. Students should be able to see round 'colonies' of bacteria growing on the agar and there will probably be some fungal colonies as well (e.g. mould).
- Activity 2.3 *Investigating Joseph Lister* in the Student's Book. This is a research activity and students will need access to secondary sources. Help students to structure their reports as a single paragraph. They should use sentences that answer the questions in the bullet points.
- Finish by asking students to draw a flow chart to show the scientific method. They should then compare their work with the flow chart on Worksheet 2.2b(1) and make corrections as necessary.

Differentiation

For less confident students, go through the flow chart on Worksheet 2.2b(1) one step at a time, ensuring that students understand the purpose of each step. Reinforce this work by writing the steps from the flow chart on cards or small pieces of paper, and challenge students to use them to recreate the flow chart.

Challenge more confident students to think up a question and then plan how to answer it using steps from the scientific method.

Homework suggestions

Ask students to copy and adapt the flow chart on Worksheet 2.2b(1) to show how Pasteur gathered evidence that microorganisms from the air spoil soup.

2.2c Decay

Students will learn:

- To describe the ecological role of microorganisms as decomposers

Glossary words

decay, decomposer

Resource preparation

Mouldy food (e.g. bread) sealed in a clear plastic bag (as used in 2.1b). Do not open the bag. Alternatively use a photo of mouldy food.

Photo of a compost heap or manure or other fertiliser made using plant or animal waste (e.g. downloaded from the internet).

Teaching and learning ideas

- Show students some mouldy food or pictures of mouldy food, and ask them what is growing on the food. Revise ideas about food going off from topic 2.1. Establish the idea that the mould growing on the food is decaying the food, and acting as a decomposer. Tell students that bacteria will be doing the same job, but they are much more difficult to spot on decaying food.
- Ask students how decay could be useful. Establish the idea that the decay of dead plants and animal wastes returns nutrients to the soil and gets rid of the waste material. Include a discussion about the role of decomposers and examples including fungi.
- Together with students, look at the 'Decay' section in the Student's Book. Encourage students to answer questions 6 and 7.
- Finish by showing students a photo of a compost heap or manure (or any other fertiliser made using plant/animal wastes). Ask students to explain why farmers/gardeners want to spread this type of material on their land, and how spreading the material helps plants to grow.

Differentiation

Before reading through the Student's Book pages, ensure that students understand that although plants make their own food they also need very small amounts of other substances (mineral salts) from the soil. These substances are released from waste materials by decomposers.

Challenge more confident students to plan a method for the investigation outlined in question 7 in the Student's Book.

Homework suggestions

Students answer the questions in topic 2.2: Microorganisms and decay in the Workbook.

Ask students to write an overview of the problems and uses of microorganisms. They should write two short paragraphs, giving examples.

Chapter 2 | Checking students' progress

End of chapter reflection

- To review the learning points of the topic
- To test understanding through answering questions

Resources

- Student's Book [End of chapter review questions]
- Workbook [Self-assessment grid, Test-style questions]
- Worksheets 2.2b(1) and 2.2b(2) [which may have already been used]

Approach

Ask students to complete the self-assessment section at the end of Chapter 2 in the Workbook. Encourage students to work together in small groups to discuss which aspects of the material are the most difficult to understand, and then have a class vote.

Use the Student's Book pages to go through aspects of the work that students have identified as difficult, using the worksheets listed above as necessary.

Ask students to complete some or all of the end of chapter review questions in the Student's Book. These can be gone through orally in class, or students could be given specific questions to answer in their books.

Ask students to individually write a question about microorganisms on the right-hand side of a slip of paper and the answer on the left. Students then cut or tear the slips of paper into two. Ask them to place all the questions in one box and all the answers in another box. Mix the pieces of paper in each box and then ask each student to take a random question and a random answer. Ask one student to stand and read out their question. The person with the answer then stands and reads out the answer. Establish that this is the correct answer and then ask that student to read out their question. Sometimes, more than one student will stand with the correct answer. Where this happens, check that both answers are correct and then choose just one student to ask their question. The other student can stand again later on. Continue until all the questions and answers have been used. Correct misconceptions in the questions and in the answers as they arise.

Finish by asking students to complete the test-style questions at the end of Chapter 2 in the Workbook. Provide feedback on students' answers, and work with students to identify areas that still need more work.

Cambridge Lower Secondary Biology
Stage 7

Chapter 3 | Classification

Chapter overview

In this chapter students will investigate variation within animals and plants. They will learn about species and how organisms are classified into groups. This chapter builds on students' skills of observation used to group living and non-living things in earlier stages of their education. Students will learn how to identify organisms using biological keys.

Topic title	Number of 40-minute periods	Learning Objectives	Thinking and Working Scientifically Learning Objectives
3.1 Classifying organisms	1	7Bp.01 Describe the seven characteristics of living organisms. 7Bp.02 Discuss reasons for classifying viruses as living or non-living. 7Bp.03 Describe a species as a group of organisms that can reproduce to produce fertile offspring.	7TWSc.01 Sort, group and classify phenomena, objects, materials and organisms through testing, observation, using secondary information, and making and using keys.
3.2 Biological keys	1	7Bp.04 Use and construct dichotomous keys to classify species and groups of related organisms.	7TWSc.01 Sort, group and classify phenomena, objects, materials and organisms through testing, observation, using secondary information, and making and using keys.
End of chapter questions	1	Check students' progress	

Background science

Please note: the background science notes are designed to provide teachers with an overview of the science concepts students may have already been taught earlier in their education, are likely to be taught in this unit and are likely to be taught in later stages. They are not a checklist of the content to be covered by the teacher in each unit.

The background science notes also serve to provide the teacher with some understanding of the background science needed in order to deliver the content of each chapter.

Organisms are classified into different groups using common features. The largest groups are called kingdoms and at this level students should be aware of the five kingdoms: animals, plants, fungi, prokaryotes (bacteria) and protista/protists/protoctists (the students do not need to know details of this last group as it can often be confusing). The animal kingdom may then be split into vertebrates (have a backbone or spinal column) and invertebrates (no backbone). The vertebrates are then grouped into classes, called fish, amphibians, reptiles, birds and mammals. There are many sub-groups of invertebrates but students should learn about the arthropods, which include insects and spiders (arachnids).

Grouping organisms means they can be identified using biological keys. Students will gain experience of using dichotomous keys to classify species. This system of classification was initially developed by Carl Linnaeus, a Swedish scientist whom students will have the opportunity to find out about using secondary sources of information.

The definition of species at this level should be the idea that a species is a group of organisms that can breed to produce offspring that are also able to reproduce. This definition is not entirely accurate and it is now more common to define a species by their DNA. However, this idea is not necessary at this level as it can get very complicated.

To investigate variation with a species, we make making observations about how members of a species are similar or different. Variation within a species is caused by genes, the environment, or a combination of both. At this stage it is not necessary to discuss genetic or environmental effects. Students will look at variation in more detail in Stage 9.

Viruses are extremely small infectious agents that are usually only visible using powerful electron microscopes. They can assume a wide range of shapes but a single virus particle (which is called a 'virion') generally has an outer layer of fat covering a protein coat inside which is a strand or strands of genes.

Viruses are unable to reproduce independently, they can't move on their own or grow bigger. They have to use proteins in the host cell and the cell's respiration to provide energy for replication. They don't excrete waste and it is not clear if viruses can detect changes in their surroundings. These factors mean that there is debate between scientists about whether viruses are living organisms. Some scientists believe that the combination of virus and host cell makes the virus a living organism, and that the virus particle outside a cell is just a step involved in the virus being able to spread once it enters the host cell.

Topic overview

		Student's Book	Workbook	Downloadable material
3.1a	**Starting point** This short activity provides the opportunity for students to demonstrate their understanding of the word variation and to make observations of variation	Starting point table		
3.1b	**Variation of characteristics** This activity provides the opportunity for students to study individuals of a single type of organism and observe variation between them	Questions 1–2		Practical notes 3.1b Worksheet 3.1b
3.1c	**Kingdoms** This activity provides the opportunity for students to study the main kingdoms and reasons why we group organisms	Questions 3–6	Questions 1–4	Practical notes 3.1c Worksheet 3.1c
3.1d	**Vertebrates and invertebrates** This activity focuses on the difference between vertebrates and invertebrates and how these groups can be further split	Questions 7–19	Questions 5–8	Practical notes 3.1d Worksheets 3.1d(1), 3.1d(2)
3.1e	**Carl Linnaeus**	Activity 3.1		
3.1f	**Species** This activity provides the opportunity for students to find out about one species of animal that interests them	Questions 24–27 Activity 3.2 Question 28	Questions 9–12, 14	Worksheet 3.1f
3.1g	**Viruses** This activity allows students to develop an understanding of why viruses are difficult to classify as living things	Questions 29–32	Question 13	

Learning Objectives

- 7Bp.01: Describe the seven characteristics of living organisms
- 7Bp.02: Discuss reasons for classifying viruses as living or non-living
- 7Bp.03: Describe a species as a group of organisms that can reproduce to produce fertile offspring
- 7TWSc.01: Sort, group and classify phenomena, objects, materials and organisms through testing, observation, using secondary information, and making and using keys

- 7SIC.01 Discuss how scientific knowledge is developed through collective understanding and scrutiny over time.
- 7SIC.02 Describe how science is applied across societies and industries, and in research.
- 7SIC.03 Evaluate issues which involve and/or require scientific understanding.
- 7SIC.04 Describe how people develop and use scientific understanding as individuals and through collaboration, e.g. through peer review

Science in context

- The Science in context: Is a virus alive? box in Topic 3.1 of the Student's Book covers the following learning objectives:
  - 7SIC.01 Discuss how scientific knowledge is developed through collective understanding and scrutiny over time.
  - 7SIC.02 Describe how science is applied across societies and industries, and in research.

Cambridge Lower Secondary Biology
Stage 7

- — 7SIC.03 Evaluate issues which involve and/or require scientific understanding.
- — 7SIC.04 Describe how people develop and use scientific understanding as individuals and through collaboration, e.g. through peer review
- Scientists use a process called 'evaluation' to answer questions such as 'is a virus alive or not?' Other issues that require scientific understanding to evaluate include 'will we ever cure cancer for good'? or 'are we alone in the universe?'

Links to other topics

- The content of this chapter is built upon in Stage 9, when students consider the causes of variation (Chapter 3 Topic 1) and then how variation can affect how well organisms survive when conditions change (Chapter 3 Topic 5).

Common misunderstandings

- Many students think that 'plants' and 'animals' are the only two kingdoms. Remind them of their work in Chapter 2 on microorganisms, and point out that fungi and bacteria are in their own kingdoms (they are neither plants nor animals).

3.1a Starting point

Resource preparation

Image of a group of animals; they should be of the same type (species) and familiar to the students.

Show students an image of a group of animals. Ask the students to work in small groups. They should list the features (characteristics) of the animals, dividing the list into two groups: features that are similar, features that are different. Use their ideas to discuss how individuals in a group of animals of the same type can be very similar but they do have features that make them look different. Establish with students that differences in features are called variation.

3.1b Variation of characteristics

Students will learn:

- To use sources of information to classify organisms based on their characteristics
- To make careful observations
- To use information from secondary sources

Glossary words

cell, classification, characteristic, nucleus, variation

Resource preparation

For Worksheet 3.1b: images of different animals and plants or examples of plants showing variation

Worksheet 3.1b

Practical notes 3.1b

Teaching and learning ideas

- Ask students what word we use to describe differences between things. Remind students of the word 'variation'.
- Together with students, look at the section titled 'Variation of characteristics' in the Student's Book. Ensure that students understand the term 'characteristic'. Encourage students to answer questions 1–2.
- Activity – Ask students to look at sets of images around the room of different animals and plants. They should work in pairs to aid discussion. Each set should show images of two or more organisms from the same species. Students use Worksheet 3.1b to make observations and answer questions about the organisms. See Practical notes 3.1b.
- Ask each pair to report back to the class about the observations they have made.
- Challenge students to suggest whether there is more variation between organisms of the same type or organisms of different types.
- Finish by showing students some of the images again (or new images) and ask students to point out characteristics and variation between those characteristics.

Differentiation

Less confident students may need some help when making their observations; before starting the activity they could be given a list of features to look for, for example, size, colour, number of leaves on a plant.

More confident students could be asked to look at the images and design their own tables to show characteristics and variation in those characteristics.

Homework suggestions

Ask students to list the variation in characteristics that they see within their family, and how are they similar and different from each other. Be aware that family may not be a good choice for some students so alternatives could be simply the people they share a home with or their friends.

3.1c Kingdoms

Students will learn:

- To use sources of information to classify organisms based on their characteristics
- To make careful observations
- To use information from secondary sources

Glossary words

animal kingdom, kingdom, plant kingdom

Resource preparation

Images or specimens of different animals and plants that can be used to group organisms into kingdoms.

Access to secondary sources of information about the classification of organisms (e.g. internet, books).

Worksheet 3.1c

Practical notes 3.1c

Teaching and learning ideas

- Together with students, look at the first section of the Student's Book, down to the 'Vertebrates and invertebrates' section. Encourage students to answer the questions.
- Show students an image of an animal they would not be familiar with. Ask students which kingdom they would put it in and why. Repeat with an image of a plant.
- Discuss the idea of the five kingdoms of organisms that are commonly used – animals, plants, fungi, prokaryotes (bacteria) and protists/protoctists. Discuss the idea that fungi are organisms like mushrooms and mould that feed on dead parts of plants and animals and their wastes. Point out that all bacteria are in the prokaryotes kingdom, which only contains single-celled organisms that do not have nuclei. The protist/protoctist kingdom is made up of many single-celled organisms and seaweeds, and is not covered in these resources. You could, however, challenge some students to find out more about the features of this kingdom.
- Activity – Ask students to look at the examples around the room of different organisms. They should work in pairs to aid discussion. The examples show images of different organisms that the students then put into the main kingdoms. Students use Worksheet 3.1c to make observations and answer questions about the organisms. See Practical notes 3.1c.
- Challenge students to suggest why fungi were once classified in the plant kingdom. The answer they might find on the internet is that they were considered to be plants because they grew in soil and their cells have cell walls.
- Finish by asking students to draw up a table to show the main features of the plant and animal kingdoms.
- Challenge some students to add information about the fungus and prokaryote (bacteria) kingdoms.

Differentiation

Less confident students should be able to identify the animals and plants but may need some help with classifying the organisms into the other kingdoms. They should be given specimens from the animal or plant kingdoms and some familiar fungi examples such as mushrooms.

More confident students should be given examples of bacteria to group.

Homework suggestions

Workbook questions 1–4 in topic 3.1: Classifying organisms.

3.1d Vertebrates and invertebrates

Students will learn:

- To use sources of information to classify organisms based on their characteristics
- To make careful observations

Glossary words

amphibian, arachnid, arthropod, bird, echinoderm, fish, insect, invertebrate, mammal, mollusc, reptile, vertebrate

Resource preparation

Images or specimens of locally occurring vertebrates that can be put into groups.

Practical notes 3.1d

Worksheets 3.1d(1), 3.1d(2)

Teaching and learning ideas

- Ask students to work in small groups to list as many animals that they can think of that live in your country. They should try to do this at species level if possible using local common names. Then the students should divide their organisms into groups, so that each group of organisms is linked by a common feature. They should feed back their ideas to the class. The activity should result in similar lists but the way students group them may be different.
- Together with students, look at the 'Vertebrates and invertebrates' section in the Student's Book. Encourage students to answer question 7.
- Ask students to work in groups and go back to their lists of local animals. They should split them first into vertebrates and invertebrates. Correct misconceptions as they arise.
- Together with students, look at the 'Vertebrates' section in the Student's Book. Encourage students to answer questions 8–15. Tell students that they can use a mnemonic (such as MRFAB) to remember the names of the five different groups (or 'classes') of vertebrate. Then ask students to sort their vertebrates into these five main groups.
- Activity – In groups, ask students to look at the examples around the room of different organisms. They should work in pairs to aid discussion. The examples show images of different vertebrates, which the students then put into the main classes. Students use question 1 on Worksheet 3.1d(1) to make observations and answer questions about the organisms. See Practical notes 3.1d.
- Challenge students to explain, using the animals' features, why sharks and dolphins are not both in the same class of vertebrates.
- Together with students, look at the 'Invertebrates' section of the Student's Book. Encourage students to answer questions 16–19.
- Discuss the idea that the arthropods can be further split into smaller groups that include insects and arachnids. Ask the students if they know any differences between insects and arachnids (the main difference being insects have six legs and arachnids have eight). Students complete the second section on Worksheet 3.1d(1) (invertebrates).
- Finish by asking students to write down the names of all the different groups of animals that they have met and describe the features of each.

Differentiation

Less confident students may need some help with classifying the organisms into the different vertebrate groups (or 'classes'). They should be given specimens that they are familiar with. Specimens should also be obvious examples of the classes they fit into and need to show clear features.

More confident students should be given some examples that are not as clear. These could include the kiwi (a bird but does not fly and has feathers that look almost hair-like), the pangolin (a mammal that has scales), sharks (fish that have scales that look like skin), and the platypus (a mammal that lays eggs).

Homework suggestions

Workbook questions 5–9 in topic 3.1: Classifying organisms, or the extension activity below.

Worksheet 3.1d(2)

Extension ideas

Ask students to find the names of three other groups of invertebrates and to list some of their characteristics.

3.1e Carl Linnaeus

Students will learn:

- To use sources of information to classify organisms based on their characteristics
- To make observations and measurements

Glossary words

fertile, hybrid, infertile

Resource preparation

Activity 3.1 *How to do research*

Teaching and learning ideas

- Together with students, look at the section in the Student's Book on 'Classifying living things'. Discuss the work of Linnaeus and how he came to develop the idea of using classification keys. Use the search term 'Carl Linnaeus' to find further information on the internet. Also explore the classification of the millions of living organisms that live on Earth today by working down the classification system from kingdom, showing examples of how different organisms fall into different groups due to their different features (there are many classification diagrams available on the internet which you could use to support with this).

Extension ideas

Some students could use secondary sources to do some further research into the work of Carl Linnaeus, looking at the classification system that he developed and considering the different layers of this in more detail.

Homework suggestions

Students should prepare a list of the ways in which a group of students of their age could be similar or different, that is, what features could they look at to identify different individuals. For example, are they male or female?

Students can complete Worksheet 3.1b if this has not been used in class.

3.1f Species

Students will learn:

- To describe what a species is
- To make careful observations
- To use information from secondary sources

Glossary words

offspring, species

Resource preparation

Images of familiar animals, images of animals that are closely related species (e.g. leopard, lion).

Internet access, poster equipment.

Worksheet 3.1f

Teaching and learning ideas

- Tell students that the word 'species' means a specific type of organism. Ask students to list as many species as they can in 2 minutes to see who can list the most. Go through the lists, identifying correct species and different breeds/varieties that students may think are different species (e.g. breeds of cattle). Keep a record of any different breeds/varieties that students have thought were different species.
- Together with students, look at the section titled 'Species' in the Student's Book. Encourage students to answer questions 24–28.
- Show students some images of familiar animals. Explain that the images show animals that can be put into groups called 'species', and reinforce the idea of a species being a group of animals that can reproduce with one another to produce offspring that can also reproduce (fertile offspring).

- Activity – In groups, ask students to research a species of their choice. Students use Worksheet 3.1f to help them. This activity provides the opportunity to cover Learning Objectives 7SIC.02 and 7SIC.05. They should produce a presentation that will explain what is meant by the word species, which species they have chosen and some information about that species.
- Ask each group to present the information they have found to the class.
- Activity 3.2 *Classifying rare species*. Ask the students to complete Activity 3.2 in the Student's Book.
- Finish by asking random students to say what is meant by the term 'species'. Work with students to produce a final, agreed definition on the board.

Differentiation

Less confident students may need some help with their research. They could be grouped with more confident students or given information about a species that they then use to produce a poster.

Challenge more confident students to find out the names of some other hybrid animals and how they have been produced.

Homework suggestions

Ask students to answer questions in the Workbook.

Extension ideas

Ask students to explain the term hybrid and suggest why hybrids are usually the result of human interference rather than occurring naturally in the wild.

3.1g Viruses

Students will learn:

- To use sources of information to classify organisms based on their characteristics
- To explain why there is no virus kingdom

Glossary words

evaluation, host cell, replication

Teaching and learning ideas

- Viruses are extremely small infectious agents that are only visible using powerful electron microscopes. They can assume a wide range of shapes but a single virus particle (which is called a 'varion') has an outer layer of fat covering a protein coat.
- The protein coat protects the genes that contain the instructions necessary for the virus to replicate once inside a host cell.
- Viruses are unable to reproduce independently, they can't move on their own or grow bigger. They have to use proteins in the host cell and the cell's respiration to provide energy for replication. They don't excrete waste and it is not clear if viruses can detect changes in their surroundings.
- These factors mean that there is debate between scientists about whether viruses are living organisms, but because there are many types of virus, they are classified in the same way as plant and animal kingdoms.
- Using the process of evaluation, some scientists believe that the combination of virus and host cell makes the virus a living organism, and that the virus particle outside a cell is just a step involved in the virus being able to spread once it enters the host cell.
- Viruses can infect plants and animals as well as bacteria and fungi. Once inside the host cell, viruses reproduce to produce millions of multiple copies and abnormal proteins, which disrupts the host cell's normal function. This leads to diseases such as measles, ebola, small pox, flu and the common cold. Herpes is a very common virus that causes cold sores. Human Immunodeficiency Virus (HIV) causes Acquired Immune Deficiency Syndrome (AIDS).
- Viruses can be spread between organisms in water droplets in the air or in soil, or from the exchange of bodily fluids.

Homework suggestions

Students could carry out an evaluation exercise to help them decide if a robot is alive. They could draw up a table showing the characteristics of living things and compare them with those a human and a robot has. The table should look like the one below and the first example has been done for you.

Living organisms have **ALL** of the characteristics on the left hand side of the table. Is a robot a living organism? Fill in the table with **Yes** or **No** to help you decide. The first two examples have been done for you:

Characteristic	Robot	Human
Movement	yes	yes
Can it reproduce and generate offspring?	no	yes
Does it have a sense of smell, taste and can it see without being controlled by a human or a computer?		
Can it grow on its own?		
Can it breathe?		
Can it excrete?		
Can it eat and absorb nutrients?		

Once they have completed the exercise, students should answer the question: What would need to happen to the robot for it to be classified as a living organism? This is a useful end of section test to determine, using homework, if students' have understood the characteristics that make something 'alive'. It can identify those who are less confident in answering this question before moving on and is useful as a basis for classroom discussion if it appears that learning needs remain.

Extension ideas

Ask students to draw a diagram to show what happens to a virus particle when it infects a host cell. The diagram should include the words host cell, replication, virus particle and genes. Encourage students to use secondary sources to help them complete their diagrams.

3.2 Biological keys

Topic overview

		Student's Book	Workbook	Downloadable material
3.2a	**Starting point** Organisms can be placed into groups, or 'classified' based on their characteristics. This short activity introduces students to this concept by asking them to group familiar objects based upon what they look like.	Starting point table	Question 1	
3.2b	**Dichotomous keys** Students begin to use and create classification keys	Questions 1–3 Activity 3.3	Questions 2–3	Worksheet 3.2b
3.2c	**Using keys to classify plants** Using keys to classify plants. This activity introduces the use of biological keys to identify plants based on the shape of their leaves.	Question 4 Activity 3.4	Question 4	Practical notes 3.2c Worksheet 3.2c

Learning Objectives

- 7Bp.04: Use and construct dichotomous keys to classify species and groups of related organisms
- 7TWSc.01: Sort, group and classify phenomena, objects, materials and organisms through testing, observation, using secondary information, and making and using keys

- 7SIC.01: Discuss how scientific knowledge is developed through collective understanding and scrutiny over time.
- 7SIC.02: Describe how science is applied across societies and industries, and in research.
- 7SIC.05: Discuss how the uses of science can have a global environmental impact.

Links to other topics

- The importance of being able to identify species and their variations is built upon in Stage 8 Chapter 3 Topic 1 and Stage 9 Chapter 3 Topic 5.

Using models

- Biological keys can be thought of as a type of conceptual model that allows the user to identify organisms in the natural world. Biological keys consist of a list of statements or questions with associated choices. These lead the user to the correct name of the organism being identified.
- The word 'dichotomous' means 'in two parts'. This is why a dichotomous key always gives two choices at each step. In each step, the user has to decide which one of two statements applies to the organism they are trying to identify. If the correct statements are chosen at each step, the name of the organism can be revealed.

Science in context

- The Science in context: Uses of classification systems box in Topic 3.2 of the Student's Book covers the following learning objectives:
  - 7SIC.01 Discuss how scientific knowledge is developed through collective understanding and scrutiny over time.
  - 7SIC.02 Describe how science is applied across societies and industries, and in research.
  - 7SIC.05 Discuss how the uses of science can have a global environmental impact.
- Look out for opportunities to use local organisms in the work in this topic.
- If there are conservation organisations working in your country or near you, consider using their work as a way to introduce the importance of being able to identify species quickly and easily.

Cambridge Lower Secondary Biology Stage 7

3.2a Starting point

Ask students to work in groups of three. Each student should find five items from their pencil case or bag and place them in the centre of the table. Next, ask students to sort the items into groups. Some students may want more direction than this, asking you to state the groups. Try to resist giving them any more information; they should be able to decide within their groups of three how to group the items. To support, you could prompt them to group the items according to some of their similarities.

Once students have grouped their items, ask them to explain to the rest of the class why they have grouped their items in the way that they have. Once all groups have explained their ideas, bring them together as a class, highlighting the main ideas that students have come up with when grouping items. It is likely that many will have grouped the items according to similarities, for example, these can all be used for writing, these can all be used to store things in.

To extend from here, students can be asked to write a series of questions, which must have yes/no answers, which other people could follow so that they could group their items in the same way, for example, does it leave a mark when rubbed on paper? – yes/no.

Students could swap their questions with another group to see if their questions could work for a different set of items. Review and discuss to bring out student ideas about classification.

3.2b Dichotomous keys

Students will learn:

- To use and construct biological keys for classification
- To make observations and measurements

Glossary words

dichotomous key

Resource preparation

Activity 3.3 *Identifying people in your class*

Plain paper to draw classification keys on.

Scissors and glue if requiring students to stick images onto their classification keys.

Worksheet 3.2b

Teaching and learning ideas

- To start, give students Worksheet 3.2b. Students should look at the pictures of the six animals on this sheet and consider the similarities and differences between them. They are then required to write five yes/no questions which would help them to work out which animal they are identifying. Ask students to write five different questions considering the different animals, rather than all five about one animal. This should help students begin to consider ways of working out which animal is which via questioning, which will support their ability to construct a classification key. Review with students by asking them to share their similarities and differences between animals as well as their five questions.
- Work through the Student's Book section on 'Dichotomous keys'. Ask students to look at the two different types of dichotomous classification key and work through questions 1–3.
- Ask students to return to Worksheet 3.2b. Students should work in pairs using the questions that they constructed in question 2 on Worksheet 3.2b to help and they should try and form a classification key of their own. Students should start by drawing a branching classification key and once this is completed they could convert this into a statement key if time allows. Students could cut out the images on Worksheet 3.2b to stick onto their keys for reference if required.
- Together with students, read through Activity 3.3 *Identifying people in your class*, in the Student's Book. Ask students to work through the activity, creating their own classification key for the group of students shown in the picture. This activity not only supports students in creating their own classification key, it also encourages them to evaluate their keys, considering how adaptable they are and whether they can be applied to other situations. Point

out that some questions are more useful than others in classification keys. You could then ask students to answer questions 2–4 in the Workbook.

- Once students have completed Activity 3.3, ask them to spend a few minutes considering which questions from their keys were the most useful for separating people into different groups. Once students have had a chance to consider this individually, initiate a discussion so that students can share their ideas about the 'usefulness' of different question types when writing a classification key.

- To finish, ask students to swap their classification keys from Worksheet 3.2b with another pair. Each pair can then test the key they have been given. One member of the pair selects one of the six animals and the other asks them the questions given in the key in order to identify which animal their partner has chosen.

Differentiation

Some students will need support when working through the different classification keys. Work individually or in a small group with these students showing them clearly how to follow the key through. Students may also need support when developing their own keys. For this it may help if you give some question starters as prompts.

Challenge more confident students to choose six more animals (or plants) and see if they can alter/add to their classification keys to incorporate these extra species.

Homework suggestions

Students should prepare a list of the ways in which a group of students of their age could be similar or different, that is, what features could they look at to identify different individuals. For example, are they male or female?

Alternatively, students could complete Worksheet 3.2b if this has not been used in class.

3.2c Using keys to classify plants

Students will learn:

- To use and construct biological keys for classification
- To make observations and measurements
- To choose the best way to present results

Resource preparation

Activity 3.4 *Classifying leaves*. Plant classification key (if required), selection of leaves from different species of plant.

See teacher and technician practical support notes for further support with this.

Worksheet 3.2c

Teaching and learning ideas

- To start, ask students to write a definition of the term classification. They should do this individually to start with, without looking at any books or other sources. Once students have written their ideas they can then use the Student's Book or other secondary sources to check their definition and alter/develop it where required. To review, students should share their definitions with a partner.

- Together with students read through the 'Using keys to classify plants' section in the Student's Book. Following on from this, ask students to complete Activity 3.4 *Classifying leaves*. The start of this activity simply asks students to draw a dichotomous key for the leaves shown in the image. Students are then required to collect some leaf samples of their own, identify them and then construct their own classification key. If it is not possible for students to go into the school grounds and collect their own leaf samples, students can be given a selection of leaves that have already been collected prior to the learning episode. Worksheet 3.2c could be used to support students when working through this activity.

- To finish, ask students to return to their starting point activity where they had to work together to group the items from their pencil cases and bags. Students should return to this activity and, using their highlighted similarities, work in small groups to draw a classification key.

Differentiation

Less confident students may require extra support creating their own classification keys. Providing some example questions or question starters may help (e.g. 'Does this leaf have…'). It may also be helpful to show the students some examples of other keys to give them some ideas. You could challenge more confident students to create a classification key for some students within their own class. It is very important, however, that you give clear guidelines and boundaries for this activity as it could potentially lead to some difficult comments or cause upset regarding features or looks.

Homework suggestions

Students choose from the six leaves on Worksheet 3.2 c. They should devise a simple game in which one student pretends a plant that has this leaf. Other students have to use questions they have devised as part of the homework task to identify what type of plant the student is pretending to be. Only 'yes' or 'no' answers are allowed as responses to the questions. Questions should all be based upon observations of what the leaves look like.

Chapter 3 | Checking students' progress

End of chapter reflection
- To review the learning points of the topic
- To test understanding through answering questions

Resources
- Student's Book [End of chapter review questions]
- Workbook [Self-assessment grid, Test-style questions]
- Worksheets 3.1b, 3.1c, 3.1d(1), 3.1d(2), 3.1g, 3.2b, 3.2c [all of which may have already been used]

Approach

Use the end of chapter 'Check your progress' box and end of chapter questions in the Student's Book as a way of recapping on the main learning points.

Key word definition game. Place at least 15 key words on the board. Students draw a grid 3 × 3 and choose nine key words to write into the spaces on the grid. The teacher reads out definitions of the words in a random order. The students cross out a word when they hear the teacher read out a definition for which it is the correct answer. They shout 'Line!' when they have crossed out a line of three words on the card. The line can be across, down or diagonally. Or they have to cross out all nine words before they can shout 'Finished!'.

Place a list of organisms that students will be familiar with on the board (or provide pictures). Ask the students to group them into kingdoms. Then they should take those they put into the animal kingdom and further group them as far as possible.

Students also complete the diagnostic information from the self-assessment checklist in the Workbook. The teacher response in the Workbook end of chapter section can be completed to give students feedback on next steps. You may wish to revisit some learning outcomes again if students find any areas particularly challenging.

Chapter 4 — Structure and properties of materials

Chapter overview

In this chapter, students will learn about physical and chemical properties of substances, using pH as a measurement of a chemical property. They will show how particles are arranged in solids, liquids and gases and use the particle model to explain their properties. They will be introduced to elements, compounds and mixtures and explore the properties of metals and non-metals. This chapter builds on content covering Properties of materials taught in in earlier stages of their education.

Topic title	Number of 40-minute periods	Learning Objectives	Thinking and Working Scientifically Learning Objectives
4.1 Physical and chemical properties	1–2	7Cp.01 Understand that all substances have chemical properties and physical properties.	7TWSc.07 Collect and record sufficient observations and/or measurements in an appropriate form.
4.2 Acidity and indicators	5–6	7Cp.02 Understand that the acidity or alkalinity of a substance is a chemical property and is measured by pH. 7Cp.03 Use indicators (including Universal Indicator and litmus) to distinguish between acidic, alkaline and neutral solutions.	7TWSp.05 Know the meaning of hazard symbols, and consider them when planning practical work. 7TWSc.01 Sort, group and classify phenomena, objects, materials and organisms through testing, observation, using secondary information, and making and using keys. 7TWSc.07 Collect and record sufficient observations and/or measurements in an appropriate form.
4.3 The particle model	3–4	7Cm.01 Understand that all matter is made of atoms, with each different type of atom being a different element. 7Cm.05 Describe a vacuum as a space devoid of matter. 7Cm.06 Describe the three states of matter as solid, liquid and gas in terms of the arrangement, separation and motion of particles.	7TWSm.01 Describe the strengths and limitations of a model.
4.4 Elements and the Periodic Table	2	7Cm.01 Understand that all matter is made of atoms, with each different type of atom being a different element. 7Cm.02 Know that the Periodic Table presents the known elements in an order.	7TWSm.02 Use symbols and formulae to represent scientific ideas.
4.5 Elements, compounds and mixtures	3–4	7Cm.04 Describe the differences between elements, compounds and mixtures, including alloys as an example of a mixture. 7Cm.07 Use the particle model to represent elements, compounds and mixtures. 7Cp.06 Understand that alloys are mixtures that have different chemical and physical properties from the constituent substances.	

Cambridge Lower Secondary Chemistry
Stage 7

| 4.6 Properties of metals, non-metals and alloys | 4–5 | 7Cm.03 Know metals and non-metals as the two main groupings of elements. 7Cp.05 Describe common differences between metals and non-metals, referring to their physical properties. 7Cp.06 Understand that alloys are mixtures that have different chemical and physical properties from the constituent substances. 7Cp.07 Use the particle model to explain the difference in hardness between pure metals and their alloys. | 7TWSp.03 Make predictions of likely outcomes for a scientific enquiry based on scientific knowledge and understanding. 7TWSc.01 Sort, group and classify phenomena, objects, materials and organisms through testing, observation and using secondary information, and making and using keys. 7TWSa.03 Make conclusions by interpreting results and explain the limitations of the conclusions. |
| End of chapter questions | 1 | Check students' progress | |

Background science

Please note: the background science notes are designed to provide teachers with an overview of the science concepts students may have already been taught earlier in their education, are likely to be taught in this unit and are likely to be taught in later stages. They are not a checklist of the content to be covered by the teacher in each unit.

The background science notes also serve to provide the teacher with some understanding of the background science needed in order to deliver the content of each chapter.

All substances have chemical properties and physical properties. Some substances are corrosive, which means that they can burn skin and eyes and cause damage to other substances. Some are irritants, which means they can cause eyes and skin to itch and blister, but are not as dangerous.

If a substance has the potential to cause harm, its container will have a hazard symbol on it.

Weak acids and alkalis are found in many common household substances. Strong acids and alkalis are found mainly in science laboratories. Hydrochloric acid is a common laboratory acid and sodium hydroxide is a common laboratory alkali.

The pH scale goes from 0 to 14. The pH of a solution depends on how strong or weak an acidic or alkaline solution is, or if the solution is neutral. The most commonly used indicators are litmus and universal indicator. Litmus turns red in acids and blue in alkalis. Universal indicator will turn into a range of colours, depending on the pH of the solution.

A strongly acidic solution has a pH of 0–3. A weakly acidic solution has a pH of 4–6. A neutral solution has a pH of 7. A weakly alkaline solution has a pH of 8–10. A strongly alkaline solution has a pH of 11–14.

All matter is made up of atoms. These may exist as single atoms or as groups of atoms, called molecules. For younger students, it is easier for them to understand the concept of particles, where no distinction is made as to whether the material is made up of atoms or molecules. Matter can exist in one of three forms: solid, liquid or gas. The state that a material is in will depend on its temperature. Pure substances have defined melting and boiling points. If the temperature is below its melting point, the material will be in the solid state; between melting and boiling point and it is a liquid, and above its boiling point it will be a gas. Some materials do not exist as a liquid, but instead turn directly from a solid to a gas when heated. This change in state is called sublimation. Changes of state was covered in Stages 4 and 6.

Changes in state are physical changes – they are reversible.

Particles are arranged differently when in each state of matter. They also move differently. This is called the particle model and can be used to explain the different properties of solids, liquids and gases. Students may already have covered the use of the particle model to explain changes of state in earlier stages of their education. This content will also be revisited at IGCSE.

Elements are pure substances – they only contain one type of particle. They are listed on the Periodic Table in order of atomic number. Elements can react in chemical reactions to form compounds. The atoms in a compound are strongly bonded together; they cannot easily be separated to form their constituent elements. The substances in a mixture are not bonded together so they can be separated easily.

Chapter 4: Structure and properties of materials

Topic overview

		Student's Book	Workbook	Downloadable material
4.1a	**Starting point** Discussion about students' prior knowledge of the topic and common everyday examples of acids and alkalis that students may be aware of	Starting point table		
4.1b	**Different properties** This activity allows students to recognise examples of chemical properties and physical properties	Questions 1–4 Activity 4.1	Questions 1–8	

Learning Objectives

- 7Cp.01: Understand that all substances have chemical properties and physical properties
- 7TWSc.07: Collect and record sufficient observations and/or measurements in an appropriate form

- 7SIC.01: Discuss how scientific knowledge is developed through collective understanding and scrutiny over time.
- 7SIC.04: Describe how people develop and use scientific understanding as individuals and through collaboration, e.g. through peer review

Links to other topics

- Students know from Stage 2 *Properties of materials* that a property is a characteristic of a material, and they understand that materials can have more than one property.
- Students know from Stage 6 *Properties of materials* that melting point, boiling point, mass, electrical and thermal conductivity are properties of a substance.
- Students will learn about concentration of solutions and solubility in Stage 8 Chapter 5 *Solutions and solubility.*
- Students will learn about physical and chemical properties in elements and compounds with different structures in Stage 9 Chapter 6 *Structure, bonding and the properties of matter.*

Science in context

- The Science in context: Alchemy box in Topic 4.1 of the Student's Book covers the following learning objectives:
  - 7SIC.01 Discuss how scientific knowledge is developed through collective understanding and scrutiny over time.
  - 7SIC.04 Describe how people develop and use scientific understanding as individuals and through collaboration, e.g. through peer review

Common misunderstandings

- Students may be uncertain as to what 'properties' are. Explain that a property is a description of what something is like – one of its characteristics. For example, eye colour, height, type of material, what happens if you put a substance in water.

4.1a Starting point

Teaching and learning ideas

Ask students to examine one or more objects on the table top, such as their pen and ruler. What properties can be observed in these objects? Which of these properties could be measured? Are there any hidden properties that could be observed through an experiment?

4.1b Different properties

Students will learn:

- Understand that all substances have chemical properties and physical properties
- To collect and record sufficient observations in an appropriate form

Glossary words

boiling point, chemical property, melting point, physical property

Resource preparation

For the demonstration: eye protection, gloves, tweezers or forceps, sharp knife, filter paper, large trough, white tile, copper foil or small lump of copper, lithium.

For Activity 4.1: graph paper.

Teaching and learning ideas

- Demonstrate the properties of lithium and copper. Place a piece of copper foil on a white tile. Show its observable physical properties (e.g. colour, hardness, resistance to cutting), then drop it in a trough of water. Observe whether any chemical reaction can be seen (there will be none, showing that copper is unreactive towards water). Remove the oil from a piece of lithium (smaller than pea-sized) using filter paper. Place the small piece of lithium on the tile. Show its observable physical properties (e.g. colour, hardness, resistance to cutting), then drop it in a trough of water. Observe whether any chemical reaction can be seen (there will be steady bubbling until the lithium disappears, showing that lithium is reactive towards water). Note that the copper should sink and the lithium will float, showing that copper is denser than water and lithium is less dense than water.
- The students should record the observed properties in a suitable table, dividing the properties into chemical properties and physical properties.
- Eye protection should be worn by all in the laboratory. Wear gloves to avoid skin contact with lithium. Return any unused lithium to its container. Leave the forceps, knife and white tile in the water so that any remaining lithium reacts safely.
- Activity 4.1 *Measuring the boiling point of water* (see the Student's Book). To engage the class, you could show them a kettle boiling and ask them what is happening inside.
- Refer to the Student's Book and questions 1–4.
- Discuss examples of chemical and physical properties, and the differences between them.
- Discuss how the densities of copper and lithium could have been determined without using water.
- Discuss why lithium is stored in oil but copper is not.

Differentiation

Students may be uncertain as to what chemical properties are. Explain that a chemical property can only be observed when a substance reacts (or fails to react) with another substance. Give everyday examples such as gas burning on a cooker and a bicycle chain rusting: you cannot determine how the gas or steel will react until the reaction itself happens.

Extension ideas

Ask students to research the existence and properties of unusual forms of substances, such as plasmas and superfluids.

Homework suggestions

Cooking involves changing the physical and chemical properties of food. Prepare a simple meal. Observe and record the physical and chemical changes that happen to the food.

4.2 Acidity and indicators

Topic overview

		Student's Book	Workbook	Downloadable material
4.2a	**Starting point** Discussion about students' prior knowledge of the topic and common everyday examples of acids and alkalis that students may be aware of	Starting point table		
4.2b	**Hazard symbols** This activity allows students to look at everyday and laboratory substances, and to decide what hazards are associated with them and how to handle them safely	Questions 1–4 Activity 4.2	Questions 2, 4	Practical notes 4.2b Worksheet 4.2b
4.2c	**Indicators** This section allows students to look at litmus indicator: how it works and what it shows you about solutions	Questions 5–7	Questions 1, 5, 6	
4.2d	**The pH scale** This section allows students to look at the pH scale, and the use of universal indicator to estimate the pH of a solution	Questions 8–15	Questions 3, 7–10	Worksheet 4.2d
4.2e	**Investigating indicators** This section allows students to make and test their own indicator solution, and to plan an investigation into acids and alkalis in solution	Activity 4.3		Practical notes 4.2e Worksheets 4.2e, 4.2e(2)

Learning Objectives

- 7Cp.02: Understand that the acidity or alkalinity of a substance is a chemical property and is measured by pH
- 7Cp.03: Use indicators (including Universal Indicator and litmus) to distinguish between acidic, alkaline and neutral solutions
- 7TWSp.05: Know the meaning of hazard symbols, and consider them when planning practical work

- 7TWSc.01: Sort, group and classify phenomena, objects, materials and organisms through testing, observation, using secondary information, and making and using keys
- 7TWSc.07: Collect and record sufficient observations and/or measurements in an appropriate form

Links to other topics

- Students know from Stage 6 Life processes that human defence mechanisms include stomach acid.
- Students will learn about the reaction of acids with alkalis (neutralisation) and pH in Chapter 5 Topic 3 *Neutralisation* in this book.
- Students will learn about the reactions of acids with metals and metal carbonates in Stage 9 Chapter 7 Topic 3 *Methods for making salts*.

Common misunderstandings

- Students may know that acids are sour and alkalis are bitter. Explain to the students that these are descriptions of properties of acids and alkalis, but they are not scientific definitions.
- Students may think that all acids are dangerous. Discuss with the students why it is safe to use acidic substances such as vinegar and lemon juice on food.
- Students may think that alkalis are not dangerous. Consider showing the students photographs of skin damage due to contact with wet cement or concrete, or eye damage from contact with an alkaline solution.

Cambridge Lower Secondary Chemistry Stage 7

- Students may confuse acid with acidic, and alkali with alkaline. The words with 'ine' on the end show that they are to do with something. Give everyday examples such as cat and feline, dog and canine, and cow and bovine. Point out the confusion with acids and alkalis may arise because the beginning of each pair of words is the same.
- Students may think that there is only one type of indicator, when there are other indicators, some of which can be used to determine the strength of an acidic or alkaline solution. Demonstrate different indicator solutions, such as litmus and universal indicator, being added to acidic, alkaline or neutral solutions.

4.2a Starting point

Teaching and learning ideas

Ask students to discuss what they think acids and alkalis are. Ask prompting questions such as: What is an acid? What is an alkali? How can you tell whether it is acidic or alkaline? What is an indicator? Do you know any examples of household acids?

4.2b Hazard symbols

Students will learn:

- To recall and use hazard symbols
- To know the meaning of hazard symbols

Glossary words

acid, alkali, corrosive, hazard symbol

Resource preparation

For the demonstration: common CLP hazard symbols with their meaning. CLP stands for the Classification, Labelling and Packaging Regulation (EC) No 1272/2008. Put each hazard symbol on its own card, with its meaning on the back. Suitable symbols include moderate health hazard, toxic, corrosive, flammable, oxidising, explosive, hazardous to the environment and serious health hazard.

For Activity 4.2: examples of laboratory items with hazard symbols on for students to choose from. (Alternatively, give the student some ideas of substances to use.)

Worksheet 4.2b

Practical notes 4.2b

Teaching and learning ideas

- Demonstrate the common laboratory hazard symbols. For each one, ask the students to discuss in pairs or small groups what they think it means, then agree their answer amongst themselves. Select one or more pairs or groups to feed back their answer to the class, then turn the card over to show the meaning of the hazard symbol.
- Activity 4.2 *Hazard symbols* (see the Student's Book). To engage the class, you could show them an example of a hazardous substance, and model the activity the first time through as a class. See Practical notes 4.2b and Worksheet 4.2b. Eye protection should be worn; avoid skin contact.
- Discuss the advantages of using hazard symbols, with or without written warnings and advice.
- Refer to the Student's Book and questions 1–4.
- Discuss suitable ways that dangerous substances could be handled safely.

Differentiation

Some students may need help distinguishing between the symbols for flammable and oxidising. The oxidising symbol looks like an O with flames.

Extension ideas

Ask students to research the use of road signs and their designs. Warning signs are mostly triangular but signs giving instructions or orders are mostly circular. The students could evaluate the ease of understanding warning signs.

Homework suggestions

Workbook question 2.

Design your own hazard symbol for a hazard not covered in the lesson. This does not need to be a laboratory hazard.

Chapter 4: Structure and properties of materials

4.2c Indicators

Students will learn:

- To understand acidity and alkalinity and how it is measured
- To classify materials through testing and observation
- To collect and record sufficient observations in an appropriate form

Glossary words

acidic, alkaline, indicator, litmus, neutral, range, pH scale, universal indicator

Resource preparation

For demonstration: solid ethanedioic acid (oxalic acid), solid calcium hydroxide, solid sodium chloride, 3×100 cm^3 beakers, glass rod, spatulas, blue litmus paper, red litmus paper, white tile. Eye protection should be worn; avoid skin contact.

For practical activity: eye protection, red litmus paper, blue litmus paper, litmus solution, test tubes, test-tube rack, glass rod, dropping pipettes, white tile, range of solutions to test (acidic, neutral and alkaline solutions). Eye protection should be worn; avoid skin contact.

Teaching and learning ideas

- Demonstrate a soluble acid and an alkali, and how they dissolve in water to produce acidic and alkaline solutions. Dip the stirring rod in each solution, and test by spotting a small drop on each litmus paper. Discuss the results with students and ensure they understand that the acidity or alkalinity of a solution is a chemical property of acids and alkalis when they dissolve. Compare the results with those obtained for sodium chloride, which gives a neutral solution. Explain that litmus is an indicator. Check that the students understand the importance of washing the glass rod each time to avoid contamination.
- Students carry out a practical in which they test a range of dilute laboratory and household substances with litmus papers and solution. This could be run as a circus with individual stations for each substance. Students record their results in a suitable table. The table for question 5 in the Student's Book shows appropriate headings. The students should use their results to classify each solution as acidic, alkaline or neutral.
- Discuss the advantages and limitations of litmus, e.g. simple classification into three groups but no indication of how strongly or weakly acidic or alkaline the solutions are.
- Discuss suitable hazard symbols for these solutions, e.g. moderately harmful, corrosive.
- Refer to the Student's Book and questions 5–7.

Differentiation

Some students may need help distinguishing between the terms acid and acidic, alkali and alkaline. The first word in each pair describes the type of substance and the second word describes its properties.

Extension ideas

Ask students to find out why litmus is called a single indicator, and to find the names and colour changes of other single indicators.

Homework suggestions

Workbook question 1, 5, 6.

Find out how litmus indicator is made.

4.2d The pH scale

Students will learn:

- To understand acidity and alkalinity and how it is measured
- To classify materials through testing and observation
- To collect and record sufficient observations in an appropriate form

Glossary words

pH scale, universal indicator

Cambridge Lower Secondary Chemistry

Stage 7

Resource preparation

For demonstration: dilute hydrochloric acid, dilute sodium hydroxide solution, deionised water, glass rod, test tubes, test-tube rack, universal indicator solution, universal indicator paper, pH colour chart, white tile. Eye protection should be worn; avoid skin contact.

For practical activity: eye protection, universal indicator solution, universal indicator paper, test tubes, test-tube rack, glass rod, dropping pipettes, white tile, range of solutions to test (acidic, neutral and alkaline solutions). Eye protection should be worn; avoid skin contact.

Teaching and learning ideas

- Discuss with the students the limitations of litmus:
    - it can only classify solutions as acidic, neutral or alkaline;
    - it gives no idea of how strong or weak these solutions may be;
    - two different litmus papers are needed to determine whether a solution is neutral.
    - Introduce the idea of the pH scale. Refer to the Student's Book.
- Demonstrate how to use universal indicator paper and solution. Discuss the reasons for using a small spot of test solution on the paper and leaving a 30 s interval before matching the colour obtained to the pH colour chart.
- Students carry out a practical in which they test a range of dilute laboratory and household substances with universal indicator paper and solution. This could be run as a circus with individual stations for each substance. Students record their results in a suitable table. The students should use their results to order the solutions from most strongly acidic to most strongly alkaline, identifying any neutral solutions.
- Refer to the Student's Book and questions 8–15.
- Discuss with the students the advantages and limitations of universal indicator:
    - only one paper is needed to determine whether a solution is acidic, neutral or alkaline;
    - it can show whether a solution is strongly or weakly acidic or alkaline;
    - it only gives an estimate of pH because it can be difficult to exactly match the colours.

Differentiation

Some students may need help understanding that acidic solutions become stronger as their pH decreases, and alkaline solutions become stronger as their pH increases. Neutral solutions are not acidic or alkaline, so the weakest acidic or alkaline solutions are found near to pH 7 (the pH of neutral solutions).

Extension ideas

Ask students to find out about the development of the pH scale, and what the term **pH** means.

Homework suggestions

Worksheet 4.2d.

Workbook questions 3, 7–9.

4.2e Investigating indicators

Students will learn:

- To understand acidity and alkalinity and how it is measured
- To know the meaning of hazard symbols, and consider them when planning practical work

Glossary words

acidic, alkaline, indicator, neutral

Resource preparation

For the activity on making their own indicator: eye protection, red cabbage, Bunsen burner, three clean test tubes, stirring rod, pipette, gauze, water, heat-resistant mat, scissors, tripod, 250 cm^3 beaker, substances to test, test-tube rack.

For Activity 4.3, students will need: shampoo, vinegar, orange juice, toothpaste, tap water, an indigestion tablet.

Worksheets 4.2e, 4.2e(2)

Practical notes 4.2e

Teaching and learning ideas

- Show students two solutions, both colourless – how could you tell which was acidic and which was alkaline?
- Worksheet 4.2e is a practical activity that students could do to make their own indicator with red cabbage. This could then be tested with some household substances. The results and effectiveness of the indicator could be compared with litmus (section 4.2c) and/or universal indicator (section 4.2d).
- Activity 4.3 *Planning an investigation – is it acidic or is it alkaline?* See Worksheet 4.2e(2). Students are asked to write a plan for an investigation using step-by-step questions. Have a class discussion on the activity – you could ask students to think about it on their own for 1 minute, then discuss it in a pair for 2 minutes, and then discuss it as a whole class.
- Students then make their predictions and prepare their plan. Make sure the students consider the hazards and hazard symbols involved.

Differentiation

The practical activity involves a multi-step method that some students may find challenging. It may help if you split the activity into four sections: breaking up the cabbage, heating in water, cooling sufficiently to be safe, testing the solutions. Pause at the end of each section to check that the students are ready for the next one. Students who are ahead a little could help the slower students, provided their Bunsen burner is turned off.

Extension ideas

Ask students to find out about how pH is measured, rather than just how it is estimated using universal indicator.

Homework suggestions

Workbook question 10.

Worksheet 4.2e(2) could be completed as a homework.

4.3 The particle model

Topic overview

		Student's Book	Workbook	Downloadable material
4.3a	**Starting point** In this short activity students classify everyday materials as solids, liquids or gases. This activity allows you to see what they already know about states of matter	Starting point table		Worksheet 4.3a
4.3b	**The particle model** Students learn about particles, and carry out a circus of activities looking more deeply at the properties of solids, liquids and gases	Questions 1–3 Activity 4.4	Questions 1–3	Practical notes 4.3b Worksheet 4.3b
4.3c	**Using the particle model to explain the properties of solids, liquids and gases** Students explore the strengths and weaknesses of the model. They will use the particle model to explain these properties and understand what a vacuum is		Questions 4–7	

Learning Objectives

- 7Cm.05: Describe a vacuum as a space devoid of matter
- 7Cm.06: Describe the three states of matter as solid, liquid and gas in terms of the arrangement, separation and motion of particles
- 7TWSm.01: Describe the strengths and limitations of a model
- 7SIC.02: Describe how science is applied across societies and industries, and in research.

Links to other topics

- In Chapter 10 Topic 4 students will use the particle model to explain the changes of state that take place during the water cycle.
- In Stage 8 students will learn about the structure of an atom.

Using models

- Particle model is introduced in this topic. It is a fundamental conceptual model that students will use to explain the properties of solids, liquids and gases.
- Students will be given the opportunity to further develop their skills in evaluating models, by describing the strengths and limitations of the particle model. This provides the opportunity to cover 7TWSM.01 describing the strengths and limitations of a model.

Science in context

- The Science in context: Breathing in space box in Topic 4.3 of the Student's Book covers the following learning objective:
  - 7SIC.02 Describe how science is applied across societies and industries, and in research.

Common misunderstandings

- Particles are inside materials rather than materials being made up of particles. This can be challenged by asking if this is true, what else is in the material? If students think that particles are suspended in air you can discuss the fact that air is also made up of particles.
- Gases do not consist of particles. Students may think that gases, such as air, do not consist of atoms because they cannot be seen. This can be challenged by asking students to squeeze a balloon full of air so they can feel that there is matter inside pushing back.
- The particles in a liquid are only moving when the liquid itself is moving.

4.3a Starting point

Teaching and learning ideas

Provide the class with a selection of materials that are easy to classify as solids, liquids and gases. Some good examples are: a bottle of water, lemonade, oil, honey, liquid soap (liquids), a balloon filled with air (gas), wood, soap, ice, candle (solids).

Ask them to work in groups and give each group a piece of paper; then ask them to draw a results table and fill it in to show what state each material is in.

Ask groups to share their results, and check that students agree with their choices.

As an optional challenge activity ask students to complete Worksheet 4.3a.

4.3b The particle model

Students will learn:

- To describe the three states of matter using the particle model
- To describe the strengths and limitations of a model
- To use a scientific model to construct explanations

Glossary words

model, particle model, boiling, condensation, freezing, melting

Resource preparation

For demonstration: a model, preferably of a familiar object, made from interlocking plastic building blocks.

For Worksheet 4.3b: three small sealed plastic syringes without needles, a beaker full of coloured water, an empty container, e.g. empty margarine tub, a beaker full of rice, solid rigid objects of different shapes, e.g. blocks of wood, plastic rods, ice.

Practical notes 4.3b

Teaching and learning ideas

- Assign each student with a state of matter (solid, liquid or gas). Ask them to describe to a partner the properties of that state. Ask the class for feedback and listen to the students to make sure that they are using scientific terminology (can be compressed, can flow, etc.) rather than the simple words (hard, squashy, etc.). Correct terminology when necessary. You might like to build up a bank of suitable words that students should use and display these on the board/large piece of paper so the class can refer to them throughout the learning episodes.
- Tell the students that they will now be learning why the states of matter have different properties. Show them a model made from building blocks. Question the class:
  - What is the model made from? (*Lots of blocks stuck together.*)
  - Describe the properties of the model. (*It is solid, hard.*)
  - How does what the model is made from give it these properties? (*the blocks are hard and stuck together*).
- Tell the class that all objects on Earth are made up of building blocks like the model. These are called particles. The particles are too small to be seen, unlike the model. However, like the model, how they are arranged will give the object different properties.
- The class now complete a circus of activities, filling in their findings on Worksheet 4.3b. This will give them an opportunity to explore further the properties of solids, liquids and gases, while formulating their own ideas of a particle model. Refer to Practical notes 4.3b for information.

- Refer to Student's Book and ask the students to read through the information on the particle model. Ask them to compare their models with this. How are they similar? How are they different?

Differentiation

Some students may have heard of atoms and question what the difference is between atoms and particles. Explain that particles can be single atoms, or groups of atoms stuck together (molecules).

With less confident students you may wish to divide up the circus activities, and give them instructions on how to carry out each rather than let them explore independently. They may also need guidance on designing a model.

Extension ideas

Ask students to design a demonstration or experiment that can be used to prove that particles exist.

Homework suggestions

Ask students to find out what a model is in science, and some examples of models and what they are used for.

4.3c Using the particle model to explain the properties of solids, liquids and gases

Students will learn:

- To describe the three states of matter using the particle model
- To describe the strengths and limitations of a model

Glossary words

model, vacuum

Resource preparation

For demonstration: A simple model, e.g. a toy car or animal

For Activity 4.4: spherical objects such as beads, polystyrene balls or dried peas, as well glue or modelling clay and an empty plastic bottle with a lid.

Teaching and learning ideas

- Review the learning from the last learning episode and ask students to draw a 2D model to show how the particles are arranged in a solid, liquid and gas.
- Ask students to form groups and assign each group a question:
  Why are solids hard?
  Why can liquids flow?
  Why do gases take up the space of the whole container?
  Why can liquids and gases be compressed but solids can't?
  Why can you put your hand through liquid water but not through ice?
  Why can you see through a gas?
  Why do solids expand (get bigger) when they are heated?
  Groups discuss their question and come to an agreed explanation. They can draw diagrams as part of their explanation. Then ask groups to share their question and explanation with another group.
- Students answer questions 1 and 2 in the Student's Book. Question 3 is a Challenge question.
- Tell the students to imagine that they are in space. What surrounds them? Does space contain particles? Introduce the term 'vacuum' as a space that contains no particles. Ask students why they can't breathe in space. Use the Science in Context box to discuss why scientific understanding of what a vacuum is has been important for scientists working in space exploration.
- **Challenge:** Tell students that in the future people might live on the Moon. However, there is no air on the Moon. Can they design homes and vehicles that will overcome this problem?
- Discuss with the students that a strong model represents all the parts of the real phenomenon it is describing. Start by using a toy car, or model animal as a simple example, and them to point out the strengths and limitations of the model.

- Now, ask them to discuss what a strong particle model would show. Listen to their ideas. They may suggest that the ideal particle model would show: how the particles are arranged, the strength of the forces in between the particles, how the particles move, that the particles are all the same, that the particles are 3D spheres (not 2D discs). Ask them to discuss how strong the particle model in the Student's Book is.
- **Challenge:** students complete Activity 4.4 *Building a model* in the Student's Book. Supply students with the equipment listed above to build their own models of solids, liquids and gases showing how the particles are arranged and how they move. This helps students to visualise particles in 3D, rather than as 2D diagrams. Ask students to evaluate each other's models by describing their strengths and limitations.

Differentiation

The group discussion questions above are ordered by difficulty, easiest first. You may like to group students so each group contains students with a mixture of attainments.

Extension ideas

'Gold is hard because gold particles are hard.'

Ask students to write down why this misconception is incorrect, and a correct version.

Homework suggestions

In preparation for the next topic, ask students to write down what an element is, with five examples.

4.4   Elements and the Periodic Table

Topic overview

		Student's Book	Workbook	Downloadable material
4.4a	**Starting point** In this activity students use an analogy to visualise how small atoms are	Starting point table		
4.4b	**Atoms and elements** Students observe a range of elements and describe their properties	Activity 4.5		Practical notes 4.4b Worksheet 4.4b
4.4c	**Symbols and the Periodic Table** Students are introduced to the Periodic Table and use a range of activities to use the symbols of the first 20 elements	Questions 1–2	Questions 1–7	Worksheet 4.4c

Learning Objectives

- 7Cm.01: Understand that all matter is made of atoms, with each different type of atom being a different element
- 7Cm.02: Know that the Periodic Table presents the known elements in an order
- 7TWSm.02: Use symbols and formulae to represent scientific ideas

- 7SIC.02: Describe how science is applied across societies and industries, and in research.
- 7SIC.04: Describe how people develop and use scientific understanding as individuals and through collaboration, e.g. through peer review
- 7SIC.05: Discuss how the uses of science can have a global environmental impact.

Links to other topics

- In Stage 8 students will revisit the Periodic Table to discover how the position of an element relates to its structure and properties.

Using models

- There is an opportunity here to address learning objective 7TWSm.01 where the students are asked to discuss the strengths and limitations of the textbook models.
- 7TWSm.02 can also be covered by using the symbols and formulae to represent the element and compounds used in this topic.
- The Periodic Table is introduced as a model used to arrange the elements in an order.

Science in context

- The Science in context: Using indium box in Topic 4.4 of the Student's Book covers the following learning objectives:
  - 7SIC.02 Describe how science is applied across societies and industries, and in research.
  - 7SIC.04 Describe how people develop and use scientific understanding as individuals and through collaboration, e.g. through peer review
  - 7SIC.05 Discuss how the uses of science can have a global environmental impact.
- You could approach this topic from a historical prospective, looking at how and why the number of known elements has increased over time, and why new elements are still being added to the Periodic Table today.

4.4a Starting point

Remind the class that everything on Earth is made up of atoms. It is very difficult to understand just how small atoms are. Tell them this narrative. Students can close their eyes to help them visualise it: Imagine you are sitting on a beach. Look up and down the beach at all the sand. Pick up a handful of sand and let the grains slowly trickle through your fingers. Some grains will stay stuck to your hand. Take a close look at a single grain of sand and think about how small it is. This grain of sand is made up of atoms. There are around the same number of atoms in this grain of sand as there are grains of sand on the whole beach. That is how small atoms are.

4.4b Atoms and elements

Students will learn:

- To understand that all matter is made of atoms, with each different type of atom being a different element
- To make careful observations
- To interpret data from secondary sources

Glossary words

element

Resource preparation

For the demonstration: Model made out of interlocking plastic building bricks. The bricks should all be the same colour and size.

For Activity 4.5: sealed containers or photographs of elements, access to the internet or books on the elements.

Worksheet 4.4b

Practical notes 4.4b

Teaching and learning ideas

- Show the class the brick model. Ask them to write down their observations about the model, for example, it is a solid, all the bricks are the same. Share their thoughts and introduce the idea of an element as being like the model. Just like the model is made up of bricks that are the same, elements are made up of the same type of atom. Explain that the 'Lego' model works well to show atoms of different elements, but that, in reality, atoms are spherical.
- Use figure 4.19 in the Student's Book to show the class diagrams of atoms inside two elements: silver and helium. Make sure students understand that not all elements are solids.
- Break up the model, showing that groups of bricks are the same substance as the whole model. In the same way, you cannot break down an element into a simpler substance – it will always be an element until you get to the individual atoms of that element. An atom is the smallest part of an element.
- Students complete Activity 4.5 *Exploring elements* in the Student's Book. Refer to practical notes 4.4b for more information. Students work in small groups to observe elements and describe their physical properties. They then try and group them. Students should be provided with a range of different elements (metals and non-metals) in different forms (solids, liquids and gases).
- Ask each group to describe one way they grouped the elements and explain why.
- If possible, supply students with secondary sources of information, such as books or the internet. They should find out additional information about one of the elements. For example, its uses, melting point and boiling point.
- Ask students to complete Worksheet 4.4b. They classify particle diagrams as elements.
- **Challenge:** Students can complete the challenge question on Worksheet 4.4b.

Differentiation

You might like to supply less confident students with the exact pages from a book or with a useful website when they carry out their secondary research.

More confident students can complete the challenge activity.

Cambridge Lower Secondary Chemistry
Stage 7

Extension ideas

Ask students to find out why the number of elements known has increased over time. Which elements have we known about since ancient times and which are a more recent discovery? Can they explain why?

Homework suggestions

Students can use the information they gathered about an element in the lesson, plus additional information, to create a poster or information leaflet about that element.

4.4c Symbols and the Periodic Table

Students will learn:

- To know that the Periodic Table shows elements in an order
- To interpret data from secondary sources
- To use symbols and formulae to represent scientific ideas

Glossary words

chemical symbol, Periodic Table

Resource preparation

Scrap paper, small container.

Worksheet 4.4c

Teaching and learning ideas

- Use figure 4.21 in the Student's Book to explore how the element name 'silver' is different in different languages. Ask students if they know any other examples of element names in different languages.
- Discuss the fact that each element is represented by a symbol. The symbol can consist of one, two or three letters although students at this stage are unlikely to know about elements with three-letter symbols. The first letter is always upper case, and the second (and third) are lower case.
- Tell them that the symbol for silver is Ag. This is not similar to the element name in many languages, like English, but is similar to some such as argent in French. Explain that the symbol comes from the Latin word 'argentum', which is related to the Sanskrit word 'arjuna', which means light.
- Use figure 4.22 in the Student's Book to introduce students to the Periodic Table. Explain that it is a list of all the elements, in order of size. Show them that hydrogen atoms are the smallest, then helium. Ask students to trace their fingers across the rows to show the order of the atoms. Explain that each is given a number, so hydrogen is number 1.
- Give each student Worksheet 4.4c, which contains a blank copy of the Periodic Table. Ask them to fill in the symbols and numbers for the first 20 elements.
- If possible, students complete task 3 on Worksheet 4.4c. Give students access to the internet and allow them to use secondary sources to research where the symbols for some other elements came from. Ask students to use the internet to find out why some elements were given their names. They can research francium, cobalt, promethium, helium and mendelevium.
- Students complete questions 1 and 2 in the Student's Book.
- Play Periodic Table bingo with the class to help them learn the symbols. Ask each student to draw a 3 × 3 grid on a piece of paper and choose nine symbols from the first 20 elements of the Periodic Table to write in their grid. Meanwhile, you will need to write the element symbols on 20 small pieces of paper, fold them up and place them in a container. Take pieces of paper from the container, one at a time, and read out the element name (not symbol) to the class. If the student has this element, they can cross it off their grid. The first student to cross off all the symbols wins.

Differentiation

Help less confident students by supplying them with useful websites for their secondary research on the internet. More confident students can use search engines and judge how useful different websites are.

Extension ideas

Ask students to find out the name of the scientist who first created a Periodic Table, and compare it to the modern version.

They can also suggest why it has changed, and if they think it will change in the future.

Homework suggestions

Ask students to make up words using just the chemical symbols, for example SOCK or CaN.

Alternatively, they can make up crosswords or word searches using the element names.

4.5 Elements, compounds and mixtures

Topic overview

		Student's Book	Workbook	Downloadable material
4.5a	**Starting point** Students compare a model of an element to a model of a compound to start to formulate their own ideas of what a compound is	Starting point table		
4.5b	**Compounds and formulae** Students use names of a range of compounds, formulae and particle diagrams to form ideas about compounds and how they are different to elements	Questions 1–5		Practical notes 4.5b Worksheet 4.5b
4.5c	**Making mixtures** Students learn about mixtures and use particle models to show the difference between mixtures and pure substances. They are introduced to the concept of alloys	Questions 6–7 Activity 4.6	Questions 1–10	

Learning Objectives

- 7Cm.04: Describe the differences between elements, compounds and mixtures, including alloys as an example of a mixture
- 7Cm.07: Use the particle model to represent elements, compounds and mixtures
- 7Cp.06: Understand that alloys are mixtures that have different chemical and physical properties from the constituent substances
- 7SIC.01: Discuss how scientific knowledge is developed through collective understanding and scrutiny over time.

- 7SIC.02: Describe how science is applied across societies and industries, and in research.
- 7SIC.03: Evaluate issues which involve and/or require scientific understanding.
- 7SIC.04: Describe how people develop and use scientific understanding as individuals and through collaboration, e.g. through peer review

Links to other topics

- Students will learn how compounds are formed during chemical reactions and use the particle model to represent them in this topic.
- Solutions as a type of mixture is covered in Stage 8. Students will also use particle model to represent solutions.
- Also in Stage 8, students will revisit the difference between pure substances and mixtures.

Using models

- 7TWSM.01 - The particle model can be used to show how the particles are arranged in an element, compound or mixture. A model of an element would only contain particles which are all of the same shape, colour and size. A model of a compound would contain two or more particles which are different in shape, colour or size but which are clearly joined together. A model of a mixture would contain two or more particles of a different shape, colour or size and which are not joined together.
- 7TWSm.02 - A model of using symbols and formula to represent elements and compounds is also introduced in the Topic.

Common misunderstandings

- When water boils, the compound breaks down to form hydrogen and oxygen gas. You can remind students that water boiling to form water vapour is a change in state, not a chemical reaction, by showing them that the steam condenses on a cold surface to form liquid water.
- Chemical reactions always involve two reactants. In fact, some involve the breakdown of one reactant into products.
- Only elements can react together.
- A chemical reaction always happens when two substances are mixed.
- A chemical change is irreversible. Chemical changes can be reversible.

4.5a Starting point

Show the class the building brick model that represents an element as used in the previous section. Now, show them a similar model that contains two different colour bricks. Ask students to describe how the two models are different. Introduce the new model as representing a compound. Tell the class that a compound is made up of atoms of different elements. The atoms are strongly held together.

4.5b Compounds and formulae

Students will learn:

- To describe the differences between elements and compounds
- To use symbols and formulae to represent scientific ideas

Glossary words

alloy, compound, formula

Resource preparation

Samples of compounds, for example water, sodium chloride, carbon dioxide, copper oxide, iron oxide (haematite), lead sulfide (galena) and silicon dioxide (quartz). Each should be labelled with their name.

Worksheet 4.5b

Practical notes 4.5b

Teaching and learning ideas

- Remind the class that everything in the Universe is made up of atoms. However, there are only around 100 different elements. Ask them to use what they learnt in the starting point activity to explain how this is possible. Students can check their answer by reading the start of the section 'Compounds' in the Student's Book.
- Provide students with particle diagrams of compounds and their names. Have examples of each compound to show the class, if possible. Ask students to suggest what elements are found in each compound. Discuss how some compounds, such as water, are given common names as well as chemical names.
- Discuss why it is difficult to break up compounds into their elements (the atoms are strongly joined together; you can use the building-block model to show this – the bricks are strongly linked together).
- Ask students to complete the first activity on Worksheet 4.5b. They complete a table to name compounds, write their formula and state what the formula shows.

Cambridge Lower Secondary Chemistry
Stage 7

- Students answer questions 1–4 in the Student's Book.
- **Challenge:** Students can complete the challenge question 5 in the Student's Book.

Differentiation

To help less confident students, complete the first few rows of the table on Worksheet 4.5b as a class, with you modelling the thought process used to complete each missing answer.

Extension ideas

You might like to introduce more confident students to how compounds are named. For example, the name of the metal in a compound goes first, the name of the non-metal changes from oxygen to oxide, sulfur to sulfide, etc.

Homework suggestions

Ask students to write a list of some compounds that they can find at home. They should use the chemical names and could look on the labels of foods, medicines, cleaning products, etc. More confident students could also name the elements each compound contains.

4.5c Making mixtures

Students will learn:

- To describe the differences between elements, compounds and mixtures
- To sort, group and classify materials through careful observation

Glossary words

alloy, mixture, pure

Resource preparation

For the activity (each pair): a set of interlocking building bricks of different colours and sizes.

For Activity 4.6: range of elements, compounds and mixtures: sealed test tube of air, beaker of water, bottle of mineral water, sodium chloride, soil, copper, sulfur, sugar, bottle of shampoo.

Teaching and learning ideas

- Use the examples in the Student's Book to show the class different everyday examples of mixtures. Ask students to work in small groups to come up with some more examples of mixtures. Go through these as a class, using their ideas to build up a list of mixtures on the board.
- Discuss the difference between pure substances and mixtures.
- **Challenge:** Ask students why mineral water is not pure.
- Remind students of the building-block model used to represent elements and compounds in previous activities. Give small groups a set of bricks. Ask them to use them to represent a mixture of different elements, a mixture of different compounds, a mixture of elements and compounds.
- Consolidate understanding by asking students to write down the meanings of the terms elements, mixtures and compounds. Allow them to check their answers by using the glossary in the Student's Book.
- Students answer questions 6 and 7 in the Student's Book.
- **Challenge:** Students can complete the challenge question 8 in the Student's Book.
- Show the class an object or image of an object made from an alloy, e.g. bronze or steel. Ask them to suggest why this metal is not listed in the Periodic Table. After hearing their suggestions, explain that it is an alloy. Alloys are mixtures which may contain either two or more different metal elements, or one or more metal element and a non-metal element.
- Students complete Activity 4.6 *Element, compound or mixture?* in the Student's Book. Students should be provided with a range of different substances (elements, compounds and mixtures). Examples of elements that could be used include oxygen, carbon, iron, sulfur and magnesium. Examples of compounds that could be used include water and sodium chloride. Examples of mixtures that could be used include air, orange juice and a mixture of sand, iron and water.
- To check understanding from this learning episode, ask students to draw particle diagrams to represent: pure copper, air (a mixture of gases), bronze (an alloy of tin and copper), salt solution (salt particles dissolved in water).

Differentiation

Less confident students can complete Activity 4.6 in pairs or small groups and discuss the answers together.

In the first teaching and learning ideas activity above, challenge more confident students by asking them to think of examples of mixtures in which all the substances are gases, liquids or solids and then examples that are a mixture of a solid and a liquid, liquid and a gas, and gas and a solid.

Extension ideas

Ask students to find out the names of some alloys, what elements they contain, their properties and how these properties are linked to their uses.

Homework suggestions

Students can complete questions 1–9 in the Workbook.

Topic overview

		Student's Book	Workbook	Downloadable material
4.6a	**Starting point** In this activity students consider objects that contain metal, and the function of the metal. This will elicit any prior knowledge of the physical properties of metals	Starting point table		
4.6b	**The properties of metals and non-metals** Students use the properties of metals and non-metals to group materials	Questions 1–2 Activity 4.7		
4.6c	**Conduction of heat** Students carry out an investigation to find out which materials are the best conductors of heat	Activity 4.8	Questions 1, 3, 5, 6	Practical notes 4.6c Worksheet 4.6c
4.6d	**Conduction of electricity** Students carry out an investigation to find out what types of materials conduct electricity	Activity 4.9 Questions 3–5	Questions 2, 4	Practical notes 4.6d Worksheet 4.6d
4.6e	**Alloys** Students carry out their own research into alloys, and their uses. They use particle model to explain the difference in hardness between pure metals and their alloys		Question 7	

Learning Objectives

- 7Cm.03: Know metals and non-metals as the two main groupings of elements
- 7Cp.05: Describe common differences between metals and non-metals, referring to their physical properties
- 7Cp.06: Understand that alloys are mixtures that have different chemical and physical properties from the constituent substances
- 7Cp.07: Use the particle model to explain the difference in hardness between pure metals and their alloys

- 7TWSp.03: Make predictions of likely outcomes for a scientific enquiry based on scientific knowledge and understanding
- 7TWSc.01: Sort, group and classify phenomena, objects, materials and organisms through testing, observation and using secondary information, and making and using keys
- 7TWSa.03: Make conclusions by interpreting results and explain the limitations of the conclusions
- 7SIC.02: Describe how science is applied across societies and industries, and in research.

Links to other topics

- The concept of electrical conductivity is revisited in Chapter 9.
- In Stage 8 students will discover that metals have different chemical properties when they learn about the reactivity series.

Using models

- Using a particle model of a pure metal compared to an alloy will help students to explain why alloys are harder than pure metals. A model of a pure metal would contain rows of particles which are all the same colour, size and shape. At this level the delocalised electrons would not have to be shown.
- A model of an alloy would contain some rows of particles of the same colour, shape and size but would also contain some other atoms of different sizes which interrupt the rows.

- Students could be asked to describe the strengths and limitations of these models to cover 7TWSm.01
- Students can be extended by asking them to use a model of the particles in a metal to explain why metals conduct heat and electricity. Delocalised electrons are not introduced until Stage 9 or later.

Science in context

- The Science in context: Metals and non-metals in the Burj Khalifa tower box in Topic 4.6 of the Student's Book covers the following learning objective:
  - 7SIC.02 Describe how science is applied across societies and industries, and in research.
- Look out for opportunities to discuss new and innovative metals or non-metals that are being developed by scientists for novel uses

Common misunderstandings

- All metals are magnetic. Magnetism is not covered in this topic but you might like to review this misconception by showing the students that the only magnetic metals are iron/steel, nickel and cobalt.
- All metals have high melting points, are hard, strong, etc. All non-metals have low melting points, cannot conduct electricity, etc. There are properties that are common to most metals/non-metals but there are always exceptions. Some of these are outlined in the Student's Book.
- Students may think that alloys are elements. Some common alloys they may know include steel, bronze and brass. Explain that these are mixtures so are not listed in the Periodic Table.

4.6a Starting point

Give students one minute to write down as many objects that contain metals as they can think of.

Invite a student to give one example from their list. They then choose another student to ask what the function of the metal is in the object. For example, they may say bridge. The function of the metal in a bridge could be to ensure the bridge is strong and does not bend when vehicles are travelling over it.

4.6b The properties of metals and non-metals

Students will learn:

- To describe the differences in physical properties between metals and non-metals
- To understand that alloys are mixtures that have different chemical and physical properties from the constituent substances
- To sort, group and classify materials through careful observation
- To make conclusions from results using scientific understanding

Glossary words

Periodic Table, physical properties

Resource preparation

For Activity 4.7: a range of metals/metal objects, e.g. iron nail, coin, copper sheet, paper clip, steel cutlery, aluminium foil; a range of non-metals, including some that are 'metallic', e.g. metallic paper, metallic plastic, ceramic tile, graphite (from the inside of a pencil), wood, salt, sealed test tube labelled 'oxygen', water, rubber band, plastic cutlery.

Teaching and learning ideas

- Inform the class that all materials are either metals or non-metals. Ask them to think of some materials that are non-metals. Use the section 'Metals and non-metals on the Periodic Table' from the Student's Book to show the class how metals and non-metals are organised in the Periodic Table. Say the name of an element and ask students to use the Periodic Table to say whether it is a metal or a non-metal.
- Ask the students to read through the information 'Testing the properties of metals and non-metals' in the Student's Book. Ask them to list the physical properties of metals and non-metals. Discuss the metals and non-metals that are exceptions to these rules.

- Tell the class that rope can be made of both metal, and non-metal. If possible, show them images of each type. Ask them to discuss in pairs:
  - What properties of each material make it good at this function?
  - Why are some ropes made of metals and some are made from non-metals?
  - Examples of where each type of rope might be used.
- Refer to Activity 4.7 *Metal or non-metal?* in the Student's Book. Supply students with the materials listed above. They should try and group the materials as metals or non-metals based on the physical properties they can observe. Students should be asked to consider properties such as solid at room temperature, high melting point, shiny appearance, malleable, hard and strong.
- Compare the groups created by the students to see if they agree with each other. Discuss any objects that they grouped differently and discuss why. Talk about why it is difficult to group materials based just on their appearance.
- **Challenge:** ask students to use secondary sources, such as books and the internet, to research more properties of metals.

Differentiation

Provide less confident students with additional properties of metals: ductile, good conductor of electricity and heat, sonorous. Ask them to use secondary sources to find out what they mean. You may like to provide suitable URLs or book pages.

More confident students will be able to guide their research themselves.

Extension ideas

Ask students to find out the properties of the metals in column 1 of the Periodic Table and explain why this shows that they are not typical metals.

Homework suggestions

Ask students to choose an object that has both metal and non-metal parts. They should draw the object, label the parts and what they are made of and explain why they are made of these materials in terms of their properties.

4.6c Conduction of heat

Students will learn:

- To describe the differences in physical properties between metals and non-metals
- To make predictions of likely outcomes for a scientific enquiry based on scientific knowledge and understanding.
- To make conclusions by interpreting results

Glossary words

physical properties

Resource preparation

For demonstration: cup of hot water/tea/coffee, metal spoon.

For activity: boiling water (this can be taken from an electric kettle), Ingenhousz apparatus with rods made of different materials (wood, plastic, glass, metal), stopwatch/stopclock, petroleum jelly, drawing pins.

Worksheet 4.6c

Practical notes 4.6c

Teaching and learning ideas

- Demonstrate to the students stirring a hot liquid with a metal spoon. Ask them to write down a prediction:
  - What will happen to the spoon if you leave it in the liquid?
  - Can you suggest a reason why?
- Go through their answers and introduce the term 'conductor of heat' as a physical property of materials. Explain that heat can pass through materials that are conductors quickly, for example the spoon. Ask students to add 'conductor of heat' to their glossary.
- Refer to Activity 4.8 *Testing conduction of heat* in the Student's Book. Ask students to read through the method and study the results. They should then answer the questions.

- Alternatively, students can carry out a similar investigation themselves. They will need Worksheet 4.6c. Refer to Practical notes 4.6c for more information.
- Introduce the term 'insulator' to describe materials that are poor conductors of heat. Discuss with students what materials are good conductors (metals) and which are insulators (most non-metals).
- **Challenge:** ask students to explain why many saucepans are made of metal with wooden or plastic handles. They should include information about conduction of heat in their answer.

Differentiation

Less confident students may need more guidance on carrying out the investigation.

Extension ideas

Ask students to find out why metals are good conductors of heat.

Homework suggestions

Students could do questions 1, 3, 5 and 6 from the Workbook.

4.6d Conduction of electricity

Students will learn:

- To describe the differences in physical properties between metals and non-metals
- To make predictions of likely outcomes for a scientific enquiry based on scientific knowledge and understanding
- To make careful observations including measurements
- To make conclusions by interpreting results

Glossary words

control variable, dependent variable, physical properties, prediction, variable

Resource preparation

For demonstration: 1.5 V batteries, insulated wires, 1.5 V lamps.

For Activity 4.9: a range of materials to test, e.g. wooden toothpick, rubber band, glass microscope slide, pencil that has been sharpened at both ends to reveal the graphite inside, iron nail, paperclip, coin; 1.5 V batteries, insulating wires, 1.5 V lamps.

Worksheet 4.6d

Practical notes 4.6d

Teaching and learning ideas

- If the equipment is available, show the class a simple electrical circuit containing a cell and lamp with insulated wires. Explain that the lamp lights because the circuit is complete. Ask them to predict what will happen if you remove the wire from one end of the cell and to explain why. Demonstrate this. Explain that the circuit is no longer complete.
- Tell them that your idea is that the wires are made of plastic, so plastic must be a good conductor of electricity. It lets the current pass through it. Tell them that they are going to test your idea.
- If you have the equipment, allow students to carry out Activity 4.9: Testing conduction of electricity. Supply groups with a simple circuit with a gap in it. They place different materials into the gap and record if the material is a conductor of electricity (the lamp will light up) or an insulator (the lamp will not light up). Give each student Worksheet 4.6d. Refer to Practical notes 4.6d for more information.
- Alternatively, refer students to Activity 4.9 in the Student's Book. They can analyse the results given in the table to answer the questions.
- Ask students to use your evidence to state whether your idea is correct. They will realise that the wires cannot be made from plastic as plastic is an insulator. Ask them what material they think is inside the plastic – it is a metal, most likely copper as copper is a very good conductor.
- Discuss the use of testing conduction of heat and electricity as a good way to identify materials as metals or non-metals, since all metals conduct heat and electricity. Ask them to add 'conductor of electricity' to their glossary.
- Students answer questions 3–4 in the Student's Book.
- **Challenge:** ask students to answer the challenge question (question 5) in the Student's Book.

Cambridge Lower Secondary Chemistry Stage 7

Differentiation

When carrying out the investigation, provide less confident students with a table to fill in.

More confident students can carry out the extension activity on Worksheet 4.6d.

Extension ideas

Ask students to find out why metals are good conductors of electricity.

Homework suggestions

Students could answer the remaining questions (2 and 4) from the Workbook.

4.6e Alloys

Students will learn:

- To understand that alloys have different chemical and physical properties from the constituent substances
- To interpret data from secondary sources
- To use a model in an explanation

Glossary words

alloy, compound, mixture, physical properties

Resource preparation

For demonstration: range of objects made from alloys, or images.

Teaching and learning ideas

- Ask students to draw particle diagrams to show a pure metal and an alloy. Use these to check that they understand that an alloy is a mixture of a metal with another element.
- Ask them to explain why alloys are mixtures, not elements or compounds.
- Students can complete question 6 in the Student's Book.
- Show the class a range of objects made from alloys or images of them. Tell them the names of the alloys and the elements they contain.
- Divide the class into groups and give each group a different alloy to research (from amalgam, brass, bronze, duralumin, nitinol, solder, steel). They can use books or the internet. They should find out:
    - What elements the alloy contains
    - A use of the alloy
    - Why an alloy is used, rather than the pure metal
  Groups can present their findings to the rest of the class.
- Tell the class that pure iron rusts. Adding other elements (mainly chromium) changes the chemical property of the iron so it no longer rusts. This is called stainless steel. Ask the class where stainless steel is useful and why, e.g. cutlery.
- Ask the class to read through the section 'Explaining physical properties' in the Student's Book.
- Use figures 4.39 and 4.40 to discuss why alloys are harder than pure metals.
- Students can complete question 7 in the Student's Book.

Differentiation

Provide less confident students with a suitable page in a book or a URL for their research.

Group less confident with more confident students.

Students may need to visualise a 3D model to understand the physical properties of alloys. Ask them to imagine layers of small balls on top of each other – the balls can slide over each other. Now, place a large ball in the middle of the layer – can they visualise why the small balls will no longer slide over each other?

Extension ideas

Ask students to find out how the amount of carbon added to steel affects its properties and uses.

Homework suggestions

See above for extension idea.

Students could answer the remaining questions from the Workbook.

Chapter 4 | Checking students' progress

End of chapter reflection
- To review the learning points of the topic
- To test understanding through answering questions

Resources
- Student's Book [End of chapter review questions]
- Workbook [Self-assessment grid, Test-style questions]
- Worksheets 4.4b, 4.7

Approach

Ask students to complete the self-assessment checklist at the end of Chapter 4 in the Workbook. Encourage students to work together in small groups to discuss which aspects of the material are the most difficult to understand, and then have a class vote. You may wish to revisit some Learning Objectives again if students find any areas particularly challenging. Use the Student's Book text and questions to revisit these aspects. Go through the answers orally in class. Take note of whether giving the answer appears to resolve students' uncertainty or not, and work through further examples.

As a short revision activity, ask students to complete Worksheet 4.4b, which asks them to classify particle diagrams as elements or compounds.

The teacher response in the Workbook can be completed to give students personalised feedback on next steps. Students could be asked to answer specific end of chapter review questions in their books. Alternatively go through some or all of the end of chapter review questions in the Student's Book orally in class.

Use the Context worksheet (Worksheet 4.7) as a framework for students to conduct their own research enquiries about the properties and uses of metals. This activity provides the opportunity to cover Learning Objectives 7SIC.02 and 7SIC.03. For example, students could focus on how ideas about the uses of new alloys such as memory alloys or how superconductors are used in magnetic levitation.

Finish by asking students to complete the test-style questions at the end of Chapter 4 in the Workbook. Provide feedback on students' answers, and work with students individually to identify areas that still need more work.

Chapter 5 | Chemical changes and reactions

Chapter overview

In this chapter, students will learn about recognising evidence that chemical reactions have taken place, the formation of precipitates, and neutralisation reactions. They will use the particle model to represent chemical reactions, and they will have an opportunity to plan and carry out an investigation. This chapter builds on topics in Structure and properties of materials in Stage 7 of the Cambridge Lower Secondary Science curriculum framework.

Topic title	Number of 40-minute periods	Learning Objectives	Thinking and Working Scientifically Learning Objectives
5.1 Making compounds	3	7Cp.04 Use tests to identify hydrogen, carbon dioxide and oxygen gases. 7Cc.01 Identify whether a chemical reaction has taken place through observations of the loss of reactants and/or the formation of products which have different properties to the reactants (including evolving a gas, formation of a precipitate or change of colour). 7Cc.03 Use the particle model to describe chemical reactions.	7TWSm.01 Describe the strengths and limitations of a model. 7TWSc.05 Carry out practical work safely. 7TWSc.07 Collect and record sufficient observations and/or measurements in an appropriate form. 7TWSp.05 Know the meaning of hazard symbols, and consider them when planning practical work.
5.2 Forming precipitates	1–2	7Cc.02 Explain why a precipitate forms, in terms of a chemical reaction between soluble reactants forming at least one insoluble product. 7Cc.03 Use the particle model to describe chemical reactions.	7TWSm.01 Describe the strengths and limitations of a model. 7TWSc.05 Carry out practical work safely. 7TWSc.07 Collect and record sufficient observations and/or measurements in an appropriate form.
5.3 Neutralisation reactions	2–3	7Cc.03 Use the particle model to describe chemical reactions. 7Cc.04 Describe neutralisation reactions in terms of change of pH.	7TWSc.05 Carry out practical work safely. 7TWSc.07 Collect and record sufficient observations and/or measurements in an appropriate form. 7TWSc.02 Decide what equipment is required to carry out an investigation or experiment and use it appropriately. 7TWSc.03 Evaluate whether measurements and observations have been repeated sufficiently to be reliable. 7TWSp.04 Plan a range of investigations of different types, while considering variables appropriately, and recognise that not all investigations can be fair tests.
End of chapter questions	1	Check students' progress	

Background science

Please note: the background science notes are designed to provide teachers with an overview of the science concepts students may have already been taught earlier in their education, are likely to be taught in this unit and are likely to be taught in later stages. They are not a checklist of the content to be covered by the teacher in each unit.

The background science notes also serve to provide the teacher with some understanding of the background science needed in order to deliver the content of each chapter.

Chemical reactions involve the interaction of reactants to form products. All chemical reactions involve energy transfers and these may be observed as temperature changes. Other evidence that a chemical reaction has happened include a gas being produced (often seen as bubbling) and a change from one colour to another. Insoluble substances called precipitates form when some solutions are mixed, and these are seen as white or coloured cloudiness in the reaction mixture.

The pH of a solution can be measured using a pH meter or estimated using universal indicator and a pH colour chart. Neutralisation happens when an acid reacts with an alkali. If an acid is added to an alkali, the pH of the reaction mixture decreases and may pass through pH 7. If an alkali is added to an acid, the pH of the reaction mixture increases and may pass through pH 7.

5.1 Making compounds

Topic overview

		Student's Book	Workbook	Downloadable material
5.1a	**Starting point** Discussion about students' prior knowledge of the topic and observations that show chemical reactions happening	Starting point table		
5.1b	**Modelling reactions** Students carry out simple chemical reactions, and model them using the particle model	Questions 1–4		
5.1c	**Evidence for reactions** Students recognise evidence of chemical reactions happening, and test for hydrogen	Question 5		Practical notes 5.1c Worksheet 5.1c
5.1d	**Testing for gases** Students test for oxygen and carbon dioxide gases, and identify hazards and risks	Questions 6–7 Activity 5.1	Questions 3, 6	

Learning Objectives

- 7Cp.04: Use tests to identify hydrogen, carbon dioxide and oxygen gases
- 7Cc.01: Identify whether a chemical reaction has taken place through observations of the loss of reactants and/or the formation of products which have different properties to the reactants (including evolving a gas, formation of a precipitate or change of colour)

- 7Cc.03: Use the particle model to describe chemical reactions
- 7TWSm.01: Describe the strengths and limitations of a model
- 7SIC.02 Describe how science is applied across societies and industries, and in research.

Links to other topics

- Students know from Stage 2 *Properties of materials* that a property is a characteristic of a material, and they understand that materials can have more than one property.
- Students know from Stage 6 *Changes to materials* that reactants interact to form products, and that a gas being produced, colour change or a change in temperature is evidence for chemical reactions happening.
- Students know from Chapter 4 Topic 3 *The particle model* in this book that the particle model can describe solids, liquids and gases.
- Students will learn about endothermic and exothermic reactions, and the relative reactivities of metals in Stage 8 Chapter 6 *Chemical changes*.
- Students will learn about displacement reactions and making salts in Stage 9 Chapter 7 *Chemical changes*.

Using models

- A word equation is a simple scientific model that shows the names of the reactants and products in a reaction.
- In this Topic, students should begin to use the particle model to represent the rearrangment of particles in a chemical reaction, and describe its strengths and limitations. This allows students to access the learning objective 7TWSm.01.

Science in context

- The Science in context: Industrial reactions box in Topic 5.1 of the Student's Book covers the following learning objectives:
  - 7SIC.02 Describe how science is applied across societies and industries, and in research.

- Look out for opportunities to show students everyday or industrial examples of evidence that chemical reactions have happened. For example, baking a cake or toasting bread are examples that may be seen in the home. Industrial examples include bubbling in the manufacture of aluminium, colour changes during the production of dyes, and the precipitation of aspirin during its manufacture.

Common misunderstandings

- Students may confuse the bubbles produced when a solid is warmed gently in a liquid with the bubbles produced by a chemical reaction in a solution. Show or explain to students that they may easily tell the difference by gently shaking the test tube or other reaction container. Bubbles due to a chemical reaction will continue to form after the existing ones have been shaken off.

5.1a Starting point

Teaching and learning ideas

Ask students to think about chemical reactions in pairs or small groups. What is a chemical reaction, how can you tell a reaction is happening, and what happens in chemical reactions? The students agree on their answers and feed back to the class. Identify misconceptions and strengths in the students' understanding.

5.1b Modelling reactions

Students will learn:

- To identify whether a chemical reaction has taken place
- To describe the strengths and limitations of a model
- To carry out practical work safely
- To collect and record sufficient observations in an appropriate form

Glossary words

compound, model, product, reactant

Resource preparation

For the practical to observe magnesium burning: eye protection, heat-resistant mat, Bunsen burner, tongs, magnesium ribbon

For the demonstration of potassium reacting with water: eye protection, gloves, safety screen, tweezers or forceps, sharp knife, filter paper, large trough, white tile, potassium

Teaching and learning ideas

- Students carry out a short practical in which they burn magnesium ribbon in air. They should record their observations and identify changes that show a reaction has happened. The students should wear eye protection, and view through a 1 mm gap in their fingers or a welding filter lens.
- Demonstrate the reaction of potassium with water. Remove the oil from a rice-grain sized piece of potassium using filter paper. Add a few drops of universal indicator to a trough of water, then drop the potassium into the water. Observe the chemical reaction (the potassium will ignite with a lilac flame, rapidly decrease in size and disappear with a pop at the end of the reaction, the indicator in the water will turn purple). Discuss the evidence that a reaction has happened. Name the reactants (potassium and water) and the products (potassium hydroxide and hydrogen).
- Eye protection should be worn by all in the laboratory. Place a safety screen between the trough and the students. Wear gloves to avoid skin contact with potassium. Return any unused potassium to its container.
- Refer to the Student's Book and questions 1–4.
- Identify the elements (magnesium, oxygen, potassium, hydrogen) and compounds (magnesium oxide, water and potassium hydroxide) in the reactions seen in the lesson.
- Explain how to use the particle model to represent chemical reactions, including the ones seen in the lesson. Use circles to represent each atom, which may be coloured and/or labelled with the symbol for each element. Compare and contrast word equations and the particle model in representing chemical reactions.

Cambridge Lower Secondary Chemistry
Stage 7

Differentiation

Students may be unsure about the difference between elements and compounds. Use their observations in the practical to show that magnesium oxide is very different in its properties to the magnesium and oxygen from which it was formed, and is not a simple mixture of these two substances.

Extension ideas

Ask students to research the structure and bonding in metals such as magnesium and potassium, molecular substances such as oxygen and water, and ionic compounds such as magnesium oxide and potassium hydroxide.

Homework suggestions

Write a revision page to summarise the lesson in a way that a Stage 6 student would be able to understand.

Draw particle diagrams to model the reactions seen in the lesson.

5.1c Evidence for reactions

Students will learn:

- To identify whether a chemical reaction has taken place
- To use a test to identify hydrogen gas
- To describe the strengths and limitations of a model
- To carry out practical work safely
- To collect and record sufficient observations in an appropriate form

Glossary words

precipitate

Resource preparation

For the demonstration of the hydrogen test: eye protection, test tube, test-tube rack, heat-resistant mat, Bunsen burner, wooden splints, dropping pipettes, calcium

For the practical to investigate evidence for chemical reactions and to test for hydrogen: eye protection, test tubes, test-tube rack, heat-resistant mat, Bunsen burner, wooden splints, dropping pipettes, magnesium ribbon, dilute hydrochloric acid, dilute silver nitrate solution, dilute sodium chloride solution

Worksheet 5.1c

Practical notes 5.1c

Teaching and learning ideas

- Demonstrate how to test for hydrogen. Place one small piece of calcium in a test tube quarter filled with water. Place a lighted splint into the mouth of the test tube after bubbling has started. Explain how the test works. Eye protection should be worn.
- Students carry out a practical activity in which they observe and record the changes that occur in chemical reactions:
    - magnesium and dilute hydrochloric acid (magnesium disappears, bubbles of gas produced)
    - silver nitrate solution and sodium chloride solution (white precipitate of silver chloride forms)
    - magnesium and silver nitrate solution (magnesium becomes coated with black silver).

    The students carry out the test for hydrogen in the reaction where bubbles are seen. The students should wear eye protection. Students use Worksheet 5.1c.
- Refer to the Student's Book and question 5.
- Explain that the reaction between silver nitrate solution and dilute hydrochloric acid produces a precipitate of solid silver chloride in a solution of sodium nitrate. The formation of a precipitate is evidence of a chemical reaction. Outline that a precipitate is a solid formed when two solutions are mixed and react together, and that they will learn more about precipitates in later lessons.
- Students use the particle model to model the chemical reactions they have carried out.

Differentiation

Some students may be nervous about carrying out the hydrogen test. Work with them in a small group, or ask competent students to work alongside them.

Students may need help to begin their particle diagrams. Provide the students with a list of products formed in these reactions (magnesium chloride, hydrogen, silver chloride, sodium nitrate, magnesium nitrate, silver). This will help them to work out the products for each reaction. In particle diagrams, show how all the reactants and products can be represented by two different joined circles, except for magnesium and silver (single circles) and hydrogen (two identical circles).

Extension ideas

Ask students to research the reasons why the test for hydrogen produces different sounds, depending on how much hydrogen and air is present.

Homework suggestions

Write a report about the reactions in this lesson and previous lesson, and the evidence that each reaction had happened.

Make a table with two columns, one for the types of evidence of a chemical reaction, and one for examples of these types of evidence.

5.1d Testing for gases

Students will learn:

- Use tests to identify oxygen gas and carbon dioxide gas
- To carry out practical work safely
- To collect and record sufficient observations in an appropriate form
- To know the meaning of hazard symbols, and consider them when planning practical work

Glossary words

hazard, calcium hydroxide (limewater), risk

Resource preparation

For the demonstration of the oxygen test: eye protection, gas jar of oxygen, heat-resistant mat, Bunsen burner, wooden splints

For the practical to test for oxygen: eye protection, boiling tube, test-tube rack, dropping pipette, spatula, <18 vol hydrogen peroxide solution, solid potassium iodide

For the practical to test for carbon dioxide: eye protection, boiling tubes, delivery tube and bung to connect to a boiling tube, test-tube rack, heat-resistant mat, Bunsen burner, wooden splints, dropping pipettes, small lumps of calcium carbonate, dilute hydrochloric acid

Teaching and learning ideas

- Demonstrate how to test for oxygen. Place a glowing splint inside a gas jar of oxygen and observe that it relights. Explain how the test works. Eye protection should be worn.
- Students carry out a practical activity in which they produce oxygen, and carry out the test for oxygen. They add about 2 cm^3 of hydrogen peroxide solution to a boiling tube in a test tube rack, then add a small amount of potassium iodide as a catalyst. The students then test for oxygen using a glowing splint. The students should wear eye protection.
- Discuss their observations with the students, and how they provide evidence for chemical reactions.
- Students carry out a practical activity in which they produce carbon dioxide, and carry out the test for carbon dioxide. They add calcium hydroxide (limewater) to a boiling tube in a test-tube rack. They add a small amount of calcium carbonate to a second boiling tube, then some dilute acid, and insert the bung with its delivery tube. The students place the open end of the delivery tube in the calcium hydroxide (limewater). The students should wear eye protection.
- Discuss their observations with the students, and how they provide evidence for chemical reactions.
- Discuss the hazards and risks of the two practical activities, including suitable precautions to reduce the risk of harm.
- Refer to the Student's Book and questions 6–7.
- Students carry out Activity 5.1: Identifying risks from the Student's Book.

Differentiation

Some students may be nervous about carrying out the oxygen test. Work with them in a small group, or ask competent students to work alongside them.

Some students may need help with the carbon dioxide practical, in particular in ensuring that the reactants remain in the bottom of the boiling tube. Demonstrate how to use the apparatus in a 'dry run' without the substances involved.

Extension ideas

Ask students to research the chemical composition of calcium hydroxide (limewater) and why carbon dioxide turns it milky.

Homework suggestions

Make flashcards for the three chemical tests studied in this lesson and the previous one. Write the name of the gas on one side, and the test on the other (what you do, and what you observe).

Complete Activity 5.1 *Identifying risks*.

Cambridge Lower Secondary Chemistry
Stage 7

Forming precipitates

Topic overview

		Student's Book	Workbook	Downloadable material
5.2a	**Starting point** Discussion about students' prior knowledge of observations that provide evidence for reactions happening	Starting point table		
5.2b	**Precipitation reactions** Students learn about precipitation reactions and investigate how to make precipitates	Questions 1–3 Activity 5.2	Questions 4–8	Practical notes 5.2b Worksheet 5.2b

Learning Objectives

- 7Cc.02: Explain why a precipitate forms, in terms of a chemical reaction between soluble reactants forming at least one insoluble product
- 7Cc.03: Use the particle model to describe chemical reactions
- 7TWSm.01: Describe the strengths and limitations of a model

- 7SIC.02: Describe how science is applied across societies and industries, and in research.
- 7SIC.05: Discuss how the uses of science can have a global environmental impact.

Links to other topics

- Students know from Stage 6, *Changes to materials*, that chemical reactions involve reactants interacting to form products.
- Students will learn that reactions do not always lead to a single pure product and that sometimes a reaction will produce an impure mixture of products in Stage 8 Chapter 6 Topic 2 *Pure substances and mixtures*.
- Students will learn about ions and ionic bonding in Stage 9 Chapter 6 *Structure, bonding and the properties of matter*.

Using models

- This Topic gives students opportunities to develop their knowledge and understanding of using the particle model to represent chemical reactions.

Science in context

- The Science in context: Removing mercury box in Topic 5.2 of the Student's Book covers the following learning objectives:
  - 7SIC.02 Describe how science is applied across societies and industries, and in research.
  - 7SIC.05 Discuss how the uses of science can have a global environmental impact.
- Look out for opportunities to show students everyday or industrial examples of precipitation reactions. For example, mixing milk with cola, and sodium carbonate (washing soda) with magnesium sulfate (Epsom salts), are two examples of precipitation reactions that can be demonstrated at home. Industrial examples include the use of aluminium sulfate in the production of drinking water, and in the removal of mercury and other heavy metals from waste water.

Cambridge Lower Secondary Chemistry
Stage 7

5.2a Starting point

Teaching and learning ideas

Ask the students to identify the ways in which they can tell that a chemical reaction has happened. Collect their answers, for example on the board. For each type of observation (temperature change, colour change, production of a gas, formation of a precipitate) ask the students to give one or more example in pairs or small groups. The students agree on their answers and feed back to the class. Lead on to the purpose of the topic, which is to study the formation of precipitates and to explain why they form.

5.2b Precipitation reactions

Students will learn:

- To explain why a precipitate forms
- To describe the strengths and limitations of a model
- To carry out practical work safely
- To collect and record sufficient observations in an appropriate form

Glossary words

insoluble, precipitate, soluble, solution

Resource preparation

For the demonstration to show precipitation reactions: small beakers, silver nitrate solution, sodium chloride solution, potassium iodide solution

For the practical to investigate precipitation reactions: eye protection, test tubes, test-tube rack, dropping pipettes, sodium hydroxide solution, solutions of different metal compounds: iron(II) sulfate, iron(III) sulfate, copper(II) sulfate, zinc chloride

For investigating the predictions made in Activity 5.2 (as a demonstration): two small beakers, barium chloride solution, sodium sulfate solution.

Worksheet 5.2b

Practical notes 5.2b

Teaching and learning ideas

- Demonstrate the reaction between solutions of silver nitrate solution and sodium chloride, and between solutions of silver nitrate and potassium iodide. Explain that each reaction produces a cloudy, insoluble precipitate, and that different precipitates can be white or coloured (silver chloride is white and silver iodide is yellow). Link to the test in which a white precipitate forms when carbon dioxide dissolves in calcium hydroxide (limewater) and reacts with it. This word equation models the reaction:

  calcium hydroxide + carbon dioxide $\rightarrow$ calcium carbonate + water

- Students carry out a practical activity in which they produce precipitates. They follow the instructions on Worksheet 5.2b to produce insoluble metal hydroxides using solutions of sodium hydroxide and metal salts. Students follow the instructions carefully and write down their observations. Practical notes 5.2b give more information.
- Use figure 5.13 in the Student's Book to show the class the particle diagram for a precipitation reaction. Students draw particle diagrams for one or more of the reactions they have seen.
- Compare and contrast word equations and the particle model in representing precipitation reactions.

- Activity 5.2 *Predicting precipitation reactions* in the Student's Book. Test the students' predictions by demonstrating what happens when barium nitrate solution is mixed with sodium sulfate solution (a white precipitate of barium sulfate forms).
- Refer to the Student's Book and questions 1–3.

Differentiation

Some student may have difficulty in working out what happens in precipitation reactions. To help them, write the metal and non-metal parts of each compound on separate cards. Show the students how to join the cards together to make the compounds in the reactants. To show the chemical reaction, split up the cards and rearrange them to form the products.

Extension ideas

Ask students to research uses of precipitation reactions in medicine to treat poisoning.

Homework suggestions

Workbook questions 4, 5, 8.

Design an experiment to show that precipitates are insoluble.

Cambridge Lower Secondary Chemistry
Stage 7

5.3 Neutralisation reactions

Topic overview

		Student's Book	Workbook	Downloadable material
5.3a	**Starting point** Quick quiz to determine the students' prior knowledge of acids, alkalis, the pH scale and indicators	Starting point table		
5.3b	**What is neutralisation?** Students learn about neutralisation reactions and what happens during neutralisation	Questions 1–8	Questions 1, 3, 4 and 5	
5.3c	**Investigating neutralisation** Students plan and carry out an investigation into the amount of acid in different acidic solutions	Activity 5.3	2, 6	Practical notes 5.3a Worksheet 5.3a

Learning Objectives

- 7Cc.03: Use the particle model to describe chemical reactions
- 7Cc.04: Describe neutralisation reactions in terms of change of pH
- 7TWSc.05: Carry out practical work safely
- 7TWSc.07: Collect and record sufficient observations and/or measurements in an appropriate form
- 7TWSc.02: Decide what equipment is required to carry out an investigation or experiment and use it appropriately.

- 7TWSc.03: Evaluate whether measurements and observations have been repeated sufficiently to be reliable.
- 7TWSp.04: Plan a range of investigations of different types, while considering variables appropriately, and recognise that not all investigations can be fair tests.
- 7SIC.02: Describe how science is applied across societies and industries, and in research.

Links to other topics

- Students may know from their previous studies that human defence mechanisms include stomach acid.
- Students learn about the pH scale and indicators in Chapter 4 Topic 2 *Acidity and indicators* in this book.
- Students will learn about the reactions of acids with metals and metal carbonates in Stage 9 Chapter 7 Topic 3 *Methods for making salts*.

Using models

- This Topic gives students opportunities to develop their knowledge and understanding of using the particle model to represent chemical reactions.

Science in context

- The Science in context: Indigestion tablets box in Topic 5.2 of the Student's Book covers the following learning objectives:
  - 7SIC.02 Describe how science is applied across societies and industries, and in research.
- Look out for opportunities to show students examples of neutralisation reactions. The use of indigestion remedies (covered in this topic) is an example of home use of neutralisation. Industrial examples include the use of lime to reduce the acidity in farmers' fields, and the manufacture of salts for use as fertilisers.

5.3a Starting point

Teaching and learning ideas

Give the students a quick quiz about acids, alkalis, the pH scale and indicators. The students could answer individually, in pairs or in small groups. Discuss their answers and correct any misconceptions.

5.3b What is neutralisation?

Students will learn:

- To understand what neutralisation means
- To describe neutralisation in terms of change of pH
- To carry out practical work safely
- To collect and record sufficient observations in an appropriate form

Glossary words

acid, acidic, alkali, alkaline, neutral, neutralisation, indicator, pH scale, universal indicator

Resource preparation

For the demonstration to show a neutralisation reaction: eye protection, pH meter, various acidic, neutral and alkaline solutions, beakers, dropping pipettes, universal indicator paper, pH colour chart, 0.05 M sulfuric acid and 0.1 M ammonia solution

For the practical to investigate a neutralisation reaction: eye protection, test tube, test-tube rack, dropping pipettes, universal indicator solution, pH colour chart, 0.05 M ethanoic acid and 0.05 M sodium hydroxide solution

Teaching and learning ideas

- Demonstrate measuring pH with a pH meter, and estimating pH using universal indicator paper. Discuss the differences between these two methods to determine pH. Demonstrate what happens to the pH of dilute sulfuric acid when ammonia solution is added to it in portions. The use of ammonia solution (ammonia is a weak alkali) ensures that the students will observe pH 7 being approached rather than just quickly exceeded, as would happen with a strong alkali such as sodium hydroxide.
- Student carry out a practical activity in which they neutralise dilute ethanoic acid with dilute sodium hydroxide solution. They add about 2 cm^3 of ethanoic acid and a few drops of universal indicator solution to a test tube. The students then add sodium hydroxide solution drop by drop, observing and recording the colour and pH each time. The students should wear eye protection.
- The use of ethanoic acid (a weak acid) ensures that the students will observe pH 7 being approached rather than just quickly exceeded, as would happen with a strong acid such as hydrochloric acid.
- Discuss other ideas about neutralisation as a class – what do you do if you are stung by a wasp? What do you do if you are stung by a bee? Why does toothpaste need to be slightly alkaline?
- Refer to the Student's Book and questions 1–8.

Differentiation

Students may find it difficult to use the dropping pipette to deliver solutions drop by drop. The practical activity could be varied by increasing the volumes used. For example, adding 25 cm^3 of acid to a beaker, then adding the alkali contained in a full dropping pipette (usually about 2 cm^3).

Cambridge Lower Secondary Chemistry
Stage 7

Extension ideas

Ask students to research the reactions of metals, metal oxides and metal carbonates with acids. They should compare the products formed and the evidence for each reaction taking place.

Homework suggestions

Workbook questions 1, 3, 4 and 5.

Research examples of neutralisation being useful in everyday life. Produce a report on your findings, including the sources of information used.

5.3c Investigating neutralisation

Students will learn:

- To understand what neutralisation means
- To describe neutralisation in terms of change of pH
- To choose and use a range of equipment correctly
- To evaluate whether measurements and observations have been repeated sufficiently to be reliable
- To carry out practical work safely
- To collect and record sufficient observations in an appropriate form
- To identify variables within an investigation
- To plan fair test investigations

Glossary words

control variable, dependent variable, independent variable, reliable, variable

Resource preparation

TV advert or video on indigestion

For Activity 5.3: eye protection, three acids of different strengths, indigestion tablet

Worksheet 5.3a

Practical notes 5.3a

Teaching and learning ideas

- To engage the class, you could show a television advert on indigestion which shows what is happening inside the stomach.
- Activity 5.3 *Investigating neutralisation* in the Student's Book. Ensure that students understand what neutralisation means by asking questions.
- Discuss with students the meaning of the terms: variable, dependent variable, independent variable, control variable. Choose examples that are not related to neutralisation, such as how does the length of a hanging rubber band change when different weights are added to it? Discuss ways to ensure that results are reliable, for example by repeating the experiment more than once and calculating mean values (ignoring anomalous results).
- Carry out Activity 5.3 *Investigating neutralisation* in the Student's Book. Worksheet 5.3a can be used as a template to fill out while planning the investigation. Note that students should wear eye protection if actually completing the experiment.
- Ask groups to work together to follow the experiment and compare results – how do they know neutralisation has happened? What would they do if they went 'too far' and went past neutralisation? How do they know which solution contained the most acid?

Differentiation

Students may not fully understand the idea of fair testing. Explain that in a fair test, the thing you are trying to measure (the dependent variable) should change only because you deliberately change something else (the independent variable). Nothing else (the control variables) should cause the thing you are trying to measure to change. Give a simple example, such as investigating the pH of a substance depends on the volume of water added to it. Ask the students to discuss (in pairs or in groups) what they will measure (pH and volume of water), what the independent variable is (volume of water because they will deliberately change it), what the dependent variable is (pH of the substance), what the control variables may be (e.g. volume of substance at the start, type of substance). Take feedback, discuss remaining or new misconceptions, and pose more examples if necessary.

Cambridge Lower Secondary Chemistry
Stage 7

Extension ideas

Ask students to research the use of titration to determine the concentration of acids and alkalis.

Homework suggestions

Workbook questions 2 and 6.

Research the symptoms and causes of indigestion, and the remedies used to treat it.

Complete the investigation plan for the next lesson.

Cambridge Lower Secondary Chemistry
Stage 7

Chapter 5 Checking students' progress

Resources
- Student's Book [End of chapter review questions]
- Workbook [Self-assessment grid, Test-style questions]
- Worksheet 5.4

Approach

Use the 'Key facts' and 'Check your skills progress' boxes in the Student's Book for each topic in this chapter as a way of recapping on the main learning points.

Ask students to complete the self-assessment checklist at the end of Chapter 5 in the Workbook. Encourage students to work together in small groups to discuss which aspects of the material are the most difficult to understand, and then have a class vote. You may wish to revisit some Learning Objectives again if students find any areas particularly challenging. Use the Student's Book text and questions to revisit these aspects. Go through the answers orally in class. Take note of whether giving the answer appears to resolve students' uncertainty or not, and work through further examples.

The teacher response in the Workbook can be completed to give students personalised feedback on next steps. Students could be asked to answer specific end of chapter review questions in their books. Alternatively go through some or all of the end of chapter review questions in the Student's Book orally in class.

Use the Context worksheet (Worksheet 5.4) as a framework for students to conduct their own research enquiries about the evidence for reactions in industrial processes, the use of precipitation reactions and/or neutralisation reactions. This activity provides the opportunity to cover learning objectives 7SIC.02, 7SIC.03 and 7SIC.05. For example, students could focus on how ideas about emissions of sulfur dioxide by vehicles and some power stations, and how these emissions are a major source of acid rain. They could look at how sulfur dioxide is removed at source by flue gas desulfurisation, how excess acidity in rivers, lakes and soils is reduced, and the global environmental impact of acid rain.

Finish by asking students to complete the test-style questions at the end of Chapter 5 in the Workbook. Provide feedback on students' answers, and work with students individually to identify areas that still need more work.

Chapter 6 — Energy

Chapter overview

Students will build on their previous knowledge from earlier stages of their education of energy as something that makes things happen, recalling energy's role in food chains and the Sun's place as the initial source of food energy.
In this chapter, they will develop their knowledge of:

- energy sources
- energy transfers
- ways of storing energy
- energy's usefulness and that it dissipates, thus becoming less useful.

Topic title	Number of 40-minute periods	Learning Objectives	Thinking and Working Scientifically Learning Objectives
6.1 Energy at work	3–4	7Pf.01 Describe changes in energy that are a result of an event or process.	7TWSm.01 Describe the strengths and limitations of a model. 7TWSa.05 Present and interpret observations and measurements appropriately.
6.2 Energy dissipation	3–4	7Pf.02 Know that energy tends to dissipate and in doing so becomes less useful.	7TWSm.01 Describe the strengths and limitations of a model. 7TWSp.03 Make predictions of likely outcomes for a scientific enquiry based on scientific knowledge and understanding. 7TWSp.04 Plan a range of investigations of different types, while considering variables appropriately, and recognise that not all investigations can be fair tests. 7TWSa.01 Describe the accuracy of predictions, based on results, and suggest why they were or were not accurate. 7TWSa.02 Describe trends and patterns in results, including identifying any anomalous results. 7TWSa.03 Make conclusions by interpreting results and explain the limitations of the conclusions.
End of chapter questions	1	Check students' progress	

Background science

Please note: the background science notes are designed to provide teachers with an overview of the science concepts students may have already been taught earlier in their education, are likely to be taught in this unit and are likely to be taught in later stages. They are not a checklist of the content to be covered by the teacher in each unit.

The background science notes also serve to provide the teacher with some understanding of the background science needed in order to deliver the content of each chapter.

Energy is widely spoken about in modern life. So, students should already have the idea that energy is needed to make things happen. You will be helping them to recognise and describe the driving role that energy *changes* have in all the events and processes they come across, and to describe how energy is being transferred, e.g. by doing mechanical work or by heating.

You will also be helping them to focus on the usefulness of energy. They may already recognise energy as something that cannot be created or destroyed, but you will be helping them to trace where it goes, and to introduce the idea that energy *dissipates* and becomes less useful after every use we make of it.

To be able to grasp why it is that energy always tends to dissipate and become less useful, you may find it helpful to think about the degree of control we have when accessing energy and directing its flow. When energy is neatly packaged and contained, either in the motion of an object we can control or in an electrical/chemical store like a battery, then we can easily direct what happens next. You can allow water held back by a dam to flow out, or you can close a switch on an electric circuit and allow current to flow.

But once energy has been transferred into the wider environment and become dispersed, our options become much more limited. In particular, once energy has become dispersed into the random thermal motions of the many particles that make up a substance, all we can do is detect a rise or fall in an object's temperature. If the object is very hot or very cold in comparison with another nearby object, we can enable some of that stored thermal energy to be transferred to the nearby object. But once thermal energy finds its way into objects that are near ambient temperature, there is little we can do with it. Even though the quantity of energy stored in the object may be huge, dispersed over a large mass, like the mass of air in a room, or the mass of the ocean, it is no longer useful for making things happen. (However, if we can make use of another energy source – for example, using electric power to run a refrigerator or a heat pump – then we can move thermal energy from one place to another.)

The mechanisms by which thermal energy gets transferred, and the direction in which it naturally flows, are topics that students will cover in Stage 9. Also at Stage 9, ideas of energy conservation that have been implicit since Stage 4 of the new Cambridge Science curriculum framework will be formulated into a Principle that can be used quantitatively to solve problems.

Note: As energy has become more central to our modern lives, our scientific ways of talking about it have been changing, too. The new Cambridge Primary and Lower Secondary Science curriculum framework has deliberately steered clear of adopting any specific model for teaching energy, preferring to allow teachers and textbook authors the choice of model, and indeed the opportunity to highlight to students the fact that a model is being used, and to discuss with them how useful the model is.

So, in this course we have moved away from naming energy types, and instead focused on energy sources, energy transfers and the various ways in which energy can be stored. This, we hope, will enable you as teachers to exercise the freedom that the curriculum framework designers have intended you to have, choosing your own energy model and approach. In making that choice you will want to consider the language and ideas your students are likely to meet when they move on to prepare for Cambridge IGCSE or equivalent and other higher qualifications.

'Potential energy' is a term that students often find rather odd and confusing. 'Potential for what?' they may wonder, or, 'Is this actual energy or just a possibility?' One way of looking at it is using a 'stores and transfers' model, in which potential energy is described as 'stored energy' or an 'energy store'. This stored energy could be *elastic* – stored in a stretched or squashed material, or *gravitational* – stored by moving a mass upwards as the force of gravity, and able to be recovered by letting the mass fall back down. (Because gravity is dealt with in a later chapter in this book, we have been cautious about using the word 'gravitational', and have just talked about energy stored in an object due to its height.) There can be value in delaying the use of the term *gravitational potential energy*, as it can be difficult for learners to understand at this level. But this term will become important for them to know at IGCSE or equivalent level. At higher levels students will learn about other fields of force – *electrostatic* or *magnetic* – and that *potential* energy can similarly be stored by changing the position of an object in those fields.

Other 'energy stores' in the 'stores and transfers' model include *kinetic* energy, *thermal* energy, *chemical* energy and *nuclear* energy. In the old language, they were all 'energy types'. IGCSE also introduces the term *internal* energy, which is a 'catch-all' for the total energy stored in a system, an important idea, but something which cannot be directly measured. Only *changes* in internal energy can be determined. So, getting your students used to talking about *changes* in energy is helpful preparation for more advanced learning later.

In both the old and the new language, *heating* and *doing work* are ways of transferring energy. *Heating* occurs when *thermal* energy is either the input or the output of the transfer. *Work is done* whenever a force moves through a distance. Students at this level need to recognise that we can store energy by applying a force and making something move; and that this stored energy can be recovered if an object then pushes back and begins to move itself – either due to its elasticity or just due to its weight making it fall. (They do not yet need to talk about force and displacement as being vector quantities.)

Heating does not always cause a temperature rise. Sometimes the thermal energy transferred into a material is used to do work, for example the work of separating and rearranging molecules to turn them from solid to liquid state – ice melting at 0 °C without a temperature rise – or the work of expanding the volume of a gas by heating it. (Students will not explore such examples as these in any detail until later in their studies.)

What is quite different between the new 'stores and transfers' model and the old 'energy types' approach, is the way in which they describe energy in wave motion. Waves, like *sound* and *light*, carry energy from one object and place to another, when they are simple travelling waves. This is how students at this level usually experience sound and light. So, in this book, we have used the 'stores and transfers' approach of describing *sound* and *light*, along with a flow of *electric current*, as ways of transferring energy. This will hold good for students in their later studies, although they will also learn how standing waves can be stores of energy. By contrast the old language for teaching about energy calls electrical, light and sound energy 'energy types'. That is something we have avoided doing in this book; nor have we called these things 'energy sources'. Rather, we have pointed, beyond the means by which energy is being transferred, to a source from which it is coming – e.g. light from the Sun. This seems to fit better with the language and ideas about energy that students will meet at IGCSE or equivalent level and beyond.

6.1 Energy at work

Topic overview

		Student's Book	Workbook	Downloadable material
6.1a	**Starting point** These activities are to refresh students' understanding of energy as 'something that makes things happen', to check their skills in recording information in a table and to begin to focus on energy sources and energy changes.	Starting point table Activity 6.1 Activity 6.2		Practical notes 6.1a
6.1b	**Energy sources and energy changes** Students recognise the role of energy sources in driving changes, and link this to topics in other chapters.	Questions 1–2	Questions 1 and 3–5	
6.1c	**Energy stored due to motion or temperature** Students discuss how energy can be stored by using forces to stretch, lift or increase the speed of objects. They make use of the Particle Model to understand how raising the temperature of an object is also storing energy in the motions of molecules.	Questions 3–5	Questions 2, 6, 8 and 10	Worksheet 6.1c
6.1d	**Energy transfers** Students revisit their notes from Activity 6.2 and use flow diagrams to describe their observations and to identify energy transfers, recognising examples of 'doing work' and 'heating'.	Questions 6–10	Questions 7 and 9	

Learning Objectives

- 7Pf.01: Describe changes in energy that are a result of an event or process
- 7TWSm.01: Describe the strengths and limitations of a model
- 7TWSa.05: Present and interpret observations and measurements appropriately
- 7SIC.02: Describe how science is applied across societies and industries, and in research
- 7SIC.05: Discuss how the uses of science can have a global environmental impact

- 7SIC.01: Discuss how scientific knowledge is developed through collective understanding and scrutiny over time.
- 7SIC.02: Describe how science is applied across societies and industries, and in research.
- 7SIC.04: Describe how people develop and use scientific understanding as individuals and through collaboration, e.g. through peer review
- 7SIC.05: Discuss how the uses of science can have a global environmental impact

Links to other topics

- The Particle Model of solids, liquids and gases will also be discussed in Chapter 4 Topic 3 *The particle model*.
- Many topics in Lower Secondary Science utilise the idea of energy transfer, for example how food can be used as a store of energy by animals and how energy is transferred in food chains (Stage 7 Chapter 2 Topic 2); how the stored energy is released by respiration (Stage 8 Biology); how plants use energy from the Sun, through photosynthesis. (Stage 9 Biology); how waves transfer energy from one object and place to another (Stage 7 Chapter 8 *Sound*, Stage 8 Chapter 9 *Light*); how chemical reactions transfer energy between the reaction mixture and the surroundings (Stage 8 Chapter 6 Topics 3 and 4); how renewable and non-renewable energy resources are used to generate electricity (Stage 8 Chapter 11 Topic 3); how thermal energy gets transferred from one object and place to another (Stage 9 Chapter 8 Topics 2 and 3).
- In Stages 8 and 9 in *Earth and Space: Cycles on Earth*, students will study the impact on our climate and natural environment caused by increasing demand for energy for human use since the beginning of the industrial revolution.

Cambridge Lower Secondary Physics
Stage 7

Using models

- The Particle Model of how particles are arranged in solids, liquids and gases is used in this topic to understand how energy is stored in the thermal motions of molecules. Ask students to comment on the model's usefulness, drawing out the point that the same model explains both changes of state between solid, liquid and gas and how energy is transferred and stored in substances.

- There is an opportunity here to address learning objective 7TWSm.01 where the students are asked to discuss the strengths and limitations of the model.

- As explained above in 'Background science', there are different models for teaching energy, and teachers can choose which model to use. You could highlight to students when a particular model is being used, and challenge them to reflect on the use of such models and whether the one you are using helps them. Including diagrams or demonstrations of analogies could help this discussion.

- A visual analogy such as pouring a liquid from one watertight container to another could be used to explain the 'stores and transfers' model, in which energy is described as being in a store (e.g. a kinetic energy store, an elastic energy store, a thermal energy store). This energy may be transferred and when it is it will end up in another store.

- Ask if there are any limitations in such a model. You could point out the danger that it might make them think of energy as a 'substance' in itself rather than an idea that helps us describe and predict the outcomes of interactions (i.e. forces, motions…) between objects.

- If you use the traditional 'energy types' model, you could use the analogy of a 'reaction' with reagents and products. That also has some positive value, but does it risk obscuring from students that energy is the same before and after a change? You could get your students' feedback on that.

- You could think carefully with your students about sound and light. Is it more helpful for them to describe these two as energy 'types' or as 'ways of transferring' energy, the latter being the 'stores and transfers' model's language?

- If this seems too advanced a discussion for your group, choose to restrict it accordingly.

Science in context

- The Science in context: using water to generate electricity box in Topic 6.1 page 132 of the Student's Book covers the following learning objectives:
  - 7SIC.01 Discuss how scientific knowledge is developed through collective understanding and scrutiny over time.
  - 7SIC.02 Describe how science is applied across societies and industries, and in research.
  - 7SIC.04 Describe how people develop and use scientific understanding as individuals and through collaboration, e.g. through peer review
  - 7SIC.05 Discuss how the uses of science can have a global environmental impact

- In the search for new and better energy sources, much scientific and technological research is going into finding ways to store large quantities of energy, ready for use.

- Look out for opportunities to discuss with students how the uses of science can have a global environmental impact, for example replacing fossil fuels with biomass/biofuels as a source of energy for heating and for transport (this will be covered further in Stages 8 and 9 in *Earth and Space*).

Common misunderstandings

- Students may confuse energy transfer words with ways of storing energy. For example, they might misuse the word 'heat' as a noun to refer to the energy stored in a warm object, which is correctly called 'thermal energy'. In the Student's Book, we have used the action words 'heating' and 'doing work' to make clearer that these are actions – ways of transferring energy.

- Students may try to talk about the total amount of energy 'in' an object – for example, the amount of energy stored in a battery. But we can only measure energy *changes*, not totals. For example, when energy from a battery is used to move an electric vehicle, the quantity of energy being transferred into kinetic energy (giving it speed) and into increasing energy stored due to height too if the vehicle is climbing a hill, is called the 'work done'. Meanwhile, the energy being transferred because of electrical resistance and friction, both of which result in a temperature increase, is called 'heating'. Both the amounts of work done and heat transferred can be measured. From those energy changes (due to work being done and due to heating), we can deduce there must now be *less* energy stored in the battery, but we have no way of measuring and knowing the absolute total amount of energy in it.

- When applying the Particle Model to understand how energy is stored in warm air, students may get confused between the bulk (macroscopic) motion of air as an air current or wind and the random, sub-microscopic motions of individual air molecules. Bulk motion of air carries usable kinetic energy because the whole mass of air moves from one place to another, and this energy can be transferred by doing the work, e.g. turning a wind turbine.

Chapter 6: Energy

- Still air (e.g. in a room which has no currents or draughts) has no useful kinetic energy because, as a whole, it is not moving anywhere. Nevertheless, if you were able to see the individual molecules in this still air you would find they are all moving in random directions. Because there are as many particles moving to the left as to the right and as many going up as going down, overall the air moves nowhere. But the molecules are full of activity, bouncing off one another and off the walls of the room. We use the word 'thermal' to describe that random, invisible, microscopic motion of molecules that is out of our control and only known to us through temperature. Usable 'kinetic' energy is how we describe energy that is stored in the organised, detectable bulk motion of air, i.e. in a wind. We can cause a wind with a fan or use it to drive a turbine.

6.1a Starting point

Resource preparation

For Activity 6.1: board or large sheet of paper and suitable marker pens.

For Activity 6.2: a set of devices that use energy to make something happen, for example: clockwork toys, lamps, balloons, matches (teacher demo if appropriate), photographic negative, tin containing some dried beans.

Practical notes 6.1a

Teaching and learning ideas

- Refer to the Student's Book and introduce Activity 6.1 *What do you know about energy?* Working in groups, ask them to write on a board or large sheet all the sources of energy they know.
- When it comes to feedback time, ask the class where our energy comes from. Accept a range of valid answers, but then ask how that energy resource was generated – where did its energy originally come from? (Most of our energy has its original source in sunshine.) Prompt students to recall their knowledge of plant growth.
- Next, carry out Activity 6.2 *Observing energy changes.* Ask students to again work in groups and to carry out the activity. Afterwards, use questions and discussion with the whole class to develop the idea that it is energy *changes* that make things happen. Refer to Practical notes 6.1a for further details.

6.1b Energy sources and energy changes

Students will learn:

- To describe the energy transfers that happen in processes and events
- To make conclusions from collected data

Teaching and learning ideas

- Refer to the section in the Student's Book about 'Energy sources'. Follow up the first Link question with discussion and questions to check students' understand that sunlight is the original energy source for biomass/biofuels (such as fuels made from wood or vegetable oil) and for fossil fuels. Sunlight is also the driving energy source for weather systems, creating winds and waves.
- Follow up the second Link question with discussion and questions to check students' understand that burning is a chemical reaction, and that burning releases energy that was stored in a fuel. This is similar to how energy is released from food (respiration as a chemical reaction will be covered in Stage 8 Biology).
- Ask students to answer questions 1–2 in the Student's Book.

Homework suggestions

Students answer questions 1 and 3–5 in topic 6.1 in the Workbook.

6.1c Energy stored – due to motion or temperature

Students will learn:

- To describe the energy transfers that happen in processes and events
- To use the particle model to explain the link between energy and temperature

Glossary words

kinetic, thermal

Resource preparation

Photographs or diagrams illustrating energy stored due to motion – i.e. speed (kinetic), stretching/squeezing/bending (elastic) or height – in everyday situations that your students can recognise and relate to.

For the optional extra homework activity: cardboard, scissors, drawing pin, water tap – Worksheet 6.1c.

Teaching and learning ideas

- Refer to the section in the Student's Book about 'Motion and energy stores'.
- Ask students to look again at their results from Activity 6.2, and to identify all the devices that moved something. In which of these three ways – kinetic, elastic or height – was energy being stored in each case?
- Use photographs to explore further examples of energy linked with motion. In each case, get students to highlight the energy change that happens.
- Refer to the section in the Student's Book about 'Energy stored due to temperature'. Ask students to explain what 'thermal energy' is.
- You could ask a small group of students to stay in a confined area of the classroom and to act out the random movements of molecules in a sample of a liquid or gas. They could each hold a ball (representing an individual molecule) and move in different directions.
- Explain that the energies of individual atoms and molecules in motion cannot be measured or controlled by us. All we can sense is the temperature, which is a 'bulk' property of a very large number of particles.
- Ask students to answer the Link question about ice melting to form liquid water.
- Explain to students the example of pumped storage for hydroelectricity given in figure 6.3.

Extension ideas

Here could be a good moment for students to explore current research and development topics in energy storage (examples to suggest to students could include new types of batteries (e.g. lithium ion) and their falling costs of manufacture, research into fuel cells and the development of hydrogen as a fuel).

Homework suggestions

Questions 3–5 in the Student's Book.

Optional: Worksheet 6.1c gives students instructions for a homework activity 'Make your own turbine'.

Students answer questions 2, 6, 8 and 10 in topic 6.1 in the Workbook.

6.1d Energy transfers

Students will learn:

- To describe the energy transfers that happen in processes and events
- To use flow diagrams to represent the idea of energy changes in a process or event

Glossary words

heating, work

Resource preparation

Student's own data from investigation Activity 6.2 carried out in 6.1a. Photographs to illustrate energy transfers.

Teaching and learning ideas

- Refer to the section in the Student's Book about 'Energy transfers' and use questioning to explore with students the meaning of 'doing work' – i.e. a force causing movement of an object.
- Challenge students to explain, with the aid of a diagram, the difference between **doing work on** an object and allowing an object **to do work**, for example by falling. (You may need to prompt some of them to recognise the significance of the direction of movement.)
- Check, by questioning, that students understand when to use the action word 'heating' (for energy transfers that raise temperature) and when it is better to use the scientific name words (noun) 'thermal energy' (to describe the energy stored in a substance due to its temperature). *See the 'Note' about old and new language for teaching energy, in the 'Background science' section in this Teacher's Guide.*
- Ask students to refer to the table of results they created in Activity 6.2, and to focus on the column headed 'What process makes it work?' Working in groups, students should now try to represent each of their table line entries by a sketched flow diagram similar to those shown in figure 6.5. Whatever makes the process work should now be

labelled in the flow diagram using the appropriate transferring energy term: doing work, heating, by electric current, by light, by sound. (These simple flow diagrams will prepare students for using Sankey energy transfer diagrams in the next topic in this chapter.)

- To summarise and reinforce both recognition of energy sources and understanding of energy transfers, you could use photographs to quiz the class on the energy changes that drive a variety of everyday devices and activities.

Differentiation

Less confident students should benefit from tackling the flow diagrams in the context of group work, but you should look for opportunities to check their understanding through individual questioning and homework examples.

Homework suggestions

Answer questions 6–10 in the Student's Book.

Students answer questions 7 and 9 in topic 6.1 in the Workbook.

Topic overview

		Student's Book	Workbook	Downloadable material
6.2a	**Starting point** Recap of learning about energy changes including energy sources and ways of transferring energy from topic 6.1	Starting point table		
6.2b	**Wasted and useful energy transfers** Active demonstrations illustrate and highlight energy wastage. Students discuss findings and learn that nearly all processes that cause an energy change waste some energy by heating their surroundings	Questions 1–2	Questions 1–2	Practical notes 6.2b
6.2c	**Energy dissipates** Students discuss how to identify which energy transfers are useful and how energy is wasted. This leads to an understanding that energy dissipates and becomes less useful Students apply this new understanding to an investigation in which kinetic energy of a moving car is dissipated by friction as the car is brought to a halt	Activity 6.3	Questions 3–4	Practical notes 6.2c Worksheet 6.2c

Learning Objectives

- 7Pf.02: Know that energy tends to dissipate and in doing so becomes less useful
- 7TWSm.01: Describe the strengths and limitations of a model
- 7TWSp.03: Make predictions of likely outcomes for a scientific enquiry based on scientific knowledge and understanding
- 7TWSp.04: Plan a range of investigations of different types, while considering variables appropriately, and recognise that not all investigations can be fair tests

- 7TWSa.01: Describe the accuracy of predictions, based on results, and suggest why they were or were not accurate
- 7TWSa.02: Describe trends and patterns in results, including identifying any anomalous results
- 7TWSa.03: Make conclusions by interpreting results and explain the limitations of the conclusions
- 7SIC.03: Evaluate issues which involve and/or require scientific understanding
- 7SIC.02: Describe how science is applied across societies and industries, and in research.

Links to other topics

- In Chapter 7 *Forces*, students can apply what they have learned about energy transfer and energy dissipation to describe how air resistance, like friction, causes energy to be wasted by heating the surroundings.
- In Chapter 8 *Sound*, students can apply what they have learned about energy transfer and energy dissipation to describe how sound is absorbed by different materials.
- In Stage 9 Chapter 8 Topic 1 students will apply what they have learned about useful and wasted energy as they develop the basic idea that energy cannot be created or destroyed into a fuller understanding and applications of the Principle of Conservation of Energy.

Science in context

- The Science in context: energy efficiency box in Topic 6.2 page 140 of the Student's Book covers the following learning objectives:
  - 7SIC.02 Describe how science is applied across societies and industries, and in research.

- Look out for opportunities to highlight the environmental impacts of energy wastage (this will be covered further in Stages 8 and 9 in *Earth and Space*), and social and political impacts of energy wastage/shortage and to give examples of community initiatives to make better use of energy and hence reduce its dissipation. (For example, fuel poverty for the aged or for isolated rural communities; electricity rationing and power cuts; local community action to influence the siting of planned new power stations; community schemes to introduce small local hydro, solar or wind energy generation that avoid transmission power losses and can enable isolated communities to be energy independent or even energy exporters; grants or loans for insulation; local area heating schemes.)

Common misunderstandings

- Students may think that 'wasted energy' is lost or destroyed. They need to understand that it always appears in another, although less useful, form. Most often this will be thermal energy at a temperature near that of the surroundings.
- Without applying the Principle of Conservation of Energy quantitatively, using Sankey diagrams in this topic should help students to see that the energy input to a process may go to various destinations and become much less useful, but it is not lost or destroyed.

6.2a Starting point

Teaching and learning ideas

- Use feedback on homework from the previous session to recap the main learning outcomes from topic 6.1 about energy sources, transferring energy and storing energy. Student's Book question 6 used flow diagrams. Questions 7–10 ask for verbal descriptions. Check that students are grasping that in all cases an energy input is needed to make something happen; that energy is transferred in one or more ways; and that energy is output to be stored in new ways or new places.
- Check that students have recognised that when something happens there is usually more than one way in which energy is being transferred. You could refer students back to the results they recorded for Activities 6.1 and 6.2, or you could do a short simple demonstration – such as closing a door – where sound is produced as a by-product. This will help lead in to the next topic, where unwanted heating is seen to be widespread across many different energy change events and processes.

6.2b Wasted and useful energy transfers

Students will learn:

- To know that when energy is transferred to make something happen, some energy dissipates and becomes less useful
- To present observations using tables
- To Analyse observations to draw a conclusion

Resource preparation

For active demonstrations of energy being wasted: weights – for physical exercise; electric lamps of various types – incandescent bulb (filament bulb), fluorescent, light-emitting diode (LED); heating water in a beaker over a flame (burner or candle); electric kettle and thermometers.

Practical notes 6.2b

Teaching and learning ideas

- Refer to the Student's Book section on 'Wasted and useful energy'. Set up a series of active demonstrations of situations where some energy is wasted – see Practical notes 6.2b for details and safety warnings. Choosing to start with some physical exercises may help students then to settle down and to focus better on the academic content of the lesson.
- Ask students to draw up a table and to record for each example: the source of the energy input, the useful energy transfer, the wasted energy transfer, their observations and comments.
- As a whole class exercise, encourage the students to discuss what conclusions they have drawn from their observations. Discuss why the wasted energy in each example was a transfer of thermal energy (by heating the surroundings).
- Challenge students to explain, in each case they investigated, whether the energy wasted by heating could be reduced, and if so how.

  (Answer: In the case of heating water there are several ways to improve energy use and avoid wastage. A better heat transfer material could be used, for example a copper vessel rather than a glass beaker. The hot gases from

the flame could be ducted around the sides of the vessel. The whole 'boiler' could be surrounded by insulation to reduce the rate at which thermal energy escapes to the surroundings.

People exercising must be cooled down to keep them healthy and active. Notice that insulation can help reduce energy wastage when heating is useful, e.g. in a water heater. But insulation such as warm clothing would be dangerous for an athlete, who could become ill or die through over-heating.

You can only reduce energy wastage in an electric lamp by choosing another type of lamp that produces the same amount of lighting with less heating, e.g. fluorescent lamps waste much less than filament lamps, but LED lamps waste even less. Once thermal energy has been produced by a lamp it must be ventilated away to keep the lamp cool.)

Extension ideas

'Waste'. Here might be another good opportunity to link students' learning about energy with what they are learning in Chemistry Chapter 5.1 about chemical reactions. Sometimes, as when burning a fuel, heating is a useful output of the reaction process, though some of the energy transferred by heating always dissipates into the surroundings. As well as energy wasted by heating the surroundings, the products of chemical reactions can also count as waste if they are not useful. Ask students to give everyday examples of these – e.g. flue gases, soot, spent batteries (if not rechargeable), vehicle exhaust fumes…

Homework suggestions

Questions 1–2 in the Student's Book.

Students answer questions 1–2 in topic 6.2 in the Workbook.

6.2c Energy dissipates

Students will learn:

- To explain that when energy is transferred to make something happen, some energy dissipates and becomes less useful
- To write a plan for an investigation and choose which variables to change, control and measure
- To make a prediction using scientific knowledge and understanding
- To decide what equipment is needed to carry out an investigation
- To carry out practical work safely
- To present data using tables with column headings
- To analyse data to draw a conclusion and evaluate the accuracy of predictions made

Glossary words

- dissipate

Resource preparation

For Activity 6.3: each group will need a flat table or bench and a sloped ramp, wheeled trolley or small model car, elastic bands and a ruler.

Worksheet 6.2c

Practical notes 6.2c

Teaching and learning ideas

- Refer to the Student's Book and to the section 'Energy dissipates'.
- Recap with students the examples of wasted energy from the previous lesson's demonstrations.
- Challenge students to think of any examples where energy does *not* dissipate – that is, gradually get wasted, spread out and less useful. They might suggest objects moving in outer space, or 'frictionless' transport like a hovercraft or magnetic levitation, or the electric currents flowing in a superconducting magnet. But even each of those has a very slight and slow wastage of energy to other objects surrounding it. Even when two objects are separated by huge distances they still exert some forces on one another and can gradually waste some energy that leads to them slowing down slightly – e.g. the Earth and the Moon and energy used moving the tides etc. Examples from everyday life will show quite large wastages of energy that are hard to reduce.
- Explain that they will now be using their new understanding about energy to plan an investigation and to make predictions about the outcomes. Refer to Activity 6.3 *Investigating energy transfers* in the Student's Book. Ask students to work in small groups and to plan an investigation into the way energy transfers affect the motion of a wheeled trolley (or model car), and then put their plan into practice (see Practical notes 6.2c and Worksheet 6.2c). Remind them about the need to control variables in order to make a fair test.

- As a whole class exercise, encourage the students to discuss what predictions they made and what conclusions they have drawn from their investigation.
- Using questioning, help the class to describe the energy changes that occurred – both the initial transfer of (stored) energy, due to starting height, into kinetic energy as the trolley or car rolled down the slope, and transfer of kinetic energy into thermal energy as friction slowed it down. Draw out the correct names for the energy transfer processes – 'doing work' and 'heating'. Ensure students understand that the kinetic energy of the car becomes zero (when the car stops), that its kinetic energy is dissipated by heating, and that the thermal energy transferred to the surroundings (wheels, the ramp and the surrounding air) cannot then be usefully used because it is widely spread out and because the temperature increase is relatively small.

Differentiation

In Activity 6.3 *Investigating energy transfers*, less confident students may need help in making a prediction and then in identifying what to measure and record. You could prompt them to think about energy dissipation and to predict what factors may affect how quickly the car or trolley slows down. Prompt them to identify all the variables, and then to think about which should be varied and measured and which should be kept the same. Encourage them to design a suitable table for recording their measurements.

Extension ideas

- Highlight again that we can only measure changes in energy; we never know how much energy in total something has stored in it. Challenge students to look again at their results from the activity *Investigating energy transfers* and to explain from what zero point they decided to measure heights or distances. Why not from the floor up… or along from the end of the table? Also ask what counts as zero speed – and point out that the world is spinning and orbiting the Sun. Then ask why it did not matter where they set their zero points. (Answer: Because they were just measuring changes.)

Homework suggestions

Question 3 in the Student's Book.

Students answer questions 3–4 in topic 6.2 in the Workbook.

Chapter 6 — Checking students' progress

End of chapter reflection
- To review the learning points of the chapter
- To test understanding through answering questions

Resources
- Student's Book [Key facts, End of chapter review questions]
- Workbook [Self-assessment checklist, Test-style questions]
- Worksheet 6.3

Approach

Tell students to use the 'Check your skills progress' boxes at the end of each topic in the Student's Book as a way of recapping on the main learning points and of identifying any areas they still find difficult.

Also ask students to complete the self-assessment checklist at the end of Chapter 6 in the Workbook. Encourage students to discuss in small groups their self-assessment for each topic. Can they explain any difficult bits to one another? Are there questions that none of them feel confident to answer? If so, they should feed that back to the teacher. You may wish to revisit some Learning Objectives again if students find any areas particularly challenging. Use the Student's Book text and questions to revisit these aspects. Go through the answers orally in class. Take note of whether giving the answer appears to resolve students' uncertainty or not, and work through further examples.

The teacher response in the Workbook can be completed to give students personalised feedback on next steps. Students could be asked to answer specific End of chapter review questions in their books. Alternatively go through some or all of the End of chapter review questions in the Student's Book orally in class.

Use the Context worksheet (Worksheet 6.3) as a framework for students to conduct their own research enquiries about the ideas in this chapter. This activity provides the opportunity to cover Learning Objectives 7SIC.02 and 7SIC.05. For example, students could focus on current research and development in energy storage (such as flywheels, batteries, pumped storage, using solar energy to produce biomass) or the global environmental impact of using different energy sources and cooking devices, or reducing energy wastage.

After any group revision sessions that you have decided to give, finish by asking students to complete the test-style questions at the end of Chapter 6 in the Workbook. Provide feedback on students' answers, and work with students individually to identify areas that still need more work.

Chapter 7 | Forces and their effects

Chapter overview

In this chapter, students build on their previous knowledge of pushes and pulls, how to draw force diagrams, describing the difference between mass and weight and that gravity is a force that pulls objects towards the centre of the Earth, from earlier stages of their education, to develop their knowledge of:

- The relationship between an object's mass and its weight, and the effects of different gravitational field strengths.
- The gravitational attraction between any two objects and an understanding that each object attracts the other with the same sized gravitational force.
- The effects of air resistance on movement and an understanding of why there is no air resistance in a vacuum.

Topic title	Number of 40-minute periods	Learning Objectives	Thinking and Working Scientifically Learning Objectives
7.1 Gravity	2–3	7Pf.03 Describe gravity as a force of attraction between any two objects and describe how the size of the force is related to the masses of the objects.	7TWSm.02 Use symbols and formulae to represent scientific ideas. 7TWSc.05 Carry out practical work safely. 7TWSc.07 Collect and record sufficient observations and/or measurements in an appropriate form. 7TWSa.02 Describe trends and patterns in results, including identifying any anomalous results. 7TWSa.03 Make conclusions by interpreting results and explain the limitations of the conclusions.
7.2 Air resistance	2–3	7Pf.04 Understand that there is no air resistance to oppose movement in a vacuum.	7TWSp.03 Make predictions of likely outcomes for a scientific enquiry based on scientific knowledge and understanding. 7TWSp.04 Plan a range of investigations of different types, while considering variables appropriately, and recognise that not all investigations can be fair tests. 7TWSc.04 Take appropriately accurate and precise measurements, explaining why accuracy and precision are important. 7TWSa.02 Describe trends and patterns in results, including identifying any anomalous results. 7TWSa.03 Make conclusions by interpreting results and explain the limitations of the conclusions.
End of chapter questions	1	Check student's progress	

Cambridge Lower Secondary Physics
Stage 7

Background science

Please note: the background science notes are designed to provide teachers with an overview of the science concepts students may have already been taught earlier in their education, are likely to be taught in this unit and are likely to be taught in later stages. They are not a checklist of the content to be covered by the teacher in each unit.

The background science notes also serve to provide the teacher with some understanding of the background science needed in order to deliver the content of each chapter.

The size of the attractive gravitational force between two objects depends on the mass of both the objects involved.

In popular language mass and weight are often used to mean the same thing. However, mass is the amount of matter in an object and is measured in kilograms, and weight is the gravitational force exerted on an object that has mass and is measured in newtons. There is a link between the mass of an object and its weight. The weight of an object is a measure of how strongly that object is being pulled by gravity towards a much larger mass (usually we think of this as the Earth, but students should also consider weight on other planets or near stars, due to the gravitational pull of the planet or star). On Earth a mass of 1 kg weighs approximately 10 N. This leads to the equation

$$\text{Weight} = \text{mass} \times g$$

where g is the gravitational field strength in newtons per kilogram (N/kg). On Earth, g = 10 N/kg (approximately). On the Moon, g is about 1/6 of this value. On more massive planets than Earth, g would be greater than 10 N/kg.

When we look at the effects of gravitational forces we need to remember that while the Earth is pulling down on a falling object, that object is, at the same time, pulling the Earth upwards towards it. We do not see the Earth moving because the Earth's mass is so much greater than the mass of the falling object. If they were similar masses, we would see them move towards each other. But in practice, the attractive gravitational forces between two everyday objects (such as two people side by side) are so small that they produce no noticeable effect.

The large-scale effects of gravity – how tides are caused by the gravitational attraction between the Earth, Moon and Sun, how planets are formed and how components of the Solar System are held in orbit around the Sun – are covered within the Stage 7 Earth in Space topic.

All objects dropped from the same place will be accelerated by gravity by the same amount. Heavier objects do not fall faster: a weight 100 times bigger acts on a mass 100 times bigger so the acceleration is the same (since acceleration = force/mass). This means that all objects should take the same amount of time to fall from the same height to the ground. In practice this does not happen because there is another force in action. This force is air resistance. The direction of the force from air resistance is opposite to the force of gravity so air resistance slows down the rate of fall. The greater the area in contact with air, the greater the effect air resistance will have on its motion. Air resistance acts whenever an object is moving through air, not just when it is falling, and the direction of the force from air resistance is always opposite to the direction of attempted movement.

The area in contact with air can be increased in several ways. For example:

- by increasing the size for same shape (such as from ball bearing to football, or small parachute to large parachute).
- by changing the surface shape such as from smooth curves to sharp angles.
- by changing smooth surfaces to rough surfaces.

This is the opposite of the smooth fabrics designed for costumes worn by speed skaters, or streamlined designs for cars which have curved surfaces and no parts that stick out. In these cases, air resistance needs to be as small as possible.

The faster an object moves, the greater the amount of air resistance. This is why skydivers and other objects that fall a long distance do not keep accelerating forever. They reach a final speed, called the terminal velocity, and continue falling at this, steady, speed. Terminal velocity is reached when the upward force of air resistance equals the downward force of weight. A similar thing happens for racing cars travelling at very high speeds. They cannot increase their speed beyond the point where air resistance equals the thrust of the car engine. Students do not need to know about terminal velocity at this stage.

Resistance to movement happens when an object is moving through a liquid like water. Water produces greater resistance to motion than air does because the density of water is greater than the density of air.

Because a vacuum contains no particles, objects moving through a vacuum do not experience air resistance. This means they are not slowed down by losing energy through collisions with particles, and if something is moving at a constant speed in a vacuum (for example a rocket in space with its engines switched off, far from the gravitational influence of any planet or star) it will continue moving at that speed because there is no force to slow it down (or speed it up).

Students do not use the equations for how forces affect speed until Upper Secondary Science. However the effects of forces such as gravity and air resistance on a moving object will be covered qualitatively in Stage 8 Chapter 8.

Topic overview

		Student's Book	Workbook	Downloadable material
7.1a	**Starting point** This activity allows you to check prior knowledge and skills, emphasising that mass and weight are different and that weight is a force.	Starting point table		Worksheet 7.1a
7.1b	**Gravity, mass and weight** This section emphasises that gravity is a force. It formalises and recaps on ideas students may have met earlier and revisited in the starting point activity. This section also explores the quantitative relationship between mass and weight.	Questions 1–8 Activity 7.1 Activity 7.2	Questions 1–8	Practical notes 7.1b Worksheet 7.1b(1) Worksheet 7.1b(2)

Learning Objectives

- 7Pf.03: Describe gravity as a force of attraction between any two objects and describe how the size of the force is related to the masses of the objects
- 7TWSm.02: Use symbols and formulae to represent scientific ideas
- 7TWSc.05: Carry out practical work safely
- 7TWSc.07: Collect and record sufficient observations and/or measurements in an appropriate form

- 7TWSa.02: Describe trends and patterns in results, including identifying any anomalous results
- 7TWSa.03: Make conclusions by interpreting results and explain the limitations of the conclusions
- 7SIC.01: Discuss how scientific knowledge is developed through collective understanding and scrutiny over time
- 7SIC.02 Describe how science is applied across societies and industries, and in research.

Links to other topics

- In Earth and Space Chapter 11 Planets and the Solar System, students can apply what they have learned about gravitational attraction to how the planets formed, how they move around the Sun and how tides on Earth are affected by the gravitational forces of the Sun and the Moon.

Science in context

- The Science in context: Mars's gravitational pull box in Topic 7.1 of the Student's Book covers the following learning objectives:
  - 7SIC.01 Discuss how scientific knowledge is developed through collective understanding and scrutiny over time.
  - 7SIC.02 Describe how science is applied across societies and industries, and in research.
- Look out for opportunities to discuss how scientists have made discoveries about our Solar System based on the effect of the attraction of planets on other objects (including planets discovered in this way). The example given in the Student's Book refers to how our knowledge about Mars has developed over time and how new observations can lead to even greater knowledge and understanding.

Common misunderstandings

- Students may confuse free fall – constantly accelerating downwards motion due to gravity – with the terminal velocity achieved by falling leaves or by a parachutist. Students do not need to know about terminal velocity. In this topic, it is important that students understand that gravity (when it is not balanced by an opposing force) always causes a *change in motion*. In free fall that means a continuously increasing downwards velocity. For an object in orbit around the Earth, the object's speed does not change, but its direction is always being turned towards the Earth.

Cambridge Lower Secondary Physics Stage 7

- Students may think that a larger object exerts a bigger force on a smaller object, rather than equal size forces being exerted by each object on the other. This is because they will see small objects fall towards the more massive Earth but not see the minute effect of the same sized pull of the smaller object on the Earth. It is worthwhile repeating this whenever you have the opportunity. Students will have a better understanding later when they have met Newton's Laws of motion in iGCSE Physics.
- Many people think of mass and weight as alternative words for the same property. It is important to use the correct terminology: mass when referring to the amount of matter an object contains (measured in kg) and weight when discussing the force exerted on a mass (measured in N).
- Students may think that an object beyond the Earth's atmosphere (in space) does not experience a force of gravity. Giving examples of spacecraft orbiting the Earth, for example, space stations, and asking students to explain why they stay in orbit will help.

7.1a Starting point

Use Worksheet 7.1a with students to find out how secure their understanding of mass and weight is.

Show a newton meter and ask students to explain how it works. *(Answer: forces can also change the shape of some objects. Springs are designed so they change length when a force is applied. We can use this to show how large a force is being applied – for example, when we measure the weight (gravitational force) of a given mass.)*

7.1b Gravity, mass and weight

Students will learn:

- To describe gravity as a force of attraction between two objects
- To describe how the size of the force is related to the masses of the objects
- To describe what gravitational field strength is and how it affects weight
- To make accurate measurements of mass and force
- To carry out practical work safely
- To collect and record sufficient measurements in an appropriate form
- To take accurate readings of mass and force
- To describe trends and patterns in results and draw conclusions
- To identify anomalous results
- To use symbols and formulae

Glossary words

free fall, gravitational field strength, gravity, weight

Resource preparation

For Activity 7.1: newton meters; stands with bosses and clamps; hangers and masses, balance to measure mass.

Worksheet 7.1b(1)

Practical notes 7.1b

Students will need graph paper for Activity 7.2

Teaching and learning ideas

- Refer to Activity 7.1 *Mass and weight* in the Student's Book. Ask students to work in groups of two or three so that they all can participate. Full instructions are given on Worksheet 7.1b(1). See Practical notes 7.1b.
- Gather feedback from the students on their results from the activity. Point out that they have felt and measured the size of gravitational force.
- Refer again to the Student's Book. Explain that weight is the pull of Earth's gravity on other masses near it – the pull between a given mass and the Earth's mass.
- Challenge students to discuss the following question in pairs or small groups: what would happen to the weight of that mass if you took it to the Moon? In feedback from the groups, summarise both the effect of moving further from the Earth and the different gravitational pull from the Moon because it has a smaller mass than the Earth.
- Discuss the formula linking mass and weight, demonstrate its use and give students the opportunity to practise using it themselves.
- Explain that forces do not just appear out of nowhere. When one object exerts a force on another, we always find the two objects pushing or pulling one another in opposite directions – a pair of opposing forces. (You could use a pair of magnets of equal size suspended from string, close to each other, to demonstrate this). Ask students to give

examples where forces are pushing or pulling in opposite directions. Use this to discuss the fact that there is gravitational attraction between two objects, both objects exert the same sized force on the other object but in opposite directions. Talk through the fact that we may only see the effect of this force on the less massive of the two objects. You might use an example such as: "If I pushed this pen with a force of 20 N would you notice it move? If I pushed this lorry with a force of 20 N would you see the lorry move?"

- Activity 7.2 *Linking a planet's mass and its gravitational field strength*, reinforces the idea that gravitational field strength is different on different planets. It also gives the opportunity for students to plot graphs, handle data and spot trends and anomalies.

- During Activity 7.2 you could challenge students to discuss possible reasons for any anomalies they have identified (Answer: it is not just a planet's mass that determines its gravitational field strength, but also its size – how densely the mass is distributed).

Differentiation

Though Worksheet 7.1b(1) contains a suitable table that will contain both their observational results and their calculations, Worksheet 7.1b(2), for the same activity, does not include a table so you can encourage more confident students to think about table design themselves, as this is a valuable science enquiry skill. Some students may also need help in finding the quantitative link between mass and weight.

Some students may find it difficult to select four suitable planets to plot the graph in Activity 7.2. It may be helpful to talk through various choices with them to help steer them towards a suitable choice. The choice of four planets should bear in mind the anomalies and also a reasonable range of values of mass to plot. Venus, Earth, Saturn and Uranus would be a sensible choice.

With more confident students, ask questions such as which is bigger, the force on an apple on the Earth or of the Earth on an apple? Which exerts a bigger force, the Sun acting on the Earth, or the Earth acting on The Sun? (the same sized force, in each case)

Extension ideas

You could introduce the idea of rearranging the weight = mass × g equation (to mass = weight/g) so that mass could be calculated for known weights.

Homework suggestions

Questions 1–3 in the Student's Book.

Questions 1–8 in the Workbook.

Ask students to research Isaac Newton and write a paragraph to suggest why he is often credited with discovering gravity. They could also research Galileo and his work on gravity.

7.2 Air resistance

Topic overview

		Student's Book	Workbook	Downloadable material
7.2a	**Starting point** Students recap ideas about the direction of friction, air resistance and water resistance forces, and how these stopping forces are due to contact with solids, liquids or gases.	Starting point table		
7.2b	**Slowing down** In this section we recap ideas about friction, including air resistance and then move on to looking at the design of parachutes.	Questions 1–4 Activity 7.3	Questions 1–8	Practical notes 7.2b Worksheet 7.2b
7.2c	**Moving through particles** Here we look at the effect on air resistance of reducing the number of particles an object moves through. This leads onto the key fact that there is no air resistance in a vacuum, and what the implications of this are for motion with and without air resistance.	Activity 7.4 Questions 5–8		Practical notes 7.2c

Learning Objectives

- 7Pf.04: Understand that there is no air resistance to oppose movement in a vacuum
- 7TWSp.03: Make predictions of likely outcomes for a scientific enquiry based on scientific knowledge and understanding
- 7TWSp.04: Plan a range of investigations of different types, while considering variables appropriately, and recognise that not all investigations can be fair tests
- 7TWSc.04: Take appropriately accurate and precise measurements, explaining why accuracy and precision are important

- 7TWSa.02: Describe trends and patterns in results, including identifying any anomalous results
- 7TWSa.03: Make conclusions by interpreting results and explain the limitations of the conclusions
- 7SIC.02: Describe how science is applied across societies and industries, and in research
- 7SIC.01: Discuss how scientific knowledge is developed through collective understanding and scrutiny over time.

Links to other topics

- There is a link to the energy topic in Chapter 6 as energy is dissipated when air resistance acts against a moving object.

Using models

- There is an opportunity here to address learning objective 7TWSm.01, where the students are asked to discuss the strengths and limitations of the models.
- Activity 7.4 involves modelling the change in air resistance when the number of air particles is reduced, leading to the understanding that there cannot be any air resistance in a vacuum. In this model the students fill a tray with small polystyrene beads and try to move a toy car through from one side of the tray to the other. The higher the number of beads the more difficult it is to push the car through. The vacuum can be modelled by having no polystyrene beads in the tray although it is essential to point out to students that the model itself cannot truly model a vacuum as the surface of the tray produces friction with the wheels of the car. In a vacuum there are no air particles so an object moving through the vacuum would not experience friction or air resistance and would be able to move freely.

Common misunderstandings

- People often confuse air resistance and wind resistance. Though wind resistance obviously involves air particles air resistance is present even when there is no wind. The difference can be illustrated to students by discussing examples that show that the effect of wind resistance is different depending on whether you are travelling with or against the wind and that the wind can sometimes also make you go faster rather than resist your motion.
- Students often have little understanding of what a vacuum is. They may define a vacuum as a space where there is no air, rather than no particles at all.
- Some still need persuading that a container full of air is not the same as empty space (a complete absence of matter). This can be addressed by asking students to think about a container of air (such as a room), and to describe, or draw, the particles of gas in the air. Then ask what is between the gas particles, leading to the idea of particle-free space. Then ask them to imagine a giant pump that could remove all the particles of matter, including all the gas particles in air from the room. What would be left? A room/space with a complete absence of matter; a completely particle-free space.

7.2a Starting point

Ask students to look at the statements on the left side of the Starting point table and then draw a simple spider diagram to show how they connect to each other. This could be done as a whole class, group, pair or individual activity.

7.2b Slowing down

Students will learn:

- To describe how air resistance affects the speed of moving objects
- To understand that there is no air resistance to oppose movement in a vacuum
- To use scientific knowledge to predict the performance, and hence design of, a parachute
- To write a plan for an investigation and choose which variables to change, control and measure
- To identify appropriate evidence to collect and suitable methods of collection
- To choose appropriate apparatus and use it correctly
- To make accurate measurements of time and distance

Glossary words

air resistance

Resource preparation

For Activity 7.3: light fabric, thin tissue or plastic bags, string or thread, small masses, scissors, glue, sticky tape or adhesive putty, rulers or tape measures, stopwatch/stopclock.

Worksheet 7.2b

Practical notes 7.2b

Teaching and learning ideas

- Refer to the Student's Book and state that parachutes are a good example of using air resistance.
- Ask which two forces are involved when an object is falling through the air. *(Answer: the force of gravity (weight) and air resistance.)*
- Ask students to recall the effect the force of gravity has on a free object. *(Answer: the object falls downwards with increasing speed.)*

- Ask what factors might increase the air resistance on an object. *(Answers: its speed of travel through the air; its shape; its size.)*
- Ask what factors affect the size of the force of gravity on an object. *(Answer: its mass – do not accept weight – if a student gives this answer then remind them that weight is itself a measure of the force that gravity is exerting on an object.)*
- Ask them to deduce what combination of factors will make an object, like a parachute and its load, fall as slowly as possible.
- Introduce Activity 7.3 *Making a parachute*. Challenge the students, working in groups of two or three, to design, make and test the best parachute that takes the longest time to reach the ground, or (for more confident students), the average speed of descent. See Practical notes 7.2b. Students use Worksheet 7.2b.
- Have a feedback session in which the parachute designs from each group are compared to see which designs fall most slowly/which parachute stays in the air the longest. Note, a fair comparison can only be made if every parachute carries the same load and has the same drop height.
- Challenge students to consider what would happen if the parachute had a heavier load. They could design and/or carry out an experiment to test their ideas.

Extension ideas

Ask students to consider what would happen if air resistance was equal to the weight of the parachute and its load. *(Answer: it would reach a constant speed, which they will learn in further studies is called the 'terminal velocity'.)*

Differentiation

This open-ended activity calls for good teamwork, planning and manual skills. You may need to think in advance about the formation of the groups to include a balance of skills and abilities.

The measurement of speed and choosing methods and conditions that will give a fair test are important but quite demanding (calculating speed from distance travelled divided by time taken is Stage 8 content). Students who are less confident with mathematics could simply time the descent, or be paired with other students to help them with the calculation of speed. Intervene with the groups as needed to review their plans and prompt them with advice and explanations where needed.

Homework suggestions

Workbook topic 7.2 Questions 1–8.

Questions 1–4 in the Student's Book.

Ask students to research some examples of where air resistance might be a problem.

Ask students to make a different parachute at home which they think will work even better than the one they made in class.

7.2c Moving through particles

Students will learn:

- To describe how air resistance affects the speed of moving objects
- To understand that there is no air resistance to oppose movement in a vacuum
- To describe trends and patterns in results, including identifying any anomalous results
- To make conclusions by interpreting results

Glossary words

vacuum

Resource preparation

For Activity 7.4: tray, small polystyrene beads. Note: this activity is best done as a demonstration.

Practical notes 7.2c

Teaching and learning ideas

- Refer to Topic 7.2: Air resistance in the Student's Book. Ask students about their own experiences of air resistance – for example, riding a bicycle and feeling the breeze pushing them back; or riding in a vehicle and hearing the noise of the passing air through an open window. Ask how much air resistance there is when they are stationary or moving very slowly – none or almost none. Air resistance force increases with speed of movement.

- Conclude by comparing friction and air resistance as summarised in the table below.

	Similarities	Differences
Friction	Both push backwards against motion, to slow it down and stop movement.	Friction is highest just before something moves. Once moving, friction force stays constant.
Air resistance	Both result in 'wasted' energy and produce heat (due to doing work against friction).	For objects at rest, air resistance is zero. The force increases as speed increases.

- Move on to Activity 7.4 *Moving through different numbers of particles*, which demonstrates that reducing the number of particles an object has to move through reduces the 'particle resistance' created. Explain that in this demonstration you are modelling the effect of air resistance on moving objects. Note, this is best done as a class demonstration so you can talk through the results at each step. It is also important to try this out in advance so that you can ensure that the combination of beads, tray and vehicle that you use is suitable and that there is a difference when the number of beads is reduced. If you are not able to do this demonstration you could do it as a 'thought experiment', getting the students to predict what will happen at each stage (with reasons).
- Link the effect of air resistance on moving objects to the design of objects where maximising speed is important, for example, racing cars. Streamlined or more aerodynamic shapes reduce the number of collisions at the surface with particles in the air, so the force of air resistance is less.
- You could discuss the change in the number of air particles in a real-life context, for example, discussing the effect of air resistance on aircraft flying at different altitudes.
- Refer to the classic experiment carried out during the Apollo 15 Moon landings where a feather and a hammer were dropped together from the same height and hit the ground at the same time. You could ask students to explain why this happens leading them to the idea that this is because the Moon has no atmosphere and therefore there is no air resistance. Video clip can be found easily through an internet search and would be worth showing to students. *Also, Brian Cox recreating the hammer and feather experiment in the world's largest vacuum chamber, can be found easily online from a search engine.* Class discussion of the observations made during this experiment link to 7Pf.04.
- Make sure you state the meaning of the term 'vacuum' and, where necessary, clarify as previously suggested in Common misunderstandings. Then explain (or ask students to explain) why there cannot be any air resistance in a vacuum.

Extension ideas

Ask students to find out about the atmosphere of our Moon and other planets in our Solar System and consider whether there would be the equivalent of air resistance from their atmospheres. Is there likely to be more, less or the same effect as air resistance on Earth?

Homework suggestions

Question 5 in the Student's Book.

Ask students to write a short explanation of why there is no air resistance in a vacuum. The audience for this would be a student who missed the lesson. The format could be a written explanation, a series of slides, a cartoon or a poster.

End of chapter reflection
- To review the learning points of the chapter
- To test understanding through answering questions

Resources
- Student's Book [Key facts; End of chapter review questions]
- Workbook [Self-assessment grid, Test-style questions]
- Worksheet 7.3

Approach

Tell students to use the 'Key facts' and 'Check your skills progress' boxes at the end of each topic in the Student's Book as a way of recapping on the main learning points and of identifying any areas they still find difficult.

Also ask students to complete the self-assessment checklist at the end of Chapter 7 in the Workbook. Encourage students to discuss in small groups their self-assessment for each topic. Can they explain any difficult bits to one another? Are there questions that none of them feel confident to answer? If so, they should feed that back to the teacher. You may wish to revisit some Learning Objectives again if students find any areas particularly challenging. Use the Student's Book text and questions to revisit these aspects. Go through the answers orally in class. Take note of whether giving the answer appears to resolve students' uncertainty or not, and work through further examples.

The teacher response in the Workbook can be completed to give students personalised feedback on next steps. Students could be asked to answer specific End of chapter review questions in their books. Alternatively go through some or all of the End of chapter review questions in the Student's Book orally in class.

Use the Context worksheet (Worksheet 7.3) as a framework for students to conduct their own research enquiries about gravity or air resistance. This activity provides the opportunity to cover Learning Objectives 7SIC.01, 7SIC.02 and 7SIC.04. For example, students could focus on how ideas about gravity were developed, how the gravitational effects of 'hidden' objects in space on other objects has helped discover new planets, or how engineers design aircraft or racing cars to be more aerodynamic.

After any group revision sessions that you have decided to give, finish by asking students to complete the test-style questions at the end of Chapter 7 in the Workbook. Provide feedback on students' answers, and work with students individually to identify areas that still need more work.

Chapter 8   Sound

Chapter overview

In this chapter students will learn about how sound travels as a wave, why sound does not travel in a vacuum and why echoes occur. This chapter builds on ideas about how sounds are produced by vibrating sources from in earlier stages of the learner's education.

Topic title	Number of 40-minute periods	Learning Objectives	Thinking and Working Scientifically Learning Objectives
8.1 How sound travels	2–3	7Ps.01 Describe the vibration of particles in a sound wave and explain why sound does not travel in a vacuum.	7TWSm.01 Describe the strengths and limitations of a model. 7TWSp.02 Describe how scientific hypotheses can be supported or contradicted by evidence from an enquiry. 7TWSc.04 Take appropriately accurate and precise measurements, explaining why accuracy and precision are important. 7TWSc.07 Collect and record sufficient observations and/or measurements in an appropriate form. 7TWSa.02 Describe trends and patterns in results, including identifying any anomalous results. 7TWSa.03 Make conclusions by interpreting results and explain the limitations of the conclusions. 7TWSa.05 Present and interpret observations and measurements appropriately.
8.2 Echoes	1–2	7Ps.02 Explain echoes in terms of the reflection of sound waves.	7TWSm.01 Describe the strengths and limitations of a model. 7TWSp.04 Plan a range of investigations of different types, while considering variables appropriately, and recognise that not all investigations can be fair tests. 7TWSc.02 Decide what equipment is required to carry out an investigation or experiment and use it appropriately. 7TWSc.03 Evaluate whether measurements and observations have been repeated sufficiently to be reliable. 7TWSa.04 Evaluate experiments and investigations, and suggest improvements, explaining any proposed changes.
End of chapter questions	1	Check students' progress	

Background science

Please note: the background science notes are designed to provide teachers with an overview of the science concepts students may have already been taught earlier in their education, are likely to be taught in this unit and are likely to be taught in later stages. They are not a checklist of the content to be covered by the teacher in each unit.

The background science notes also serve to provide the teacher with some understanding of the background science needed in order to deliver the content of each chapter.

Sound is created by vibrations. Sound travels as a longitudinal wave that creates a series of compressions and rarefactions. Compressions are the areas of the wave where the vibrations are close together and rarefactions are the areas of the wave where the vibrations are further apart from each other.

In longitudinal waves, the particles vibrate in the same direction as the movement that created the wave. The wave travels parallel to the direction of vibration. In transverse waves, the wave travels at 90° to the direction of vibration. The particles vibrate about a fixed position. Students do not need to know details about longitudinal and transverse waves in Lower Secondary Science.

Sound can travel through any medium. Generally, the denser the medium, the faster and easier sound travels through it because it is easier to create compressions and rarefactions when particles are close together. How well sound is transmitted through different materials affects how loud it sounds – this explains why sounds heard through a string telephone are louder than sound at the same distance heard through the air. The solid string transfers the sound better than the air. Sound cannot travel through a vacuum. A vacuum is a completely empty space and therefore contains no particles. As there are no particles, compressions and rarefactions cannot occur so sound cannot be transmitted.

● ● ● ● ● ● ● ● ● ● ● ● ● ● ●

Normal position of air particles.

●●●● ● ● ● ●●● ● ●● ● ●●

Position of air particles when a sound is produced. Some are pushed closer together (a *compression*), others move further apart (a *rarefaction*).

● ●● ● ●●● ●● ● ●● ●●●●

The positions of the air particles changes as the particles vibrate. This creates a sound wave that travels through the air.

Echoes are produced when sound is reflected. Measuring the time delay between making a sound and hearing its echo is one way of measuring the speed of sound through air. Sound travels through air (at standard temperature and pressure) at a speed of approximately 340 m/s.

The ear detects sound as the vibrations enter the ear canal and hit the eardrum. From here, the vibrations are passed via the ossicles to the inner ear. Ultimately the vibrations are converted into electrical signals and sent to the brain via nerves. Students do not need to know details of this process.

The volume of a sound is determined by the amplitude of the sound wave. The amplitude is the maximum displacement of the particle from its resting position. The pitch of a sound is determined by the frequency of the sound wave. The higher the frequency, the higher the pitch. The link between loudness and amplitude, pitch and frequency will be covered in Stage 9. The human ear can normally detect sounds with a frequency of between 20 Hz and 20 000 Hz. Sounds with frequencies higher than this are called ultrasound. Those with a frequency below 20 Hz are called infrasound. Ultrasound has many uses, including finding distances to surfaces from reflected pulses of ultrasound (in medical imaging, for internal structures in the body and in sonar, for underwater exploration). Animals such as elephants can hear infrasound. Seismic P waves are longitudinal infrasound waves and reflection (and refraction) of seismic waves can be used to find out more about the internal structure of the Earth. Students do not need to learn these contexts.

Topic overview

		Student's Book	Workbook	Downloadable materials
8.1a	**Starting point** This short activity provides an opportunity to establish the extent of your students' prior knowledge on how sounds are made and the particle model of solids, liquids and gases	Starting point table		Worksheet 8.1a
8.1b	**How sounds travel** A short demonstration recaps that sounds are produced by vibrating sources, and that the vibrating source makes the surrounding air vibrate Students make a string telephone to show that sounds travel as vibrations through a medium Demonstration of bell jar experiment, to show that sound cannot travel through a vacuum	Questions 1–2 Activity 8.1 Activity 8.2 Questions 3–5	Questions 1–8	Practical notes 8.1b(1), 8.1b(2), 8.1b(3)
8.1c	**Modelling sound waves** Demonstration of waves using a slinky spring This activity not only demonstrates how sound travels through media by the oscillation of particles but also gives students the opportunity to consider the strengths and weaknesses of the slinky spring model of sound waves	Activity 8.3		Practical notes 8.1c

Learning Objectives

- 7Ps.01: Describe the vibration of particles in a sound wave and explain why sound does not travel in a vacuum
- 7TWSm.01: Describe the strengths and limitations of a model
- 7TWSp.02: Describe how scientific hypotheses can be supported or contradicted by evidence from an enquiry
- 7TWSc.04: Take appropriately accurate and precise measurements, explaining why accuracy and precision are important
- 7TWSc.07: Collect and record sufficient observations and/or measurements in an appropriate form

- 7TWSa.02: Describe trends and patterns in results, including identifying any anomalous results
- 7TWSa.03: Make conclusions by interpreting results and explain the limitations of the conclusions
- 7TWSa.05: Present and interpret observations and measurements appropriately
- 7SIC.01: Discuss how scientific knowledge is developed through collective understanding and scrutiny over time
- 7SIC.02: Describe how science is applied across societies and industries, and in research
- 7SIC.04: Describe how people develop and use scientific understanding as individuals and through collaboration, e.g. through peer review

Links to other topics

- The particle model of solids, liquids and gases is essential prior learning, and will be revisited in Chapter 4 Topic 3 *The particle model* at some point in this course.
- The idea of a vacuum as a completely empty space with no particles is also applied in Chapter 7 Topic 2 when discussing resistance to motion through air.
- In this Topic, students can apply what they have learned previously about energy transfer to how well different materials absorb the energy of sound waves. The more energy absorbed, the quieter the sound will be.

Cambridge Lower Secondary Physics Stage 7

Using models

- Animations or physical models (the 'slinky spring') of the movement of particles in a longitudinal wave are helpful in developing scientific understanding of how sound waves travel through air, because it is not possible to actually see sound waves travelling. The slinky spring should be stretched out as much as possible between two people.
- The person at one end of the spring should push the end of the slinky towards the other person without letting go of it.
- This pushing represents a vibration. Each of the coils in the spring will vibrate against the neighbouring coil, causing the vibrations to move along the spring, modelling the vibrations of a sound wave. The pushing of the coils together at one end of the slinky represents a compression. When these coils are released they spread out again. This spreading out represents a rarefaction.
- The particle model of how particles are arranged in solids, liquids and gases helps explain how sound travels and why sound travels at different speeds and with different amounts of energy dissipation in different media.
- In this Topic, students have the chance to comment on the strengths and limitations of the slinky spring as a physical model of a sound wave. This covers Learning Objective 7TWSp.01.

Science in context

- The Science in context: Scientists discover how sound travels box in Topic 8.1 of the Student's Book covers the following learning objectives:
  - 7SIC.01 Discuss how scientific knowledge is developed through collective understanding and scrutiny over time.
  - 7SIC.02 Describe how science is applied across societies and industries, and in research.
  - 7SIC.04 Describe how people develop and use scientific understanding as individuals and through collaboration, e.g. through peer review
- Look out for opportunities to discuss examples of how science is used in products that reduce sound levels, for example, double-glazed windows reduce the amount of external sound that enters a building because there is a vacuum between the two glazing panels so sound cannot be transmitted through the window.

Common misunderstandings

- Students may think that sound can travel through a vacuum. Using the description of sound travelling by means of vibrating particles and emphasising that a vacuum is a completely empty space containing no particles will help to clarify this.
- Some students may also think that when sound is travelling through a medium each particle just pushes into its neighbour and does not oscillate and return to its original position, rather like a line of dominoes falling after the first is pushed. Looking at the movement of individual coils of the slinky spring whilst modelling a sound wave will help to address this misconception.
- Students may also think that sound does not travel through solids. This may be because they are familiar with the idea of echoes and echoes rely on solid surfaces reflecting sound rather than transmitting it. They may also think about thick walls masking sound from the other side. Discussing the fact that while some sound may be reflected, some will also be transmitted through the solid; allowing students to experience hearing sounds that have travelled through solids for themselves will help to address this. (For example, making a string telephone or putting their ear to a wall to listen to sounds being made in the next room.)

8.1a Starting point

Resource preparation

For demonstration 1: a range of objects that can be used to create sounds (empty test tubes, elastic bands, metal and wooden rulers, beakers partly filled with water, balloons, newspapers). Ideally, include some objects that can be used to make sounds in more than one way, for example tubes that can be tapped or blown through.

Worksheet 8.1a

Teaching and learning ideas

- Ask students to write down five things they know about sound. This could be done individually, in pairs or in small groups. Alternatively, ask students to volunteer answers as a whole-class activity, each student asked to share one thing that they know. This will help to elicit prior knowledge and any misconceptions held about how sounds are made and how to change the volume and pitch of sounds.
- Demonstration 1: Show the class a selection of objects. Have a quick class discussion about how sound can be produced from each object and how these sounds can be changed in terms of the pitch and volume. This serves to

recap and consolidate the content taught in Stage 5. Demonstrate with each object according to the suggestions made by the students

- Refer to the section 'How are sounds made?' in the Student's Book and ask them to discuss question 1. This activity can be used as a revision exercise to remind learners of what they covered in Stage 5.
- You can use Worksheet 8.1a to find out what your students recall (from their previous studies), and any misconceptions they have, about the particulate nature of solids, liquids and gases.

8.1b How sounds travel

Students will learn:

- To describe the vibration of particles in a sound wave
- To use a model to describe how sound travels as a wave
- To explain why sound does not travel through a vacuum
- To describe how a hypothesis can be supported or confirmed as wrong by interpreting the evidence obtained from an enquiry
- To make conclusions by interpreting results
- To carry out practical work safely

Glossary words

medium, sound wave, vacuum, vibration

Resource preparation

For demonstration 1: A large length of elastic or rubber

For Activity 8.2 (for each pair): 2 plastic cups or metal cans with small holes in the bottom, 4–5 m of string

For demonstration 2: Bell in a bell jar apparatus with power supply

Practical notes 8.1b(1), 8.1b(2), 8.1b(3)

Teaching and learning ideas

- To engage students, go around the class asking each student to make a sound. Each student must use a method that has not already been used. Use this to recap that when an object vibrates to produce sound, the air around it vibrates.
- Demonstration 1: Use a large length of elastic or rubber to demonstrate how air can be made to vibrate (as shown in 'Making air vibrate' in the Student's Book and in practical notes 8.1b).
- Use tins or plastic cups with string to make and test string telephones (as described in Activity 8.1 *Making a string telephone* in the Student's Book, Practical notes 8.1b and Worksheet 8.2). This shows that sound can travel through solid media like string.
- Demonstration 2: Use the bell in the bell jar apparatus (as described in Activity 8.2 *Showing that sound cannot travel through a vacuum* in the Student's Book and in Practical notes 8.1b) to demonstrate that sound cannot travel through a vacuum.
- Challenge students to explain why sound can travel through solids but not through a vacuum.

Differentiation

Less confident students could be given reminders of the particle model for solids, liquids and gases and be referred back to Worksheet 8.1a.

Homework suggestions

Students could test how well sound travels through the walls of their home by asking someone to speak in the next room and listen with their ear right next to the wall.

Ask students to find out how astronauts speak to each other when on the Moon or when in space but outside their spacecraft, i.e. when working in a vacuum.

Students answer questions 1–8 in Topic 8.1 How sounds travel in the Workbook.

Questions 2–6 in the Student's Book also relate to this section but it might be better to address these after completing 8.1c Modelling sound waves.

Cambridge Lower Secondary Physics
Stage 7

8.1c Modelling sound waves

Students will learn:

- To describe the vibration of particles in a sound wave
- To use a model to describe how sound travels as a wave
- To explain why sound does not travel through a vacuum
- To describe the strengths and limitations of a model for sound waves

Glossary words

medium, sound wave, vibration

Resource preparation

For the demonstrations: a slinky spring and some pieces of coloured cotton which can be easily seen against the spring.

Teaching and learning ideas

- Tie a piece of coloured cotton (that is visible at the back of the class) to one coil of the slinky spring. Start by showing how a slinky can be used to make transverse waves (hold the slinky spring at both ends and then shake it up and down). Ask students to describe what happens to the coloured cotton as the spring moves. (It goes up and down but does not move left or right.)
- Then ask two students to demonstrate another way of making waves with the slinky. (They should each hold one end of the spring and then move backwards and forwards to one another. This creates a longitudinal wave.) Explain that there are two types of waves and say that, in relation to sound, it is only the longitudinal type that we are interested in. Ask students to describe what happens to the coloured cotton as the spring moves this time. (It moves backwards and forwards but not up and down.)
- After demonstrating longitudinal waves with the slinky, you can relate what you have seen the coil doing to the vibration of air particles when a sound wave passes through a medium. The diagrams in the Student's Book are a useful reference. This will also help students appreciate that to travel, sound must have particles available.
- To consolidate the idea that sound travels through the vibration of particles, students could answer Questions 2–5 in the Student's Book.
- Challenge: Question 6 is a challenge question. Students will need to think about the differences between solids, liquids and gases to answer it. They could refer back to Worksheet 8.1a to help them.

Homework suggestions

Students could try to find some other examples of waves which travel through a material due to vibrating particles, for example, seismic waves, ultrasound waves or water waves.

8.2 Echoes

Topic overview

		Student's Book	Workbook	Downloadable materials
8.2a	**Starting point** Recap of learning about sound from Topic 8.1, and prior understanding of the term 'reflection'	Starting point table		Worksheet 8.2a
8.2b	**What is an echo?** This section introduces students to echoes and the idea of reflection of sound, using some simple demonstrations to model reflection	Questions 1–2	Questions 1, 3	Practical notes 8.2b
8.2c	**Measuring the speed of sound using echoes** This activity focuses on how the speed of sound in air can be measured using an echo method	Activity 8.4 Questions 3–4	Question 4	Practical notes 8.2c Worksheet 8.2c
8.2d	**Applying ideas** Students explore uses of echoes. They also explore problems that can be caused by unwanted echoes and ways of reducing these.	Questions 5–7	Questions 2, 5–7	

Learning Objectives

- 7Ps.02: Explain echoes in terms of the reflection of sound waves
- 7TWSm.01: Describe the strengths and limitations of a model
- 7TWSp.04: Plan a range of investigations of different types, while considering variables appropriately, and recognise that not all investigations can be fair tests
- 7TWSc.02: Decide what equipment is required to carry out an investigation or experiment and use it appropriately

- 7TWSc.03: Evaluate whether measurements and observations have been repeated sufficiently to be reliable
- 7TWSa.04: Evaluate experiments and investigations, and suggest improvements, explaining any proposed changes
- 7SIC.02: Describe how science is applied across societies and industries, and in research.

Links to other topics
- The discussion of the student's understanding of the term 'reflection' will be revisited at Stage 8 Physics Chapter 9 *Light* Topic 1 *Reflection*, where the law of reflection is introduced.

Using models
- If students are not confident in their understanding of reflection, a simple model of reflection, using a ball thrown against a wall with the reflected bounce back off the wall, and/or showing reflection of a wave with a slinky spring and/or ripple tank can model the process effectively. It also gives the student the opportunity to discuss the strengths and limitations of each model.

Cambridge Lower Secondary Physics
Stage 7

Science in context

- The Science in context: Mapping underwater box in Topic 8.2 of the Student's Book covers the following learning objectives:
  - 7SIC.02 Describe how science is applied across societies and industries, and in research.
- Look out for opportunities to discuss the history of the development, and the use of sonar. The use of ultrasound reflections to produce images could also be discussed, if so, it would be best to just describe ultrasound as a type of sound wave that humans cannot hear, rather than try to explain it in terms of frequency as students will not meet this idea until later on in the course. It is also possible to involve the idea of echolocation by bats (and some whales) considering why it is important for bats to have this ability and also how it was discovered (Griffin and Galambos 1938) and further investigated. Opportunities may arise to further discuss reduction of echoes in concert halls and recording studios too.

Common misunderstandings

- Students do not study reflection of light in depth until Stage 8. Some may need help to understand the process of reflection. The demonstrations or analogies for reflection in 8.2b will help with this.
- Though students may understand that solid objects and light can reflect they may find it difficult to apply this to waves (as they are not yet aware that light travels as a wave). Modelling reflection of a wave using a slinky spring can help with this.

8.2a Starting point

Teaching and learning ideas

- Students will have already met the idea that light reflects off surfaces, and they may have done experiments to observe that a ray of light changes direction when it is reflected from a plane mirror.
- Worksheet 8.2a would make an effective way of reviewing student's prior knowledge and understanding of reflection, and also of the timing method they used in the previous topic and the terms accurate and precise. The second part of the worksheet could be done orally as a whole-class or small-group activity or answered individually. It is important to assess student's responses to ensure the class has a sound understanding to build on.

8.2b What is an echo?

Students will learn:

- To explain echoes in terms of the reflection of sound waves
- To use a physical model to show how reflection occurs at a boundary
- To describe the strengths and limitations of a model

Glossary words

echo, reflection

Resource preparation

For demonstrations: tennis ball, slinky spring, ripple tank, dipper, plane barrier

Practical notes 8.2b

Teaching and learning ideas

- Discuss echoes. Refer to figure 8.9 in the Student's Book. Ask students whether they have experienced echoes and where they were when it happened.
- Use the demonstrations outlined in Practical notes 8.2b as analogies to model the reflection of sound waves to produce echoes. Ask the students to comment on how effective was each model they have seen (how well it helped them understand the scientific idea of how an echo is produced).
- Challenge students to consider the strengths and weaknesses of each of the models you have demonstrated. Is there anything about echoes, or reflection, that the model cannot explain? For example, the first demonstration does not show the wave nature of sound.

Differentiation

Less confident students could be asked to consider other examples of reflection to reinforce the idea; for example, when playing pool or football.

More confident students could identify that in the third demonstration, the water wave is not a compression (longitudinal) wave as it is for the slinky spring; instead the particles of water move up and down as the wave passes.

Homework suggestions

Students answer questions 1–3 and 5 in topic 8.2 Echoes in the Workbook.

Ask students to research examples where reflection of sound could be useful and when it could be a problem.

8.2c Measuring the speed of sound using echoes

Students will learn:

- To explain echoes in terms of the reflection of sound waves
- To evaluate whether measurements have been repeated enough times to be reliable
- To evaluate experiments and investigations, and suggest improvements, explaining any proposed changes

Glossary words

accurate, anomaly, echo, reliable

Resource preparation

Worksheet 8.2c

Practical notes 8.2c

Teaching and learning ideas

- Ask students to work in small groups to discuss how they might use echoes to measure the speed of sound (Activity 8.4 in the Student's Book: *Using echoes to measure the speed of sound*). Bring the class back together and ask students to feed back ideas. (They could use the scenario described in question 2 to help them. If they know the distance from the girl to the cliff, and the time it takes to hear the echo, then they can work out the speed of sound.) Remind them of the method they used to measure the speed of sound in the previous lesson. Make sure they understand that the distance to use in the equation is *twice* the distance of the girl from the cliff.
- Discuss the questions in Activity 8.4 as a class. Encourage discussion of what equipment is required, and how reliability can be improved (sufficient repeats).
- Discuss how this method differs from the method they used in 8.1d. Which method do they think would produce more accurate measurements? What have they changed, and how will that make the calculated speed more accurate?
- Students may also be able to do this experiment if it is possible in your setting (see Practical notes 8.2c). Worksheet 8.2c is available for use by any groups who do not plan their own method. If there is enough equipment available, students could carry out their plan in pairs. This can also be a whole-class activity with one person making the sound and as many other students as possible timing.
- Ask students to present the conclusion to the activity to others in the class in an appropriate way (a formal presentation or a written report are just two examples).
- Challenge students to consider how they might, for example, if additional equipment were available, make their results even more accurate.

Differentiation

Worksheet 8.2c is available for use by students who were not able to make an effective plan.

Students who are less confident with mathematics could work in a group with others who are more confident.

Homework suggestions

Ask students to research examples of how echoes could be used to measure distance.

8.2d Applying ideas

Students will learn:

- To explain echoes in terms of the reflection of sound waves

Teaching and learning ideas

- Talk about the types of surfaces that reflect sound (hard, flat, stone) and everyday examples of how echoes can be reduced (such as using soft materials including carpets and rugs to reduce the sound that travels between one floor of a building to the floor below). Students can do questions 5–7 in the Student's Book.
- Discuss the Science in context box in the Student's Book, which explains how sonar is used in underwater exploration.

Extension ideas

Students could try use the particle model of solids, liquids and gases to suggest why some materials reflect sound better than others. They could consider: how close together the particles are (the closer they are the fewer gaps there are for the sound wave to travel through); how smooth the surface of the material is (the rougher the surface the more particles the sound wave will 'hit' so the more energy will dissipate).

Homework suggestions

Students answer questions 4, 6 and 7 in Topic 8.2 Echoes in the Workbook.

Chapter 8 — Checking students' progress

End of chapter reflection

- To review the learning points of the chapter
- To test understanding through answering questions

Resources

- Student's Book [Key facts, End of chapter review questions]
- Workbook [Self-assessment checklist, Test-style questions]
- Worksheet 8.3

Approach

Use the 'Key facts' and 'Check your skills progress' boxes in the Student's Book for each topic in this chapter as a way of recapping on the main learning points.

Ask students to complete the self-assessment checklist at the end of Chapter 8 in the Workbook. Encourage students to work together in small groups to discuss which aspects of the material are the most difficult to understand, and then have a class vote. You may wish to revisit some Learning Objectives again if students find any areas particularly challenging. Use the Student's Book text and questions to revisit these aspects. Go through the answers orally in class. Take note of whether giving the answer appears to resolve students' uncertainty or not, and work through further examples.

The teacher response in the Workbook can be completed to give students personalised feedback on next steps. Students could be asked to answer specific end of chapter review questions in their books. Alternatively go through some or all of the end of chapter review questions in the Student's Book orally in class.

Use the Context worksheet (Worksheet 8.3) as a framework for students to conduct their own research enquiries about sound. This activity provides the opportunity to cover Learning Objectives 7SIC.01 and 7SIC.02. For example, students could focus on how ideas about sonar were developed.

Finish by asking students to complete the test-style questions at the end of Chapter 8 in the Workbook. Provide feedback on students' answers, and work with students individually to identify areas that still need more work.

Chapter 9 | Electricity and circuits

Chapter overview

In this chapter students will construct simple circuits from circuit diagrams. They will use a model to help them understand the flow of current around a circuit. They will investigate the effects of making changes in series circuits and look at which materials conduct electricity.

Topic title	Number of 40-minute periods	Learning Objectives	Thinking and Working Scientifically Learning Objectives
9.1 Charge flow in circuits	2	7Pe.01 Use a simple model to describe electricity as a flow of electrons around a circuit. 7Pe.02 Describe electrical conductors as substances that allow electron flow and electrical insulators as substances that inhibit electron flow.	7TWSm.01 Describe the strengths and limitations of a model 7TWSp.03 Make predictions of likely outcomes for a scientific enquiry based on scientific knowledge and understanding.
9.2 Circuit diagrams	2	7Pe.04 Describe how adding components into a series circuit can affect the current (limited to addition of cells and lamps). 7Pe.05 Use diagrams and conventional symbols to represent, make and compare circuits that include cells, switches, lamps, buzzers and ammeters.	7TWSp.03 Make predictions of likely outcomes for a scientific enquiry based on scientific knowledge and understanding. 7TWSc.02 Decide what equipment is required to carry out an investigation or experiment and use it appropriately. 7TWSc.07 Collect and record sufficient observations and/or measurements in an appropriate form.
9.3 Currents in series circuits	2	7Pe.03 Know how to measure the current in series circuits. 7Pe.04 Describe how adding components into a series circuit can affect the current (limited to addition of cells and lamps).	7TWSm.01 Describe the strengths and limitations of a model. 7TWSc.07 Collect and record sufficient observations and/or measurements in an appropriate form. 7TWSc.04 Take appropriately accurate and precise measurements, explaining why accuracy and precision are important. 7TWSc.05 Carry out practical work safely. 7TWSa.02 Describe trends and patterns in results, including identifying any anomalous results.
End of chapter questions	1	Check students' progress	

Background science

Please note: the background science notes are designed to provide teachers with an overview of the science concepts students may have already been taught earlier in their education, are likely to be taught in this unit and are likely to be taught in later stages. They are not a checklist of the content to be covered by the teacher in each unit.

The background science notes also serve to provide the teacher with some understanding of the background science needed in order to deliver the content of each chapter.

An electric current is a flow of charge. Current is defined as the amount of charge (in coulombs) flowing past a point each second. Students do not need to know this now, but the idea of how much charge flows each second is useful.

Charge is carried by electrons which flow from the negative terminal of a cell or battery to the positive terminal. Conventional current is described as flowing from positive to negative. At this level it is probably best to avoid mentioning the direction of electron flow as it can cause confusion.

A series circuit consists of just one loop. The current is the same all around the circuit. The electrons lose energy as they go around the circuit, e.g. as electrons flow through a lamp energy is converted to heat and light, but the flow of electrons (current) remains the same. Parallel circuits are not covered in this topic but are referred to in order to make clear the definition of series circuits. Parallel circuits are those consisting of more than one loop. Parallel circuits will be covered in more detail in Stage 9.

Topic overview

		Student Book	Workbook	Downloadable materials
9.1a	**Starting point** This short activity allows students to reconsider a simple circuit they should have constructed before, and to ask questions about why the lamp lights	Starting point table		
9.1b	**Simple circuits** Students observe a simple series circuit in more detail and begin to formulate ideas about the flow of current. They are introduced to the rope loop model	Questions 1–3 Activity 9.1	Questions 1–3	Practical notes 9.1b
9.1c	**Conductors and insulators** Students test a range of materials in order to sort them into conductors and insulators. This is related to the flow of electrons in the material	Questions 4–7 Activity 9.2	Questions 4 and 9	Practical notes 9.1c

Learning Objectives

- 7Pe.01: Use a simple model to describe electricity as a flow of electrons around a circuit
- 7Pe.02: Describe electrical conductors as substances that allow electron flow and electrical insulators as substances that inhibit electron flow
- 7SIC.02: Describe how science is applied across societies and industries, and in research.
- 7SIC.05: Discuss how the uses of science can have a global environmental impact.
- 7TWSm.01: Describe the strengths and limitations of a model

Links to other topics

- Students learn about atoms in Stage 7 Chapter 4 Topic 3, but will not come across atomic structure until Stage 8 Chapter 4 Topic 1, so electrons will probably be new to them at this stage.
- Students may have covered Chapter 6 where they study energy changes. In this topic they meet cells as suppliers of energy. It is important that they know energy is conserved and think about what happens to the energy when a current flows.

Using models

- The use of a model can help students to understand electricity. It can be conceptually difficult as we cannot see the electrons or their flow directly.
- The model used here is the rope loop model. This is described in detail in the National Strategies teaching unit 'Explaining how electric circuits work'. In the rope loop model the teacher asks a group of learners to gently hold a loop of rope in their hands. The loop of rope models an electrical circuit.
- The teacher pulls the rope, supplying energy and modelling the cell/battery.
- When the teacher pulls the rope, the rope flows around through the learners' hands. This models the flow of current through the circuit.
- This model is discussed in the Student's Book. There are other models and it can be useful for students to compare these. This will be revisited at Stage 9 and comparisons of models made then, so it may be preferable to use just one model at this stage.
- There is an opportunity here to address learning objective 7TWSm.01 where the students are asked to discuss the strengths and limitations of the model.
- The model is described using a large rope loop. Some students may find it useful to have a small loop to use alongside circuits they make to help them visualise the charge flow.

Cambridge Lower Secondary Physics Stage 7

Science in context

- The Science in context: Keeping the water flowing box in Topic 9.1 of the Student's Book covers the following learning objectives:
  - 7SIC.02 Describe how science is applied across societies and industries, and in research.
  - 7SIC.05 Discuss how the uses of science can have a global environmental impact.
- Students should be encouraged to look at electrical appliances in the classroom and at home and ask questions about how they are powered and what materials are used in their construction. They should be reminded that mains electricity is much more powerful than the cells they are using and can therefore be hazardous.

Common misunderstandings

- Students are likely to have an idea that something flows around the circuit and refer to this as 'electricity'. This term is too vague, and it is best to establish at an early stage that it is electric charge or current which flows. Referring pupils back to the rope model as they progress through the topic will help. Discourage the use of the term electricity other than as a topic heading.
- Students often think electricity is in the cell and flows out to the lamp. The correct science is that the electric charges (carried by electrons) are in the wires and the cell provides energy to make them move. The big circuit activity helps students understand this. They often predict that the lamp will light shortly after the cell is connected as the current has to reach the lamp. Seeing the lamp light instantly challenges this. Backing this up with the rope model can help them picture the electron flow.

9.1a Starting point

Resource preparation

Set up a simple circuit with one lamp and one cell.

Teaching and learning ideas

Demonstrate to the students that the lamp lights when the circuit is connected. This will not be new to them. Ask them to work with a partner to explain why the lamp lights – encourage them to talk about both the lamp and the cell in their explanations. The aim of this is to elicit their understanding, spot misconceptions and encourage them to move on from simply what happens to an explanation of why.

Keep a record (maybe their notes) of their ideas. Looking back at these at the end of the topic can help them to see how their ideas have progressed. Explaining their own misconceptions is a useful consolidation exercise at the end of the topic.

9.1b Simple circuits

Students will learn:

- To describe electricity using a simple model

Glossary words

cell, current

Resource preparation

For the demonstration: long loop of rope, preferably marked at regular intervals (with stripes, or similar). The rope should be long enough to pass through the hands of the whole class when standing in a circle. The loop should be fastened with tape rather than a knot so it can flow smoothly. The rope should be as smooth as possible to avoid friction. Thin climbers' rope (4–6 mm diameter) is ideal.

For Activity 9.1: 1.5 V cell, lamp, switch, long wires (at least 2 m long, but preferably long enough to go round the whole classroom)

Practical notes 9.1b

Teaching and learning ideas

- Students complete Activity 9.1 *Lighting a lamp* as a reminder of previous work on electrical circuits. Encourage discussion about what is happening in the circuit and in the components of the circuit. See Practical notes 9.1b for further information.

- Show students the big circuit. Ask them to predict what will happen when the switch is closed. Discuss their ideas. Will the lamp light straight away or will there be a delay? Why? Encourage all students to express their opinion, even if only by a show of hands. Then, with a big build-up – possibly turn out the lights and have a countdown – close the switch. The students will see the lamp light instantaneously. This challenges the idea that current has to flow from the cell to the lamp before it can light.

- Tell the students that we are going to use a rope loop as a model to explain what is happening in the circuit. Explain that scientists often use models to explain things which can't be seen directly. The flow of charge in the wires is real, but the electrons are far too small for us to see.

- Have the class stand in a circle and hold the rope loosely – it should pass through everyone's hands but they shouldn't grip it. Tell them that the rope represents the charge (electrons). Say that you are going to be the cell in the circuit and ask them what your role is. They should already have the idea that the cell provides energy or makes things work. Ask how you could model this. They will suggest pulling on the rope. Demonstrate this and point out that as soon as you start to pull, the rope starts to move all round the loop. This is why the lamp lights instantaneously in the big circuit.

- Have one student model the lamp. They do this by gently gripping the rope. Ask them what they feel as the rope passes through their hands. The heat they feel due to friction is analogous to the filament of the lamp getting hot and glowing. Discuss the energy transfers taking place – how far you go with this will depend on whether the students have studied the Energy topic before this.

- Ensure that students are clear about what represents what in the model:
  - Rope = charge
  - Flow of rope = current
  - Teacher pulling rope = cell
  - Student gripping rope = lamp

- Encourage students to raise questions about the model, e.g. what happens if the student grips harder? Try these out and tell students that they will return to this model throughout the topic.

- Students answer Questions 1–3 from topic 9.1 in the Student Book. Go through the answers to check understanding.

- **Challenge:** Challenge students to use the model to answer their own questions and those of classmates.

Differentiation

Students can repeat the modelling in small groups. This allows them to take the role of the cell or the lamp, which will help embed the model. Group more confident students with those who are less confident with the model.

Ask more confident students to write questions to check understanding of the model.

Extension ideas

The idea of resistance can be introduced here. A formal definition of resistance is not needed, but the concept can be introduced by talking in terms of the student's hands resisting the flow of the rope. Resistance is not introduced until Stage 9.

Challenge students to use the model to predict and test the effects of increasing resistance.

Homework suggestions

Workbook questions 5–8.

9.1c Conductors and insulators

Students will learn:

- To describe electricity using a simple model
- To investigate which materials conduct electricity
- To make predictions of likely outcomes for a scientific enquiry based on scientific knowledge and understanding

Glossary words

conductor, electron, insulator

Resource preparation

For Activity 9.2: Each group/pair needs 1 × 1.5 V cell, 1 × 1.5 V lamp, 3 wires; a range of labelled metals and non-metals. Metals could include copper, iron, aluminium and zinc. Non-metals could include plastic, wood, glass and carbon. Carbon should be included to show there are exceptions to the general rule that only metals conduct. Wires with crocodile clips will ensure there is good contact with the test material, or students can simply hold wires against the materials.

Practical notes 9.1c

Teaching and learning ideas

- Revisit the rope model and explain that the charge which flows round the circuit is carried by invisibly small particles called electrons. Students will not have studied atomic structure at this stage. Explain that in some materials the electrons are fixed in place but in others some of them can move freely. Only those with free electrons can conduct electricity.

- Introduce the terms conductor and insulator and give the appropriate definitions. Get students to discuss how these terms can be used when talking about components in electrical circuits.

- Show the students a circuit with a lit lamp. Ask what this tells them about the materials which the wires and lamp are made of. Get them to look carefully at the lamp to see the thin wire filament and show a wire without a plug connector so they can see the copper wire inside. (If you use LED lamps, it is worth letting students see a filament lamp as the thin wire helps with the analogy.)

- Students complete Activity 9.2 *Investigating which materials conduct electricity*, to investigate conductors and insulators. When they are given the materials which they will test, get them to predict which materials will conduct. They can then plan and carry out the investigation. See Practical notes 9.1c for further information.

- Discuss the results of the investigation and ask students to answer Questions 4–7 in the Student Book.

Extension ideas

Encourage students to look at electrical appliances and identify which parts are made of conductors and which of insulators. For the conductors, get them to think about whether a low resistance wire such as copper or a higher resistance wire which will become hot is needed. For example, in a hairdryer, the casing is plastic (insulator) as are the casing of the plug and the wire covering. The wires are copper to carry the current easily, but the heating element is made of resistance wire so it will get hot to heat the air.

Homework suggestions

Workbook questions 5–8.

Cambridge Lower Secondary Physics Stage 7

Topic overview

		Student Book	Workbook	Downloadable materials
9.2a	**Starting point** This short activity allows students to demonstrate their knowledge of series and parallel circuits and circuit symbols from Stage 6	Starting point table	Questions 1 and 2	
9.2b	**Circuit symbols** Students practice drawing and interpreting circuit diagrams	Questions 1–5	Questions 3 and 4	Worksheets 9.2b(1), 9.2b(2)
9.2c	**Comparing circuits** Students predict and then test the effect of changing the numbers of cells and bulbs in a series circuit	Activity 9.3	Question 5	Practical notes 9.2c Worksheet 9.2c

Learning Objectives

- 7Pe.04: Describe how adding components into a series circuit can affect the current (limited to addition of cells and lamps)

- 7Pe.05: Use diagrams and conventional symbols to represent, make and compare circuits that include cells, switches, lamps, buzzers and ammeters

Thinking and Working Scientifically objectives

- Collect and record sufficient observations and/or measurements in an appropriate form
- Decide what equipment is required to carry out an investigation or experiment and use it appropriately

Using models

- The use of the rope model will help students make predictions about the effect of changes to the components of a circuit.

Science in context

- Point out to students that the use of standard, international symbols makes it possible for electrical engineers to understand each other's circuit diagrams without the need for translation.

Common misunderstandings

- Students often mix up diagrams with more than one cell. Make sure they know a straight line between components is a wire, so there should be a line from the positive of one cell to the negative of the next, but there should not be a line inside the cell as there is no wire there.

9.2a Starting point

Resource preparation

Have a slide ready to show a circuit diagram for a series circuit with two cells, a switch, an ammeter and a lamp.

Cambridge Lower Secondary Physics
Stage 7

Teaching and learning ideas

- This is an opportunity for students to revisit drawing circuit diagrams. Take time to make sure students draw these clearly, using pencil and ruler, and that they learn the symbols.
- Show the students the circuit diagram and ask them in pairs to explain what it shows. Discuss their explanations and explain why symbols are used and that circuits are drawn as straight lines and right angles for neatness. Remind them of the need for a complete circuit and for cells to be the same way round.

9.2b Circuit symbols

Students will learn:

- To use diagrams and conventional symbols to represent, make and compare circuits that include cells, switches, lamps, buzzers and ammeters
- To decide what equipment is required to carry out an investigation or experiment and use it appropriately

Glossary words

parallel circuit, series circuit

Resource preparation

Have available pictures of circuits and made-up circuits for students to draw. These should start with simple series circuits with a range of components but could extend to parallel circuits if appropriate.

Worksheets 9.2b(1), 9.2b(2)

Teaching and learning ideas

- Remind students of the common symbols they need to know. Get them to do the matching exercise on Worksheet 9.2b(1) either as a cut and stick exercise or by drawing the symbols into their books.
- Ask students to answer Questions 1 and 2 in the Student Book.
- Give students Worksheet 9.2b(2). They need to identify what is wrong with each circuit.

Extension ideas

Students could be given pictures, or actual circuits and asked to draw the circuit diagrams for them.

Homework suggestions

Make flashcards to help learn symbols.

9.2c Comparing circuits

Students will learn:

- To investigate the effect of changing the numbers of cells and lamps in a circuit
- To make predictions of likely outcomes for a scientific enquiry based on scientific knowledge and understanding.

Resource preparation

For Activity 9.3: each group will need 3 x 1.5 V cells, 3 x 2.5 V bulbs, 6 x wires, a small loop of rope.

Each student will also need a copy of Worksheet 9.2c

Practical notes 9.2c

Teaching and learning ideas

- Before constructing the circuits in this activity, revisit the rope model. Ideally use the rope again, though as students become more used to the model they will be able to think through a situation using the model without the physical rope.
- Demonstrate what happens when two people pull the rope (two cells). The rope will go faster, but avoid referring to speed. Instead talk about the amount of rope passing through their hands each second. This is analogous to current.
- Also demonstrate that two bulbs mean it will be harder to make the rope move so there is less current. Extend this to get the idea that with two bulbs and two cells, it is hard for the rope to move, but the extra cell gives extra pull, so the same current flows as in the circuit with one cell and one lamp.

- Students complete Activity 9.3 *Comparing circuits*. As they set up the circuits, ask them to predict before connecting each circuit how bright the lamp(s) will be. Encourage them to state this as 'I predict that in circuit b the lamp will be very bright as the two cells give a lot of pull and there is only one lamp so the current can flow easily.' See Practical notes 9.2c for further information.
- This activity gives students lots of circuits to construct, ensuring they practise and develop skills in constructing circuits from diagrams. Ask them to take turns, and to fully deconstruct each circuit before the next is built. This is good practice for when they make more complex circuits in later topics. Students generally make more mistakes trying to alter a circuit rather than starting from scratch each time.

Differentiation

Encourage students to use the rope model alongside their circuits. A small rope loop will let them try things out and will help embed the model.

Some students will find setting up circuits easier than others. It is important to ensure all students practise constructing circuits. Ensure that they take turns, constructing each circuit from scratch. Students who are very confident could be given status as experts. This means they can help others BUT they can only advise – they are forbidden to touch any of the apparatus. This ensures less confident students have to construct the circuits and helps the more confident students consolidate their learning.

Homework suggestions

Workbook question 6.

9.3 | Currents in series circuits

Topic overview

		Student Book	Workbook	Downloadable materials
9.3a	**Starting point** The rope loop is revisited and students consider how to measure the rate of flow of rope (representing current)	Starting point table	Questions 1–3	
9.3b	**Measuring current** Students measure current at different points in a series circuit	Activity 9.4	Questions 4 and 5	Practical notes 9.3b Worksheet 9.3b
9.3c	**Comparing current in circuits** Students plan and carry out an investigation into the effect on current of increasing the number of lamps in a circuit They then look at the effects of changes including swapping the direction of cells	Questions 1–2 Activity 9.5, 9.6	Questions 6 and 7	Practical notes 9.3c(1), 9.3c(2)

Learning Objectives
- 7Pe.03: Know how to measure the current in series circuits
- 7Pe.04: Describe how adding components into a series circuit can affect the current (limited to addition of cells and lamps)
- 7SIC.02: Describe how science is applied across societies and industries, and in research.

Thinking and Working Scientifically outcomes
- Describe the strengths and limitations of a model
- Take appropriately accurate and precise measurements, explaining why accuracy and precision are important

Using models
- The rope model is extended to demonstrate current as the rate of flow.

Science in Context
- The Science in context: Parallel and series circuit box in Topic 9.3 of the Student's Book covers the following learning objective:
  - 7SIC.02 Describe how science is applied across societies and industries, and in research.

Common misunderstandings

- Students frequently think that current is used up as it goes through a lamp. They need to know that the flow of charge, or of electrons is unchanged around a loop. What changes is the energy of the electrons. Energy supplied by the cell is changed to heat and light in the lamp and so the electrons returning to the cell have less energy. Ensure that students observe the flow of the rope at different points in the loop and see that this doesn't change. This will then be reinforced when they measure current in the circuit and find it unchanged.

- Students sometimes assume current can reach a lamp placed in a broken circuit if the gap is after the lamp. Discuss how this could be modelled – maybe by cutting the rope (no need to actually cut it!) Students should see that this stops any flow. This could lead to a discussion on the limitations of the model as it isn't a satisfactory analogy. In effect cutting the rope gives a long piece of rope which can still move if pulled until all the rope has passed the person pulling and ends up in a pile by the puller. This is not what happens with current. Remind students that a model is just a way of picturing a difficult situation and not reality.

  It may be useful to refer back to the big circuit model where students saw that current reached the lamp instantaneously, and breaking the circuit has the same effect.

  Students can try breaking a real circuit at different points to see that any gap stops current flowing throughout the loop.

9.3a Starting point

Resource preparation

For the demonstration: large rope loop

Teaching and learning ideas

- Revisit the rope model using the large rope loop. Explain to students that they are going to measure the current because this is more accurate than judging current by observing the brightness of bulbs. Ensure they are clear that current is the amount of charge flowing each second, represented by the amount of rope flowing each second.

- Challenge them to come up with a way of measuring the amount of rope flowing. This may lead to suggestions of measuring the length of rope flowing through their hands, or counting stripes on the rope.

- Explain that an ammeter performs this role in a circuit.

9.3b Measuring current

Students will learn:

- To know how to measure the current in series circuits
- To carry out practical work safely
- To collect and record sufficient observations and/or measurements in an appropriate form

Resource preparation

For Activity 9.4: each group will need 2 × 1.5 V lamps, 2 × 1.5 V cells, 5 × wires, an ammeter, preferably accurate to +/- 0.1 A. (A more accurate ammeter may show the change in current as the lamps get hot and this may cause confusion.)

Worksheet 9.3b

Practical notes 9.3b

Teaching and learning ideas

- Show students how to connect the ammeter. Point out that the positive and negative and show them how to connect it in a circuit. Demonstrate what happens if the ammeter is connected the wrong way round and point out that a negative sign here just tells us which way current is flowing through the ammeter.

- Students complete Activity 9.4 *Measuring the current in a series circuit*. Get students to predict what they will find and explain this using the model. They can then carry out the investigation and record the results on Worksheet 9.3b. Encourage students to take the circuit apart and make from scratch each time. See Practical notes 9.3b for further information.

- Challenge students to repeat the experiment using an analogue ammeter.

Differentiation

Some students will finish this task quickly. They could investigate whether the same pattern of results is obtained with more lamps in the circuit or using other components such as buzzers or motors.

Homework

Workbook questions 4 and 5

9.3c Comparing current in circuits

Students will learn:

- To know how to measure the current in series circuits
- To describe how adding components into a series circuit can affect the current (limited to addition of cells and lamps)
- To collect and record sufficient observations and/or measurements in an appropriate form
- To describe trends and patterns in results, including identifying any anomalous results

Resource preparation

For Activity 9.5: each group needs 2×1.5 V cells, 5×1.5 V lamps, a switch, an ammeter, 7 wires, graph paper.

For Activity 9.6: each group needs 1×1.5 V cell, 2×1.5 V lamps, a switch, an ammeter, 5 wires.

Practical notes 9.3c(1), 9.3c(2)

Teaching and learning ideas

- Explain to students that the next activity is a more detailed version of Activity 9.3. They can draw on their observations of the brightness of the lamps to help them to predict what will happen with the current.
- Get students to look at the graph of current against the number of cells and describe what it shows.
- Students can then plan and carry out Activity 9.5 *Changing the number of bulbs in a circuit*. Remind them of the different variables and get them to identify the variables for the investigation. The main control variable is that the number of cells should not be changed. Encourage students to repeat measurements and calculate a mean. They should use a range of 1–5 lamps as this will give sufficient readings for a meaningful graph.
- Challenge students to explain the curve of the graph.
- Summarise the points of learning relating to components in a series circuit, and ask students what they know about the positions of components in a circuit.
- Students should carry out Activity 9.6 *Explaining changes in a circuit* to investigate changes in circuits. Encourage students to refer back to the rope loop model, particularly when they change the cell round. See Practical notes 9.3cii for further information.

Extension

Students could carry out an investigation into the effect of increasing the number of cells on the current and compare their results to those in figure 9.14. This is chance to introduce the idea of peer reviewing and scientists checking the reproducibility of experimental results.

Homework

Workbook question 8.

Chapter 9 | Checking students' progress

End of chapter reflection
- To review the learning points of the chapter
- To test understanding through answering questions

Resources
Student Book [Key facts, End of chapter review questions]
Workbook
Worksheet 9.4

Approach

Use the Key facts and Check your skills progress boxes in the Student's Book for each topic in this chapter as a way of recapping on the main learning points.

Ask students to complete the self-assessment checklist at the end of Chapter 9 in the Workbook. Encourage students to work together in small groups to discuss which aspects of the material are the most difficult to understand, and then have a class vote. You may wish to revisit some Learning Objectives again if students find any areas particularly challenging. Use the Student's Book text and questions to revisit these aspects. Go through the answers orally in class. Take note of whether giving the answer appears to resolve students' uncertainty or not, and work through further examples.

The teacher response in the Workbook can be completed to give students personalised feedback on next steps. Students could be asked to answer specific end of chapter review questions in their books. Alternatively go through some or all of the end of chapter review questions in the Student's Book orally in class.

Use the Context worksheet (Worksheet 9.4) as a framework for students to conduct their own research enquiries about light bulbs. This activity provides the opportunity to cover Learning Objectives 7SIC.01, 7SIC.02 and 7SIC.05. For example, students could focus on how ideas about filament lamps were developed or on the global environmental impact of the development of low-energy light bulbs.

Understanding the rope loop model is important for students so have the large and small loops available for students to check things out.

Finish by asking students to complete the test-style questions at the end of Chapter 9 in the Workbook. Provide feedback on students' answers, and work with students individually to identify areas that still need more work.

Chapter 10 — The Earth and its atmosphere

Chapter overview

This chapter provides opportunities to focus on how a scientific idea (hypothesis) can be tested against evidence, and discussed and improved by scientists over time. It also offers an opportunity to discuss the use of models.

In this chapter, students will first explore the structure of the Earth and the theory of plate tectonics. They will move on to understand how earthquakes, volcanoes and some mountains are produced at plate boundaries, before considering the composition of the Earth's atmosphere and the water cycle.

Topic title	Number of 40-minute periods	Learning Objectives	Thinking and Working Scientifically Learning Objectives
10.1 The Earth's crust	3	7Esp.01 Describe the model of plate tectonics, in which a solid outer layer (made up of the crust and uppermost mantle) moves because of flow lower in the mantle.	7TWSp.02 Describe how scientific hypotheses can be supported or contradicted by evidence from an enquiry.
10.2 Earthquakes, volcanoes and mountains	5	7ESp.02 Describe how earthquakes, volcanoes and fold mountains occur near the boundaries of tectonic plates.	7TWSm.01 Describe the strengths and limitations of a model.
10.3 The Earth's atmosphere	2	7ESp.03 Know that clean, dry air contains 78% nitrogen, 21% oxygen and small amounts of carbon dioxide and other gases, and this composition can change because of pollution and natural emissions.	7TWSc.03 Evaluate whether measurements and observations have been repeated sufficiently to be reliable. 7TWSc.04 Take appropriately accurate and precise measurements, explaining why accuracy and precision are important. 7TWSa.04 Evaluate experiments and investigations, and suggest improvements, explaining any proposed changes. 7TWSa.05 Present and interpret observations and measurements appropriately.
10.4 The water cycle	2	7ESc.01 Describe the water cycle (limited to evaporation, condensation, precipitation, water run-off, open water and groundwater).	7TWSm.01 Describe the strengths and limitations of a model. 7TWSc.02 Decide what equipment is required to carry out an investigation or experiment and use it appropriately. 7TWSc.05 Carry out practical work safely.
End of chapter questions	1	Check students' progress	

Background science

Please note: the background science notes are designed to provide teachers with an overview of the science concepts students may have already been taught earlier in their education, are likely to be taught in this unit and are likely to be taught in later stages. They are not a checklist of the content to be covered by the teacher in each unit.

The background science notes also serve to provide the teacher with some understanding of the background science needed in order to deliver the content of each chapter.

This chapter covers a range of key earth sciences topics that are fundamental to later studies: plate tectonics theory and its consequences, the composition of the atmosphere, and the water cycle. There are several opportunities to describe or create models and explore their strengths and limitations.

After a brief revision of the Earth's inner structure, the development of plate tectonics via Wegener's idea of continental drift is explored. This offers an opportunity to talk about how a scientific hypothesis depends on evidence, and how scientists discuss, refine and sometimes reject ideas before they are finally accepted based on further investigations.

The consequences of the movement of Earth's tectonic plates at plate boundaries are discussed next. Earthquakes, volcanoes and fold mountains are all explored, including an activity to model a volcano. This presents an opportunity to describe the work of scientists who use observations to better predict earthquakes and their effects, including tsunami, and volcanoes and their effects. This is a good time to show how science can have a positive global impact, through the development of tsunami early warning systems and an activity encouraging students to think about practical earthquake precautions.

Describing the composition of the Earth's atmosphere affords an opportunity to explain how the percentages of different gases in a mixture can be determined experimentally. Here, the importance of accuracy and precision and the reliability of measurements are all discussed. A brief introduction to the change in atmospheric composition over time, and the role of pollutants, provides a grounding for the topic of climate change due to human activities in Stages 8 and 9. The positive global impact of science in addressing the depletion of the ozone layer is also described.

The water cycle is introduced by revising evaporation, condensation and precipitation, then the new concepts of water run-off, open water and groundwater are added to build up the full cycle. A demonstration of a model of evaporation, condensation and precipitation provides a chance for students to review their understanding of how models work and how they might be improved.

Cambridge Lower Secondary Earth and space
Stage 7

10.1 The Earth's crust

Topic overview

		Student's Book	Workbook	Downloadable materials
10.1a	**Starting point** This short discussion provides an opportunity for students to demonstrate their understanding that Earth consists mainly of rock, with surface oceans of water	Starting point table		
10.1b	**Inside the Earth** Students describe and draw a diagram of the structure of the Earth	Questions 1, 2	Question 1	
10.1c	**The movement of the crust** Students describe continental drift and the evidence for the idea	Questions 3, 4	Questions 3, 5 and 6	Worksheet 10.1c
10.1d	**Tectonic plates** Students learn about and write a timeline of the development of the theory of plate tectonics	Questions 5–7 Activity 10.1	Questions 2, 4 and 7–10	

Learning Objectives

- 7ESp.01: Describe the model of plate tectonics, in which a solid outer layer (made up of the crust and uppermost mantle) moves because of flow lower in the mantle
- 7TWSp.02: Describe how scientific hypotheses can be supported or contradicted by evidence from an enquiry
- 7SIC.01: Discuss how scientific knowledge is developed through collective understanding and scrutiny over time
- 7SIC.04: Describe how people develop and use scientific understanding, as individuals and through collaboration, e.g. through peer-review

Links to other topics

- Chemistry Stage 7 Chapter 4 Topic 3 The states of matter (solid, liquid and gas)
- Physics Stage 8 Chapter 10 Topic 1 Magnetic fields
- Earth and Space Stage 7 Chapter 11 Topic 1 Planets of the Solar System (the rocky composition of Earth)
- Physics Stage 8 Chapter 8 Topic 3 Pressure on an area (in relation to forces at plate boundaries)
- Earth and Space Stage 9 Chapter 12 Topic 1 Evidence for plate tectonics

Using models

- Discussing Wegener's model of continental drift offers numerous opportunities to discuss how models are tested against evidence and improved. In this case, additional evidence and scientific thinking resulted in the modern theory of plate tectonics.
- There are many strengths and limitations of Wegener's model, and there are similar strengths and yet still some limitations of the plate tectonics model. For example, you could discuss with students how difficult it is to get direct evidence, such as drilling deep enough to penetrate the Earth's crust, which cannot be done yet.

Science in context

- The Science in Context: Publishing scientists' work box in Topic 10.1 of the Student's Book covers the following learning objectives:
  - 7SIC.01 Discuss how scientific knowledge is developed through collective understanding and scrutiny over time.
  - 7SIC.04 Describe how people develop and use scientific understanding as individuals and through collaboration, e.g. through peer review

- Look out for the opportunities and questions that encourage students to discuss how scientific knowledge is developed through collective understanding and review over time. Closely connected with this are opportunities to describe how people develop scientific understanding, through collecting evidence and through peer review. For example, Wegener's suggestion of continental drift had some supporting evidence, but this was not enough to convince a majority of scientists that he was correct. It took decades of scientists discussing Wegener's ideas and collecting evidence for enough of them to adopt and improve his ideas to form the theory of plate tectonics.

Common misunderstandings

- The problem with discussing Wegener's hypothesis of continental drift before describing the modern theory of plate tectonics is that some students may think only (land) continents are moving plates. It is important to stress that this was a limitation of Wegener's hypothesis, and that there are plates under the oceans.
- Some students may think that movements within the crust are mostly 'up and down' (e.g. to form fold mountains or volcanoes, or as witnessed by people who have experienced an earthquake). Use every opportunity to talk about horizontal plate movement. (This is part of the reason why here we discuss fold mountains after plate boundaries, earthquakes and volcanoes.)
- Students may think that the edge of a continent must form a plate boundary; counter this with examples such as undersea plate boundaries (mid-Atlantic Ridge) and largely landlocked plate boundaries (Indian plate boundary forming the Himalayas).
- It is very difficult for students to appreciate that plate movement is mostly extremely slow, particularly when violent and rapid events such as earthquakes are used as evidence of plate motion. Emphasise how earthquakes result from the build-up of forces and energy at plate boundaries over many thousands of years, and the sudden movement is a release of that energy.
- Some students may think of the mantle as liquid rock over which the crusts 'float', but the molten mantle is a thick substance with the properties largely those of a solid that 'creeps'; it does not behave like a 'runny' liquid.

10.1a Starting point

Review students' understanding of Earth being mostly composed of rock, with surface oceans of water

Teaching and learning ideas

Ask students:

- What is the structure of the Earth? (Rocky crust, hot/molten rocky mantle, metal core)
- Where does the water on Earth appear? (Just on the surface and in the atmosphere/air)
- What is under the oceans? (Rocky crust)

10.1b Inside the Earth

Students will learn:

- To describe how Earth has a structure comprising outer rocky crust, molten mantle and solid core
- To identify what parts of the model of the Earth's structure are testable

Glossary words

core, crust, mantle

Resource preparation

For introduction to topic: Cutaway image of the inner structure of Earth, for example Student's Book figure 10.1.

Teaching and learning ideas

- Show a cutaway diagram of the inner structure of the Earth and ask students to add labels to show core, mantle and crust, as well as surface water.
- Be careful when discussing the mantle. Students may think it is liquid, like a water ocean, but in reality it is thought to be solid but able to flow to a limited degree due to the heat and pressure. (Note that pressure is not explained in this Stage, so avoid using the term; say 'forces' or 'squashing forces' instead.)
- Emphasise how the crust thickness varies between 25 and 90 km on land and between 5 and 10 km beneath the oceans. Explain how this is very thin compared to the diameter of the Earth. It is a bit like the shell on an egg.

Differentiation

- Some students may need support in recognising the relative thickness of different parts of the crust. Ask them to draw scale sketches to show the thickness on land and beneath the ocean.

Extension ideas

- Ask students to find out more about the core of the Earth and how scientists can measure some of its properties.

Homework suggestions

Students answer question 1 in Topic 10.1 in the Workbook.

10.1c The movement of the crust

Students will learn:

- To describe Wegener's hypothesis of continental drift and evidence that supported it
- To describe how a hypothesis can be tested against evidence

Glossary words

continent, continental drift, hypothesis

Resource preparation

Globe or flat map of the world

Worksheet 10.1c for continental drift, scissors (Note: it could potentially be difficult for students to cut out the shapes of the continents. To make it easier for them this worksheet could be copied and enlarged or the shapes could be cut out in advance of the lesson)

Teaching and learning ideas

- Introduce the topic by showing a globe or a flat map of the entire world, focusing on the shapes and sizes and positions of the land masses. Explain that the largest land masses are called continents, and identify the Americas, Africa, Asia and Europe.
- Describe how the shapes of west Africa and the eastern coast of South America seem to fit together. Explain how Alfred Wegener suggested that many millions of years ago, these two continents did indeed fit together, and that in fact all land masses were once joined together.
- You may wish to use Worksheet 10.1c, which has a map of the ancient continent of Pangaea, with the outlines of the present-day continents marked on it. Students can cut out the continents by following their outlines, and explore how different continents 'fit' together and how they are now positioned.
- Explain how Wegener thought the continents moved apart by what he called 'continental drift', but he could not explain what was causing the continents to move, and he could not explain what was happening to the parts of the Earth's crust that were found under the oceans.
- Discuss (briefly) the evidence for this drift: (i) matching shapes of coastlines; (ii) matching patterns of rock layers on separate continents; (iii) fossils of identical animals found on both continents, when those animals could not fly or swim. (Students will study this evidence in much greater detail in Stage 9, so it is best not to labour these points.)

Differentiation

- Limit the amount of discussion about Wegener's ideas of continental drift and focus more on the basic aspects needed to develop the theory of plate tectonics later: (i) that parts of the Earth's crust are moving sideways and (ii) this movement is very, very slow.

Extension ideas

- You could have an in-class 'debate', where half the class argues in support of Wegener's ideas and the other half represents the other scientists who questioned them. Explain to students that all scientific ideas are discussed and improved in this way.

Homework suggestions

Students answer questions 5–6 in Topic 10.1 in the Workbook.

10.1d Tectonic plates

Students will learn:

- To understand the model of plate tectonics
- To describe how the model of plate tectonics took time to be accepted by most scientists
- To describe how a hypothesis can be tested against evidence

Glossary words

peer review, tectonic plate, theory

Resource preparation

For Activity 10.1: plain paper, rulers, coloured pencils

Teaching and learning ideas

- Briefly review students' understanding of magnetism. They should be aware that like poles repel and opposite poles attract, and that magnetic materials produce a magnetic field that affects objects around them.
- Explain how some layers of rock contain magnetic materials, and that the magnetic fields of these rock layers 'line up' as the rocks form and cool. As layers of rocks build up over time, the magnetic parts of the rocks form patterns that are like a 'fingerprint'. It is possible to tell where some rocks come from just from the magnetic fields these layers produce.
- Scientists investigating these magnetic rock layers discovered more evidence that coasts of some continents were once joined together. This led to more scientists re-evaluating Wegener's ideas and developing them into a new theory: plate tectonics.
- Explain how plate tectonics is an improvement on Wegener's ideas because it says that the land found under oceans also moves, an area that Wegener's idea did not address.
- Explain how the hot rock in the mantle can flow very, very slowly, so that if the Earth's outer rocky layers form large pieces, these pieces can be pulled along by the movement of the mantle underneath.
- Ask students to carry out Activity 10.1 *Developing and testing a hypothesis*. Students will need a plentiful supply of plain paper or a large (A3 or bigger) single sheet, along with rulers and coloured pencils. Students should create a timeline of the development of the theory of plate tectonics. They should be encouraged to use a range of different sources to conduct their research, such as internet sources or textbooks.

Differentiation

- Less confident students may need support in understanding how tectonic plates move when the mantle is not liquid. Focus on a single plate and ask them to imagine the plate as a piece of cardboard sitting on top of a dessert made from jelly. The jelly is solid but if it gets warm, it can get slippery so that things can move slowly over the top of it.
- Encourage more confident students to think about the difference between continental drift and plate tectonics. Ask them to write a short description of one significant piece of evidence that plate tectonics can explain, but continental drift cannot (example: the movements of the crust under oceans).

Extension ideas

- Challenge students to describe the directions in which tectonic plates can move, particularly relative to each other. For example, they can push towards each other, or draw away from each other, or move sideways past each other. (This will be developed further in Topic 10.2b.)

Homework suggestions

Students answer questions 8–10 in Topic 10.1 in the Workbook.

Cambridge Lower Secondary Earth and space
Stage 7

Topic overview

		Student's Book	Workbook	Downloadable materials
10.2a	**Starting point** Students discuss what they know about earthquakes and volcanoes	Starting point table		
10.2b	**Plate boundaries** Students learn the different ways two plates can come together at boundaries, and how one strength of the plate tectonics model is that it explains the creation of volcanoes and earthquakes at boundaries		Question 3	
10.2c	**Earthquakes** Students learn about the causes of earthquakes and take part in an activity that requires students to think about the effects of earthquakes (including tsunami) and how to reduce their impact. Students also investigate which cities are most at risk of earthquakes	Question 1 Activity 10.2 Activity 10.3 Questions 2–5	Questions 5 and 7	Worksheet 10.2c
10.2d	**Volcanoes** Students learn about the causes and effects of volcanoes, and do an activity to model a volcano. Students also investigate where volcanoes are most likely to form	Questions 6–9 Activity 10.4 Activity 10.5	Questions 6, 8, 9 and 11	Practical Notes 10.2d Worksheet 10.2d (1) Worksheet 10.2d (2)
10.2e	**Mountains** Students learn how fold mountains form at certain types of plate boundary, and do an activity to model the formation of fold mountains	Questions 10–12 Activity 10.6	Questions 1, 2, 4 and 10	Worksheet 10.2c(2)

Learning Objectives

- 7ESp.02: Describe how earthquakes, volcanoes and fold mountains occur near the boundaries of tectonic plates
- 7TWSm.01: Describe the strengths and limitations of a model
- 7SIC.05: Discuss how the uses of science can have a global environmental impact

- 7SIC.02: Describe how science is applied across societies and industries, and in research.
- 7SIC.03: Evaluate issues which involve and/or require scientific understanding.

Links to other topics

- Physics Stage 7 Chapter 6 Topic 1 Energy at work (in relation to energy transfers).
- Physics Stage 8 Chapter 8 Topic 3 Pressure on an area (in relation to forces at plate boundaries).

Using models

- Plate tectonics and plate boundaries offer opportunities to discuss models, their strengths and their limitations. For example, the movement of plates as they come into contact at plate boundaries explains why we find significant events such as volcanoes and earthquakes so frequently in these areas. However, although the model tells us where we might expect such events to occur, it does not tell us much about exactly when they might occur and when they do, how large they will be.

- A theme through this section is the study that scientists make of earthquakes and volcanoes, in order to better understand how they occur, when they might be more likely to occur, and how to reduce the impact of their effects. All this use of past scientific data to predict future events requires complex models, which usually require large, fast computers to operate. You may wish to develop this idea further: that a scientific model is now usually written as software on a supercomputer. You could encourage students to think about the skills modern scientists need, including quite sophisticated computer modelling skills.

- In contrast, there is also an opportunity for students to build their own physical model of a volcano, and suggest how it can be improved. Encourage students to think about the limitations of such a model.

- Related to all these different types of model is the problem of time. On the one hand, models of plate tectonics are trying to show how very slow-moving events are caused and what effects they have. Remind students just how slowly tectonic plates move, perhaps 1 or 2 cm per year. On the other hand, an earthquake can cause significant movement in seconds. Both these extremes of time are hard to model.

Science in context

- The Science in context boxes 'Tsunami warning systems' and 'How vulcanologists use data' in Topic 10.2 of the Student's Book cover the following learning objectives:
  - 7SIC.02 Describe how science is applied across societies and industries, and in research.
  - 7SIC.03 Evaluate issues which involve and/or require scientific understanding.
  - 7SIC.05 Discuss how the uses of science can have a global environmental impact.

- Look out for opportunities to discuss how scientists investigating earthquakes and volcanoes make use of the evidence they find to have a global impact, such as by developing early warning systems for earthquakes and tsunami, and by predicting the effects of catastrophic events so that people are better prepared when an earthquake occurs or a volcano erupts.

Common misunderstandings

- Students may think that a coastline of a continent is always a plate boundary. This is certainly not the case, although it is occasionally true. For example, the east coast of the United States is NOT a plate boundary, but much of the west coast is. Discuss with students how they can use evidence to tell the difference (one good example is the lack of active volcanoes on the east coast, whereas there are several along the west coast).

- Students may think earthquakes are always major events to be feared, if they base their thinking on news reports. Point out that many smaller ground movements called earth tremors happen every day all over the world. Humans often cannot detect them. The large earthquakes that affect people's lives are the only ones that tend to make the news.

- Students may think that the ground 'breaks up' or 'cracks open' during an earthquake. Unlike in major films, most earthquakes do not create such massive damage. Cracks might appear in pavements, roads or buildings but these are often quite small.

- Students may think volcanoes are rare events and one-offs. However, most active volcanoes are constantly emitting gases and have a 'store' of magma underground that typically produces slow, constant lava rather than the spectacular eruptions seen in films or in the news. Such major eruptions are, as with earthquakes, due to a build-up of forces over time.

- Students may think that all volcanoes are cone-like structures on land, whereas in fact there are many active volcanoes under the oceans.

10.2a Starting point

Resource preparation

A map of the major plate boundaries on Earth along with locations of volcanoes and recent major earthquakes (for a good example, search the website of the US Geological Service (USGS.gov) for a resource entitled 'This Dynamic Planet'; there is a high-resolution map of the world here showing the features suggested)

Teaching and learning ideas

- Show a map of the world that illustrates the major tectonic plates and plate boundaries, along with the locations of recent earthquakes and volcanoes.
- Explain to students what they are looking at and what the symbols and colours represent.
- Choose one major plate boundary and zoom in on it (such as the west coast of South America) and ask the students what they see (they should describe two plates next to each other, plus a large number of volcanoes and earthquakes marked along or near to the join between the two plates).
- Explain that they are going to investigate this link between plate boundaries and events such as earthquakes and volcanoes.

10.2b Plate boundaries

Students will learn:

- To describe how the plate tectonics model explains earthquakes, volcanoes and fold mountains
- To describe how science can help predict earthquakes and volcanoes, and reduce their effects
- To understand some strengths and limitations of the plate tectonics model

Glossary words

earthquake, limitation, plate boundary, strength, volcano

Resource preparation

For short activity on tectonic plates: plain paper, coloured pencils

Teaching and learning ideas

- Ask students to draw two tectonic 'plates' of crust that are connected along a line. Ask them to describe the different ways these plates can move past each other. They can move (i) apart, leaving a gap behind, (ii) slide past each other, (iii) push towards each other and both push upwards or (iv) push towards each other and one plate is pushed downwards, the other upwards.
- You do not need to introduce the scientific terms for the different types of plate boundary (subduction, etc.) but students do need to recognise that there are different types and that the plates move towards, past or away from each other in different ways.
- If you showed a map of plate boundaries across the world in the Starting point activity, show it again and ask students to point out the plate boundaries.
- Point out examples of the different types: two pushing together so that one is pushed beneath the other (e.g. west coast of North America); two pushing together so that both push upwards (India plate where it meets the Eurasia plate); two moving apart (e.g. mid-Atlantic rift).

Differentiation

- Focus in on one example of a plate boundary and get students to model it using pieces of paper as 'plates' set flat on a smooth desk. If they push the two sheets of paper together carefully, they may find that one piece collides with the other and they both push upwards, or that one slides under the other.
- More confident students could develop their learning by describing what sort of plate boundary passes through Iceland, and suggest why Iceland has a number of active volcanoes.

Extension ideas

- Ask students to investigate how many volcanoes there are in the middle and east of South America, and compare this to the west coast. Students should be able to explain why there are many fewer in the middle, relating this to local plate boundaries and their types.

Homework suggestions

Students answer question 3 in Topic 10.2 in the Workbook.

10.2c Earthquakes

Students will learn:

- To describe how the plate tectonics model explains earthquakes
- To describe how science can help predict earthquakes and reduce their effects
- To understand some strengths and limitations of the plate tectonics model

Glossary words

assumption, fault line, tsunami

Resource preparation

- For the introduction: two magazines with square spines or thin textbooks
- For Activity 10.2: figure 10.7 (room with movable objects) from the Student's Book
- For Activity 10.3: figure 10.8 (Map of plates and plate boundaries, plus major cities) from the Student's Book, access to the internet for online research

Teaching and learning ideas

- Review briefly the learning about plate boundaries. Demonstrate two magazines, placed flat on a table back to back so the two spines form a 'plate boundary'. Place one hand on each magazine and push them together so that the magazines 'bend' upwards or one goes over the other. Ask students what you are modelling (the forces of two plates as they push together).
- Use the magazines again and push them towards each other, but with a slight sideways force so they slip past each other. They should move in small fits and jerks, not smoothly.
- Explain that plate movement, although it is slow, involves very large forces. If two plates are 'stuck' together because of friction (review friction if necessary) then the forces build up until the plates move suddenly.
- Explain to students that this sudden slipping is often what causes an earthquake. Energy is released across a wide area, and the ground can feel like it is moving up and down or side to side.
- Ask students to describe any earthquakes they have heard about in the news recently. Ask them why earthquakes can damage buildings (the shaking can cause cracks in the walls, or cause the whole building to collapse).
- Ask students to complete Activity 10.2 *Preparing for an earthquake*, in which students inspect figure 10.7 from the Student's Book and identify all the items in the room that might become dangerous during an earthquake, and suggest how five objects can be placed differently to make them more safe.
- Ask students to complete Activity 10.3 *Investigating where earthquakes occur*, in which students inspect a map of the world and its biggest cities, and determine which cities are most at risk from earthquakes (any that are on or near plate boundaries). Students should also choose one of their 'at risk' cities and research the last time there was an earthquake there, and how much damage it caused.
- Explain how scientists measuring earthquakes have collected enough data to be able to model the movement of tectonic plates and predict where earthquakes might occur. However, they do not know exactly when they might occur (a model limitation).
- Discuss the global impact of some earthquakes, particularly those that take place under the ocean and which can cause tsunami.

Differentiation

- Less confident students may need guidance locating the plate boundaries in Activity 10.3. Focus in on one plate boundary (such as that along the west coast of South America) and use online maps to highlight the cities.

Extension ideas

- Students could investigate either the 2004 earthquake that caused a tsunami in the Indian Ocean, or the 2011 earthquake near Japan that caused a tsunami there. They should find out exactly when the earthquake occurred and list some of its effects.

Homework suggestions

Students answer question 7 in Topic 10.2 in the Workbook.

Cambridge Lower Secondary Earth and space
Stage 7

10.2d Volcanoes

Students will learn:

- To describe how the plate tectonics model explains volcanoes
- To describe how science can help predict volcanic eruptions and reduce their effects
- To understand some strengths and limitations of the plate tectonics model
- To understand how scientists make predictions of likely outcomes of events

Glossary words

rift valley

Resource preparation

For Activity 10.4: Worksheet 10.2d (1), Practical Notes 10.2d, large tray (approximately 30 cm x 40 cm minimum) with tall sides, cleaned 250 or 500 ml soft drinks bottle, wet sand or soil, jug, water, baking soda (sodium hydrogencarbonate), washing up liquid, red or orange food colouring, vinegar (dilute ethanoic acid)

For Activity 10.5: Worksheet 10.2d, (2) figure 10.14 (map of major tectonic plates and their boundaries) from the Student's Book, access to the internet for research

Teaching and learning ideas

- Review briefly what students know about volcanoes. Focus on the amount of energy needed to melt rock and force ash and gases miles into the air. Check that the students understand that much of this energy can come from plate boundaries and the plate movements.
- Discuss with students the situation where two plates are moving apart. Gradually a valley forms between the plates, into which molten rock can flow. Show the mid-Atlantic ridge on a map or on screen, and ask students to find land that sits above that ridge (Iceland). Show images of some Icelandic volcanoes, as examples of when molten rock reaches the surface of the crust.
- Explain that a plate boundary is not always needed for volcanoes to form; at other places on the Earth's surface, the crust is thinner and weaker and sometimes molten rock from below can burst through a weak spot.
- Ask students to carry out Activity 10.4 *Modelling volcanoes*, Practical Notes 10.2d and Worksheet 10.2d (1). This requires plenty of space and protection for students' clothes as it can get messy!
- Ask students to complete Activity 10.5 *Investigating where volcanoes occur*, in which students inspect a map of the world and suggest where volcanoes are most likely to be found (plate boundaries). Students should also choose one of their 'at risk' areas and research the last time there was a major eruption there, and how much damage it caused.
- Explain how vulcanologists (scientists who measure volcanoes) have collected enough data to be able to model the movement of tectonic plates and predict where volcanic eruptions might occur. However, they do not know exactly when they might occur (a model limitation).

Differentiation

- Less confident students may need guidance locating the plate boundaries in Activity 10.5. Focus in on one plate boundary (such as that along the west coast of South America) and use online maps to highlight where eruptions have occurred.
- More confident students might complete Activity 10.4 quite quickly. Encourage them to describe the limitations of their model (such as: it only shows lava erupting, not ash or gases). Can they suggest ways to improve their model?

Extension ideas

- Ask students to research the effects of the biggest volcanic eruptions, such as producing so much ash it is blown around the Earth's atmosphere and can even cause the Earth's surface temperature to cool slightly, or (particularly in the case of the eruption of Eyjafjallajökull in 2010) disrupt air traffic.

Homework suggestions

Students answer questions 8, 9 and 11 in Topic 10.2 in the Workbook.

10.2e Mountains

Students will learn:

- To describe how the plate tectonics model explains fold mountains
- To understand some strengths and limitations of the plate tectonics model

Glossary words

fold mountains, vulcanologist

Resource preparation

- For Activity 10.6: Sheets of paper, A4 or A3, in at least six different colours, sheets of other materials such as greaseproof paper/baking parchment, cooking foil, thin cardboard
- Worksheet 10.2e on fold mountains

Teaching and learning ideas

- Ask students to complete Activity 10.6 *Making a model of fold mountains*, in which they use sheets of paper or other materials to create a 'layered' rock that is then pushed together and rises upwards.
- Stress the difference between timescales for the formation of fold mountains (millions of years) and 'sudden' events such as earthquakes.
- Ask students to complete Worksheet 10.2e *Fold mountains*

Differentiation

- For Activity 10.6, some students may need thicker materials such as towels or blankets to better understand how the rock layering looks and how it folds.
- More confident students could be asked to investigate how quickly the Himalayas mountains have formed.

Extension ideas

- Ask students to research areas other than the Himalayas where fold mountains have formed.

Homework suggestions

Students answer questions 4 and 10 in Topic 10.2 in the Workbook.

Topic overview

		Student's Book	Workbook	Downloadable materials
10.3a	**Starting point** This short discussion provides an opportunity to revisit students' knowledge that the atmosphere contains a mixture of different gases	Starting point table		
10.3b	**Earth's atmosphere** Students learn how the amounts of different gases in a mixture can be determined using reactions and a gas syringe Students do an activity to draw a pie chart to show the composition of the atmosphere. They also do an activity investigating accuracy and reliability	Questions 1–4 Activity 10.7 Activity 10.8	Questions 1–3, 7 and 9	Worksheet 10.3b (1) Worksheet 10.3b (2)
10.3c	**Changes in the atmosphere over time** Students learn how the composition of the Earth's atmosphere has changed over time, most recently because of pollution and natural emissions. Students discuss the effects of pollutants in the atmosphere and learn how scientific evidence of damage to the ozone layer led to global change in the use of CFCs	Questions 5–8	Questions 4–6, 8 and 10	Worksheet 10.3c

Learning Objectives

- 7ESp.03: Know that clean, dry air contains 78% nitrogen, 21% oxygen and small amounts of carbon dioxide and other gases, and this composition can change because of pollution and natural emissions
- 7TWSc.03: Evaluate whether measurements and observations have been repeated sufficiently to be reliable
- 7TWSc.04: Take appropriately accurate and precise measurements, explaining why accuracy and precision are important

- 7TWSa.04: Evaluate experiments and investigations, and suggest improvements, explaining any proposed changes
- 7TWSa.05: Present and interpret observations and measurements appropriately
- 7SIC.02: Describe how science is applied across societies and industries, and in research
- 7SIC.05: Discuss how the uses of science can have a global environmental impact

Links to other topics

Earth and Space Stage 9 Chapter 13 Topic 2 Climate change

Science in context

- The Science in context: Using inert gases box in Topic 10.3 of the Student's Book covers the following learning objectives:
  - 7SIC.02 Describe how science is applied across societies and industries, and in research.

10.3a Starting point

Teaching and learning ideas

- Remind the students of their prior learning concerning the Earth's atmosphere. They should know that air is a mixture of different gases, and that air contains oxygen that we need to live.

10.3b Earth's atmosphere

Students will learn:

- To know the percentages of the different gases in the Earth's atmosphere
- To evaluate whether measurements and observations have been repeated sufficiently to be reliable
- To present data using a pie chart
- To evaluate experiments and investigations, and suggest improvements, explaining any proposed changes
- To explain why accuracy and precision are important in measuring quantities of gases

Glossary words

accurate, gas syringe, inert, range, reliable

Resource preparation

Worksheet 10.3b (1) for taking readings from gas syringe, calculating quantities and percentages

For Activity 10.7: protractor, ruler

For Activity 10.8: Worksheet 10.3b (2) taking accurate measurements, illustrating accuracy and reliability

Teaching and learning ideas

- Explain to students the percentages of different gases in the atmosphere and the importance of nitrogen, oxygen and carbon dioxide.
- Describe the gas syringe investigation in the Student's Book, and how a reaction between oxygen in the air and copper means the amount of oxygen in the air can be measured.
- Ask students to complete Worksheet 10.3b (1), which involves them reading measurements from a gas syringe used to calculate the amount of oxygen in the air.
- Ask students to complete Activity 10.7.
- Explain how the gas syringe technique requires careful techniques, and that accuracy and reliability of measurements are important aspects of scientific investigations. Be careful to explain the difference between accuracy and reliability. A measurement is accurate if it is close to the 'real' or 'true' value. A set of measurements are considered reliable when they are fairly consistent when repeated.
- Ask students to complete Activity 10.8 and Worksheet 10.3b (2) in which they learn about accuracy and reliability.

Differentiation

- Some students will need help producing their first pie chart. You may wish to have them produce a simpler pie chart, for example from a tally chart of objects, or by using more approximate values for the percentages of the gases in the air (nitrogen = 80%, oxygen = 20%) and then increasing the precision.
- More confident students could investigate how the quantities of gases other than oxygen in the atmosphere can be measured.

Extension ideas

- Ask students to create a bar chart of the composition of gases in the Earth's atmosphere, to compare with the visual impact of a pie chart. Ask them where a pie chart might be more useful, and where a bar chart would be better.

Homework suggestions

Students answer questions 3, 7 and 9 in Topic 10.3 in the Workbook.

10.3c Changes in the Earth's atmosphere over time

Students will learn:

- To know describe how the composition of the Earth's atmosphere can change because of natural processes and human activities
- To describe the percentages of the different gases in the Earth's atmosphere
- To describe how climate modelling has led to worldwide changes in the use of particular substances

Glossary words

acid rain, fossil fuel, photosynthesis, pollutant

Resource preparation

Video or images of atmospheric pollution

Worksheet 10.3c The Earth's changing atmosphere [context worksheet]

Teaching and learning ideas

- Have a class discussion where students can come up with sources of natural emissions that could change the composition of the atmosphere. Possible sources of natural emissions include volcanoes (sulfur dioxide), wetlands/marshlands (methane) and decomposition of organic material such as animals or plants (carbon dioxide).
- Explain that the atmosphere has not always contained the same amounts of gases. There is no need to go into details but you could point out that, for many millions of years after the Earth formed, there were no living things present, and so as living things developed (particularly plants) these gradually changed the amounts of oxygen and carbon dioxide in the atmosphere.
- You could ask students to research what effects the pollutant gases carbon dioxide, sulfur dioxide and nitrogen oxides have on the environment and on people. Some of these effects are summarised in table 10.3 in the Student's Book.
- You could watch a short video of atmospheric pollution over cities, or look at a number of images, so that students can describe what they see (typically pale brown or dark orange 'haze' above buildings). Challenge students to describe how daily exposure to these air pollutants can affect people (e.g. increase frequency and severity of asthma attacks; build-up of dirt/small particles of dust in people's noses and lungs; coughs and throat infections).
- Explain how scientists have helped us recognise problems with pollutants in the past and, as a result, countries have taken action to solve the problems.

Differentiation

- Some students may struggle to appreciate how the composition of the atmosphere has changed over time. Focus in on the changes that the development of life has caused. In particular, look at how hundreds of millions of years ago there was no oxygen in the atmosphere. Very simple creatures (bacteria) developed that used sunlight, water and carbon dioxide to produce oxygen.
- More confident students could be asked to investigate why some pollutants affect areas on Earth that are far away from where they are produced.

Extension ideas

- Ask students to research more details of how the Earth's atmosphere has changed, and produce a set of four 'storyboards' that describe significant moments in the Earth's history and the composition of the atmosphere at each time. (For example, soon after the Earth formed, then two other times, then the present day.)

Homework suggestions

Students answer questions 6, 8 and 10 in Topic 10.3 in the Workbook.

Topic overview

		Student's Book	Workbook	Downloadable materials
10.4a	**Starting point** This short activity provides an opportunity for students to discuss evaporation, condensation and precipitation of water	Starting point table	Question 1	Worksheet 10.4a
10.4b	**Evaporation, condensation and precipitation** Students learn how the amounts of evaporation, condensation and precipitation depend on air temperature and winds	Questions 1–4	Question 2	
10.4c	**Water that falls on the surface of Earth** Students learn about water run-off, open water and groundwater. They undertake an activity to model evaporation, condensation and precipitation	Questions 5–8 Activity 10.9	Questions 3–8	Worksheet 10.4c Practical Notes 10.4c

Learning Objectives

- 7ESc.01: Describe the water cycle (limited to evaporation, condensation, precipitation, water run-off, open water and groundwater)
- 7TWSm.01: Describe the strengths and limitations of a model
- 7TWSc.02: Decide what equipment is required to carry out an investigation or experiment and use it appropriately
- 7TWSc.05: Carry out practical work safely
- 7SIC.01: Discuss how scientific knowledge is developed through collective understanding and scrutiny over time

- 7SIC.02: Describe how science is applied across societies and industries, and in research.
- 7SIC.03: Evaluate issues which involve and/or require scientific understanding.
- 7SIC.04: Describe how people develop and use scientific understanding as individuals and through collaboration, e.g. through peer review
- 7SIC.05: Discuss how the uses of science can have a global environmental impact.

Links to other topics

- Earth and Space Stage 9 Chapter 13 Topic 2 Climate change (and effects on water in the Earth's ice caps and oceans)

Using models

- Note that a diagram of the water cycle itself is a model, so there are opportunities to present this topic as adding steadily more layers of complexity and explanation to the water cycle model. If time permits, you may wish to explore some parts of the water cycle in more detail (e.g. how we can find and use groundwater).
- The model of evaporation, condensation and precipitation is designed to be a demonstration not a student practical. This is because it is quite difficult to set up and requires large amounts of hot (ideally, almost boiling) water. However, once set up it is a good opportunity to discuss why it is a crude/very limited model, such as the absence of winds (which are so important in modelling the Earth's atmosphere), the short timescales involved in using the model, and so on.
- There is an opportunity here to address learning objective 7TWSm.01 where the students are asked to discuss the strengths and limitations of the models

Cambridge Lower Secondary Earth and space
Stage 7

Science in context

- The Science in context: Investigating ice cores box in Topic 10.4 of the Student's Book covers the following learning objectives:
  - 7SIC.01 Discuss how scientific knowledge is developed through collective understanding and scrutiny over time.
  - 7SIC.02 Describe how science is applied across societies and industries, and in research.
  - 7SIC.03 Evaluate issues which involve and/or require scientific understanding.
  - 7SIC.04 Describe how people develop and use scientific understanding as individuals and through collaboration, e.g. through peer review
  - 7SIC.05 Discuss how the uses of science can have a global environmental impact.

Common misunderstandings

- Students may think that clouds are formed of water vapour (gas), but in fact clouds are visible because they are formed from tiny condensed water droplets.
- Students may not realise that only a very small proportion of the water on Earth is present in water run-off (rivers etc.). Keep emphasising that the largest proportion of water (over 95%) is to be found in the oceans.

10.4a Starting point

Resource preparation

Video of evaporation, condensation and precipitation or Worksheet 10.4a labelling images of E, C, P

Teaching and learning ideas

- Remind students of the processes they should already know that concern water: evaporation, condensation and precipitation. Ask students to describe what each involves.
- You might want to show a video that illustrates each process.
- Worksheet 10.4a offers a short revision opportunity, where students match each process with its definition.

10.4b Evaporation, condensation and precipitation

Students will learn:

- To describe the water cycle
- To understand a model of the Earth's water cycle
- To make conclusions by interpreting results

Glossary words

condensation, evaporation, precipitation

Teaching and learning ideas

- Discuss the oceans with students and what water processes they think are important that affect the oceans (evaporation, mainly).
- Ask the students to describe how water that has been evaporated from the oceans is carried so it is over land (winds).
- Ask students to describe how clouds form (condensation). Challenge them to name the physical quantity that is most important in terms of whether or not clouds form (temperature).
- Explain how the water droplets in clouds get larger as they cool, as more water condenses and as droplets merge together. Once the drops reach a large enough size they fall as precipitation.
- Emphasise how precipitation includes rain, snow, hail or sleet, depending on temperature.

Extension ideas

- Ask students to research the largest hailstones that have been seen.

Homework suggestions

Students answer question 2 in Topic 10.4 in the Workbook.

Chapter 10: The Earth and its atmosphere

10.4c Water that falls on the surface of Earth

Students will learn:

- To describe the water cycle
- To understand a model of the Earth's water cycle
- To describe the strengths and limitations of the model used to demonstrate evaporation, condensation and precipitation
- To choose equipment needed to carry out an investigation and use it appropriately
- To carry out practical work safely

Glossary words

glacier, groundwater, open water, water cycle, water run-off

Resource preparation

For Activity 10.9: Worksheet 10.4c and Practical Notes 10.4c
for demonstration, large bowl half-filled with hot water (ideally from a kettle), cling film/polythene wrap, ice cubes, Universal Indicator or coloured food dye

Teaching and learning ideas

- Explain to students what is meant by 'open water' (water stored in the oceans, large lakes and all rivers). Stress that this contains by far the largest quantity of water found on Earth.
- Challenge students to describe what can happen to rain that falls on the ground. Explain that most will soak into the soil or run into cracks between rocks, ending up where we cannot see it (groundwater). Explain that the rest runs over the surface, forming pools and streams, which eventually merge to form rivers that flow out towards the oceans.
- On a whiteboard or a large sheet of blank paper, sketch the basic outline of land and ocean from the Student's Book figure 10.25. Then ask students to name the different water processes and places where water is found, and get them to tell you where to place labels on the diagram to show where each occurs. Once the major items are in place, draw arrows to show the water cycle.
- Carry out Activity 10.9, which uses Practical Notes 10.4c, Worksheet 10.4c, as a demonstration. Students record their observations and comment on the limitations of the model.

Differentiation

- Some students may struggle to remember the terms water run-off, open water and groundwater. If so, focus on the cycle itself and build a basic cycle with only evaporation, condensation and precipitation marked. Then add each of the more challenging terms in, but stress the important thing for students to remember is the cycle.
- More confident students could be challenged to investigate the difference between sea (salt) water and fresh water as found in rain and water run-off. Why do the minerals in salt water not evaporate with the water?

Extension ideas

- Ask students to research how much of Earth's water is stored as ice at the Poles and in glaciers.

Homework suggestions

Students answer questions 6–8 in Topic 10.4 in the Workbook.

Chapter 10 Checking students' progress

End of chapter reflection
- To review the learning points of the chapter
- To test understanding through answering questions

Resources

Student's Book Chapter 10 [End of chapter review questions]

Workbook Chapter 10 [Self-assessment grid, Test-style questions]

Worksheets 10.1c, 10.2c (1), 10.2c (2), 10.2d (1), 10.2d (2), 10.3b (1), 10.3b (2), 10.3c (Context), 10.4a, 10.4c [all of which may have already been used]

Approach

Use the 'Key facts' and 'Check your skills progress' boxes in the Student's Book for each topic in this chapter, and the end of chapter review questions as a way of recapping on the main learning points.

Ask students to complete the self-assessment checklist at the end of Chapter 10 in the Workbook. Encourage students to work together in small groups to discuss which aspects of the material are the most difficult to understand, and then have a class vote. You may wish to revisit some Learning Objectives again if students find any areas particularly challenging. Use the Student's Book text and questions to revisit these aspects. Go through the answers orally in class. Take note of whether giving the answer appears to resolve students' uncertainty or not, and work through further examples.

The Teacher's comments section in the Workbook can be completed to give students personalised feedback on next steps. Students could be asked to answer specific end of chapter review questions in their books. Alternatively go through some or all of the end of chapter review questions in the Student's Book orally in class.

Use the Context worksheet (Worksheet 10.3c) as a framework for students to conduct their own research enquiries about the composition of the atmosphere. This activity provides the opportunity to cover Learning Objectives 7SIC.01, 7SIC.02, 7SIC.03, 7SIC.04 and 7SIC.05. For example, students could focus on how scientists can determine the proportions of gases present over many thousands of years by investigating ice cores and other evidence. Alternatively, students could research how the climate can be modelled to predict long-term trends as well as forecast the weather.

Finish by asking students to complete the test-style questions at the end of Chapter 10 in the Workbook. Provide feedback on students' answers, and work with students individually to identify areas that still need more work.

Chapter 11 | The Earth in Space

Chapter overview

This chapter provides opportunities to focus on the development of scientific understanding and technology over time, including how predictions are made and tested, and how models have strengths and limitations.

In this chapter, students will first explore the Solar System and its movements using their own observations and current scientific ideas. Then, by reviewing the history of how we learned about our Solar System, they will learn how important ideas in science must always be supported by evidence, and how scientists improve their models as they learn more.

Topic title	Number of 40-minute periods	Learning Objectives	Thinking and Working Scientifically Learning Objectives
11.1 The planets and the Solar System	4	7ESs.01 Describe how planets form from dust and gas, which are pulled together by gravity. 7ESs.02 Know that gravity is the force that holds components of the Solar System in orbit around the Sun.	7TWSp.02 Describe how scientific hypotheses can be supported or contradicted by evidence from an enquiry. 7TWSp.03 Make predictions of likely outcomes for a scientific enquiry based on scientific knowledge and understanding. 7TWSa.01 Describe the accuracy of predictions, based on results, and suggest why they were or were not accurate. 7TWSa.02 Describe trends and patterns in results, including identifying any anomalous results.
11.2 Tides	2	7ESs.03 Describe tidal forces on Earth as a consequence of the gravitational attraction between the Earth, Moon and Sun.	7TWSm.01 Describe the strengths and limitations of a model. 7TWSa.03 Make conclusions by interpreting results and explain the limitations of the conclusions. 7TWSa.05 Present and interpret observations and measurements appropriately.
11.3 Eclipses	3	7ESs.04 Explain how solar and lunar eclipses happen.	7TWSm.01 Describe the strengths and limitations of a model.
End of chapter questions	1	Check students' progress	

Background science

Please note: the background science notes are designed to provide teachers with an overview of the science concepts students may have already been taught earlier in their education, are likely to be taught in this unit and are likely to be taught in later stages. They are not a checklist of the content to be covered by the teacher in each unit.

The background science notes also serve to provide the teacher with some understanding of the background science needed in order to deliver the content of each chapter.

This chapter is primarily about the observations humans have made of the effects of gravity on Earth and the rest of the Solar System, and the patterns and ideas that explain those effects.

The history of observations of the Solar System is used to introduce the ideas of orbits and how the Sun and planets formed. Gravity is introduced in Stage 7 Topic 7.1. More detail on the measurement of distance and time, and the concepts of speed and average speed, is found in Stage 8 Topics 7.1 and 7.2.

This chapter also includes the observation of circular (and elliptical) orbits, which will be better explained at IGCSE or equivalent in terms of gravitational attraction providing the required centripetal force.

The history of the discovery of the planets and the most widely accepted theory of how the Solar System formed are presented. Early astronomers thought that the Earth was at the centre of the whole Universe. Over time, astronomers invented new devices and gathered new evidence. This story is continued to its natural conclusion, by discussing the use of space probes and the need for large international teams of scientists to deliver them.

The collection of observational data and its use to make predictions (such as the prediction of the existence of Neptune and its subsequent discovery) is explored. For now, the application of this work is limited to the Sun and planets; the existence of asteroids, and the observation of the wider Universe, are discussed in Stage 8 Topic 12.1.

At first sight, tides on Earth should be a straightforward topic to cover; the essential idea that gravitational forces of other bodies affect the Earth has already been introduced in the first section of this chapter. However, an explanation of the frequency of tides requires the introduction of inertia to explain the twin tidal bulges causing two high tides per day. The differences between solids and liquids, enabling water in the oceans to flow but holding land in position, are covered in Stage 7 Topic 4.3.

Similarly, eclipses of the Sun and Moon, and the formation of shadows in general, receive a fuller treatment in Stage 8 Chapter 9 when students will study light. For now, students only need to understand that light travels in straight lines to our eyes from light sources or from reflective surfaces, and light that is blocked creates shadows.

11.1 The planets and the Solar System

Topic overview

		Student's Book	Workbook	Downloadable materials
11.1a	**Starting point** This short discussion provides an opportunity for students to demonstrate their understanding of gravity and orbits.	Starting point table	Question 1	
11.1b	**Our Solar System** Students analyse a table of data about the Solar System to explain the years and days of the different planets.	Questions 1–4 Activity 11.1	Questions 2–4	Worksheet 11.1b Practical notes 11.1b
11.1c	**Discovering planets** Students draw a timeline of the discovery of the planets in the Solar System	Questions 5–7	Questions 5–7	Worksheet 11.1c
11.1d	**The formation of planets** Students describe the formation of the Solar System from dust and gas clouds.	Questions 8–10	Questions 8–10	Worksheet 11.1d

Learning Objectives

- 7ESs.01: Describe how planets form from dust and gas, which are pulled together by gravity
- 7ESs.02: Know that gravity is the force that holds components of the Solar System in orbit around the Sun
- 7TWSp.02: Describe how scientific hypotheses can be supported or contradicted by evidence from an enquiry
- 7TWSp.03: Make predictions of likely outcomes for a scientific enquiry based on scientific knowledge and understanding
- 7TWSa.01: Describe the accuracy of predictions, based on results, and suggest why they were or were not accurate
- 7TWSa.02: Describe trends and patterns in results, including identifying any anomalous results

- 7SIC.01: Discuss how scientific knowledge is developed through collective understanding and scrutiny over time
- 7SIC.04: Describe how people develop and use scientific understanding, as individuals and through collaboration, e.g. through peer-review
- 7SIC.02: Describe how science is applied across societies and industries, and in research.

Links to other topics

- Physics Chapter 7 Topic 1 in this book: the existence and action of gravity is essential prior learning.

Using models

- There is an opportunity here to address learning objective 7TWSm.01 where the students are asked to discuss the strengths and limitations of the models.
- If you wish to expand upon the history of the development of our understanding of the Solar System, it is helpful to research and show diagrams of previous models such as that with the Earth at the centre of the Solar System. Avoid those that go into too much detail such as planetary epicycles.
- Animations or physical models of the planets in their orbits are helpful in developing scientific understanding of the structure of the Solar System, particularly in showing the wide range of orbital periods and distances involved.
- Looking at images or videos that describe the invention and development of the telescope can help students appreciate the advancement of technology, and how that links in the development of improved models of the formation and structure of the Solar System.

Cambridge Lower Secondary Earth and space
Stage 7

Science in context

- The Science in context: Exploring space – a team effort box in Topic 11.1 of the Student's Book covers the following learning objectives:
  - 7SIC.01 Discuss how scientific knowledge is developed through collective understanding and scrutiny over time.
  - 7SIC.02 Describe how science is applied across societies and industries, and in research.
  - 7SIC.04 Describe how people develop and use scientific understanding as individuals and through collaboration, e.g. through peer review
- Look out for opportunities to place the development of scientific technology and ideas in a historical context. Students may not always appreciate the significance of observations of the night sky to all cultures around the world. For example, much of the mathematical 'apparatus' that was needed to develop and explain the formation and structure of the Solar System was developed by Persian astronomers and mathematicians before 1000 Common Era (CE).
- You may also choose to develop the theme of modern-day international collaboration in science, using the wealth of material available online concerning projects such as Juno, Cassini, Galileo, the Mars rovers and New Horizons. The NASA website, in particular, is a reliable and rich resource for this material.

Common misunderstandings

- The redefinition of the term 'planet' to exclude Pluto is recent enough that students may have old books that show the Solar System with nine planets rather than eight.
- Ancient astronomical systems often included the Moon as a planet (Luna). The Moon and the Sun both appear to revolve around the Earth. Students will need a clear explanation of why that is true for the Moon but is not true for the Sun.

11.1a Starting point

Review students' understanding of forces and gravity, and their application to the Solar System.

Teaching and learning ideas

Ask students the following questions.

- What is gravity? (A force, that depends on the mass of an object, and which is the reason why we stay on the surface of Earth.)
- What is the evidence for gravity? (Our weight.)
- Check that students appreciate the difference between an object's mass and its weight. Remind them that mass does not change, but weight depends on the gravitational field strength where the object is positioned. (For example, the weight of an object on the surface of the Moon is approximately one-sixth the weight of the same object on the surface of the Earth.)
- Ask students what they know about the Sun and the Earth. (That the Earth orbits the Sun; that the Sun is a source of light/energy; that the Sun is much bigger than the Earth.)

Draw a part of a circle representing the Sun at the left-hand edge of a whiteboard. Ask students to direct you where to draw the Earth. Add an arc passing through the Earth that represents the orbit of the Earth. Ask students to tell you what you have drawn.

- Ask how long the Earth takes to orbit the Sun. (1 year.)
- Ask why the Earth orbits the Sun. (Gravity.)

11.1b Our Solar System

Students will learn:

- To describe how planets form from dust and gas, which are pulled together by gravity
- To know that gravity is the force that holds components of the Solar System in orbit around the Sun
- To describe patterns in data about the planets and identify anomalous results

Glossary words

dwarf planet, gravity, mass, moon, orbit, planet, Solar System

Resource preparation

For introduction to topic: Image of the Sun and eight planets of the Solar System.

For Activity 11.1: Data from Table 11.1 in Student's Book (also reproduced in Worksheet 11.1b); sheets of plain A3 paper; crayons or marker pens in four different colours; calculators.

Worksheet 11.1b

Practical notes 11.1b

Teaching and learning ideas

- Show the image of the Solar System and run through the names of the different planets with the students. Ask questions to check knowledge, such as: Which is the largest planet? (Jupiter) Which planet is furthest away from the Sun? (Neptune) Which planet has huge rings? (Saturn) Where is the Earth? (Third planet out from the Sun).

- Explain how gravity due to the large mass of the Sun is the reason why planets orbit the Sun. Ask students to describe the shape of a planet's orbit. (For now it is sufficient to say the orbits are circular, or nearly circular.) Challenge students to say which planet takes the longest time to go once round the Sun (Neptune). Explain that this is because Neptune has the biggest orbit.

- Move on to describe how most planets have moons. Earth has one Moon, but some planets have many more. Challenge students to suggest why moons orbit a planet (gravity).

- In small groups, students can do Activity 11.1 *Explaining years and days*. Table 11.1 in the Student's Book, Worksheet 11.1b and Practical notes 11.1b support this. Check that students follow the 'A' instructions to produce a poster before they start answering the 'B' questions. Challenge students to justify their choice of planet. Was there a particular part of the data that they found interesting?

- Once students have completed the activity, you could stick the posters to the walls or display them on tables for all to inspect. Ask students to say what they have learned about planets and to describe the new fact that surprised them the most.

Differentiation

- Some students may need a reduced amount of data compared to Table 11.1, which is very detailed. Consider reducing the rows of data used, to focus the activity, or (once the students have chosen a planet) encourage them to cover up the other planets so they only see the data they need.

- When planning their poster, students may need guidance on how much space to use for each item.

- More confident students can be grouped with less confident students to complete the activity.

- Ask more confident students to select a row of data from Table 11.1 and produce a bar chart or scatter graph. Challenge them to describe any pattern they observe.

Extension ideas

- Ask students to find out more about Pluto. Explain that Pluto is a dwarf planet and has a different shaped orbit to the other planets. Direct them to search for information about the New Horizons probe that passed by Pluto in 2015.

Homework suggestions

Students answer questions 3–4 in Topic 11.1 in the Workbook.

11.1c Discovering planets

Students will learn:

- To describe how planets form from dust and gas, which are pulled together by gravity
- To understand that gravity is the force that holds components of the Solar System in orbit around the Sun
- To describe how predictions of new planets were tested against evidence

Glossary words

astronomer, law of gravitation, telescope

Resource preparation

For the demonstration: images of Galileo's drawings of objects seen through his telescope, such as those showing the movement of the moons of Jupiter, and images of planets taken with modern telescopes, for example, from the Hubble Space Telescope. Use a search engine to find appropriate images.

For question 5 from the Student's Book: Worksheet 11.1c

Teaching and learning ideas

- Describe some of the history of how people have been observing the stars and planets in the night sky for thousands of years. Explain how the first fully scientific observations of the planets were made possible by Galileo's development of the telescope.

- Demonstrate how some of the first astronomical observations made using the telescope were of planets and their moons. Show images of some of Galileo's drawings, such as of the movement of moons around Jupiter.

- Move on to compare Galileo's drawings with examples of images from modern telescopes, such as those of Jupiter taken by the Hubble Space Telescope.

- Explain that because the orbits of the planets are nearly circular, and stay the same, we can work out exactly where they will be at any time in the future.

- Describe how Brahe's records of the movement of the planets produced detailed evidence for the planets orbiting the Sun, and how Kepler (and later, Newton) used this evidence to write down mathematical rules that described how the force of gravity worked and how this meant the movement of planets could be predicted.

- You could develop question 5 in the Student's Book (draw a timeline of the discovery of the planets in the Solar System) into a whole-class or group activity. Use Worksheet 11.1c for this purpose. The worksheet contains some pre-populated information; if you prefer, remove this information to leave a more open-ended activity for students. The information given also includes two statements about the discovery of moons orbiting other planets; these can be left out if desired, as they are not stages in the prediction and discovery of the planets themselves.

Differentiation

- Less confident students could use the timeline included on the Worksheet, highlight the stages described in the Student's Book and add any other information they research.

- More confident students could be challenged to explain how we can see planets at night, when planets do not produce their own light.

Extension ideas

- Challenge students to research future telescopes, such as the James Webb Space Telescope or the Giant Magellan Telescope. Where will they be and when are they due to start working? How big are they?

Homework suggestions

Students answer questions 6–7 in Topic 11.1 in the Workbook.

11.1d The formation of planets

Students will learn:

- To describe how planets form from dust and gas, which are pulled together by gravity
- To understand that gravity is the force that holds components of the Solar System in orbit around the Sun
- To describe how scientific ideas can be supported or contradicted by evidence

Glossary words

meteorite, solar nebula, space probe

Resource preparation

Optional: modelling clay, Worksheet 11.1d for card sorting

Teaching and learning ideas

- Introduce the idea that a large proportion of the Universe is made from dust and gas. Explain that we can see some of this dust and gas because it is lit up by light from stars.

- Talk through the stages listed in the Student's Book that describe how the Solar System formed from this dust and gas. Emphasise that the dust and gas is brought together over time because of the force of gravity.

- You could use Worksheet 11.1d, which contains a set of 'cards' that students can cut out. Each card describes a different stage in the formation of the Solar System. Once the students have their cards ready, they should shuffle them. Challenge the students to place their cards in the correct order. Select different stages and ask the students to say why they placed the card for that stage where they did.

- Following this card sorting, discuss as a class what the correct order is.

- Highlight the difference between the four rocky inner planets and the four gaseous outer planets.

Differentiation

- Less confident students may struggle with the concept of gases being drawn together by gravitational forces. Gravity is often thought of as something that only affects large, solid objects. Explain how it takes a very long time for enough dust to stick together to form rocks, but then the rocks also start to stick together. You could ask the students to model this using small pieces of modelling clay, to gradually form a larger object.
- More confident students may ask how we can know the planets formed in this way, if it took place so long ago. Explain how, in science, evidence is key, and that we can find evidence by looking at other stars and planets in the Universe that are in the process of being formed.

Extension ideas

- Ask students to find out what the word 'exoplanet' means, and research recent news about exoplanets. Ask them to suggest why studying exoplanets can help us understand more about our own Solar System.

Homework suggestions

Students answer questions 9–10 in Topic 11.1 in the Workbook.

Topic overview

		Student's Book	Workbook	Downloadable materials
11.2a	**Starting point** This short demonstration and discussion provides an opportunity to review prior learning about the properties of solids and liquids. Students compare the water in Earth's oceans with water held in a small container.	Starting point table		
11.2b	**Water in the Earth's oceans** Students are introduced to the idea of tides as the movement of water due to gravity.		Question 1	
11.2c	**The effects of the Moon** Students analyse data about tides using a graph and describe patterns in the data.	Activity 11.2 Questions 1–3	Questions 2–4	
11.2d	**The effects of the Sun** Students describe the additional effects of the Sun on tides.	Questions 4–7	Questions 5–9	Worksheet 11.2d

Learning Objectives

- 7ESs.03: Describe tidal forces on Earth as a consequence of the gravitational attraction between the Earth, Moon and Sun
- 7TWSm.01: Describe the strengths and limitations of a model
- 7TWSa.03: Make conclusions by interpreting results and explain the limitations of the conclusions
- 7TWSa.05: Present and interpret observations and measurements appropriately

Links to other topics

- Stage 7 Chapter 4, concerning the physical properties of solids and liquids, is essential prior learning.

Using models

- Remind students that the arrangements of 'Sun', 'Earth' and 'Moon' in 11.2d 'The effects of the Sun' form a model. Use this as an opportunity to discuss which aspects of these models are representing different 'real life' objects. Encourage students to comment on whether the model is to scale.
- There is an opportunity here to address learning objective 7TWSm.01 where the students are asked to discuss the strengths and limitations of the model

Common misunderstandings

- Students may understandably think that the gravitational pull of the Moon on water in Earth's oceans means that there is only one tidal bulge, in the direction of the Moon. This then leads them to think that there will only be one high tide every 24 hours or so. Unfortunately, the reason for two tidal bulges is not straightforward to explain. Inertial mass is quite an advanced concept. See the Teaching and learning ideas below for a way to approach this.

11.2a Starting point

Resource preparation

For the opening demonstration: two laboratory beakers, water

Teaching and learning ideas

- Ask students to describe what they know about the properties of solids and liquids. Focus on the properties of movement: that solids are in a rigid structure and different parts cannot move differently to other parts, whereas liquids can flow and fill their container.
- Demonstrate this property of liquids by pouring water from one flask or beaker to another.
- Challenge students to use their observations of the demonstration to explain the difference between land and ocean on Earth.

11.2b Water in the Earth's oceans

Students will learn:

- To describe tidal forces on Earth as a consequence of the gravitational attraction between the Earth, Moon and Sun
- To present and interpret observations and measurements appropriately

Glossary words

high tide, low tide, sea level

Resource preparation

Pre-load/cache a timelapse video of the cycle of tides. Ideally use a video of a local location, but if not available, search online.

Teaching and learning ideas

- Show a timelapse video of the cycle of high and low tides, which shows the water level as it changes over the course of one day. Ask students to describe what they observe.
- Ask students to estimate the height by which the water level changes (several metres).
- Describe how this happens with all the water on the Earth's oceans, but at different times around the Earth.

Differentiation

- Less confident students may prefer a visual guide to the changes in sea level due to tides. Explore more timelapse videos and use them to reinforce the idea that tides occur in all the oceans of Earth.
- More confident students could develop their learning by thinking of other types of evidence for high and low tides. For example, challenge them to explain why, on ocean beaches, there is often a line of debris (seaweed, shells, rubbish and so on) further up the beach than the level of the water (high tides reach furthest up the beach and the water pushes solid items to this point, then the water retreats towards its low tide level).

Extension ideas

- Discuss with the class why oceans are affected by tides in a measurable way, but generally rivers are not (rivers are shallow and contain a fraction of the amount of water found in the oceans).
- Students could research larger rivers such as the Amazon and how the final part of the river before it reaches the ocean is tidal.

Homework suggestions

Students answer question 1 in Topic 11.2 in the Workbook.

11.2c The effects of the Moon

Students will learn:

- To describe tidal forces on Earth as a consequence of the gravitational attraction between the Earth, Moon and Sun
- To present measurements on a line graph
- To make a conclusion by interpreting results

Glossary words

inertia, tidal bulge

Resource preparation

For Activity 11.2: graph paper

Teaching and learning ideas

- Challenge the students to suggest how the gravity due to the Moon might affect the land and water on Earth. Will one be affected in a different way to the other? (The strength of gravitational field is very slightly larger on the side of the Earth closest to the Moon, but the solid land is not able to flow and the water is able to flow, so the effect is more noticeable on the water.)
- Draw or show an image of the Earth's tidal bulges (see figure 11.7 in the Student's Book). The main concept to establish is that the gravity due to the Moon 'pulls' the water and the land, but the water can move or 'bulge' slightly because it can flow. So this accounts for the tidal bulge nearest the Moon.
- However, students need to appreciate there are two tidal bulges, the second on the side of the Earth furthest from the Moon. This is more difficult for students to understand.
- There are two ways to approach explaining this; choose the explanation you think best for your students.
- You could describe the phenomenon of inertia (inertial mass), which describes the way in which mass resists movement. The liquid water opposite the Moon experiences a very slightly smaller attraction than the water closest to the Moon (gravitational field strength reduces due to distance). The inertia of the water is less easily overcome and so there is a 'bulge' away from the Moon as well.
- You could encourage students to visualise (or draw) a diagram and show how the gravitational force due to the Moon reduces with distance. So the water nearest the Moon is pulled more strongly than the land, and the land is pulled more strongly than the water on the side furthest from the Moon. The water is 'stretched' into an oval shape with the land of Earth in the centre.
- Now ask the students to describe what the Earth does once every 24 hours (it completes a rotation). So each point in or near the oceans of Earth passes through a tidal bulge once every 12 hours.
- Students can complete Activity 11.2, a data handling and analysis activity about observing changes in sea level due to tides. Check that students produce smoothly curving graph lines not zigzags or straight lines joining points. Summarise the learning by asking students to explain how they recognise high and low tides from the data.

Differentiation

- Less confident students may need guidance in plotting the data points and (in particular) drawing a smoothly curved graph line in Activity 11.2. Encourage more confident and less confident students to work together in this activity.
- More confident students can be challenged to extend their graph to show the actual period of high tides (12 hours 25 minutes), based on data they research or you provide. Link in with question 3 from the Student's Book.

Extension ideas

- Challenge students to explain why there are no tides on Mars (no surface water oceans) or Jupiter (gaseous planet).

Homework suggestions

Students answer questions 3–4 in Topic 11.2 in the Workbook.

11.2d The effects of the Sun

Students will learn:

- To describe tidal forces on Earth as a consequence of the gravitational attraction between the Earth, Moon and Sun
- To describe the strengths and limitations of a model

Glossary words

neap tide, spring tide

Resource preparation

Three different sized balls to represent the Sun (soccer ball/football), Earth (table tennis ball) and Moon (small marble).

Worksheet 11.2d

Teaching and learning ideas

- Ask students which other objects in the Solar System exert a 'pull' (gravitational force) due to their mass (answer: all of them).
- Discuss with students which object, apart from the Moon, produces the largest gravitational effect (the Sun). Remind students that the force due to gravity produced by an object on Earth gets smaller the further away the object is. Challenge students to suggest why, despite being so far away, the Sun still has a measurable effect on tides (gravity also depends on mass, and the Sun is hundreds of thousands of times more massive than the Earth or Moon).
- Demonstrate the relative positions of the Sun, Earth and Moon by arranging a football at one end of a large desk (Sun), a table tennis ball (Earth) near the opposite end of the desk, and near to the Earth a marble (Moon).
- Arrange the Moon so it is on the same side of the Earth as the Sun. Ask students to suggest whether we should add or subtract the gravitational force due to the Sun to/from that of the Moon (add). Ask what effect they think this will have on a high tide (makes it higher still). Name this a spring tide.
- Now repeat but place the Moon at right angles to the Earth–Sun direction. Ask the question again about what effect the gravitational force of the Sun may have on high tide (little because the Moon has a much greater effect on the water of Earth than the effect of the Sun). Name this a neap tide.
- Ask students to comment on the model used. What are its strengths? (Easy to set up, very clear visually.) What are its limitations? (Not accurate in terms of scale, not easy to visualise gravitational forces or simulate the full orbits of the Earth and Moon.)

Differentiation

- Some students will need help understanding why forces add when they are in the same direction. Explain that forces only cancel out if they are the same size and in opposite directions.
- More confident students could be asked to explain what force acts on the Moon due to the Earth (gravity), how big it is (same as force acting on Earth due to Moon, but in opposite direction) and why it is not easy to get evidence of this (no tides on Moon because there is no surface water; also, Moon is not rotating relative to Earth, the same side faces Earth all the time).

Extension ideas

- Ask students to compare the distances from Earth to (a) the Moon and (b) the Sun, and the differences in masses between the two.

Homework suggestions

Students answer questions 7–9 in Topic 11.2 in the Workbook.

11.3 Eclipses

Topic overview

		Student's Book	Workbook	Downloadable materials
11.3a	**Starting point** This short activity provides an opportunity to revisit material about the relative orbits and positions of Sun, Earth and Moon, which should have been covered in earlier years and developed in Topic 11.1.	Starting point table		
11.3b	**Solar eclipses** Students observe a short demonstration of the positions of the Sun, Earth and Moon during a solar eclipse. Students discuss how the Sun can be observed safely and create a simple piece of apparatus to assist with this.	Activity 11.3 Questions 1–3	Questions 2, 4–6, 8 and 10	Practical Notes 11.3b Worksheet 11.3b
11.3c	**Lunar eclipses** Students create a model of the Sun, Earth and Moon to show how both lunar and solar eclipses occur.	Activity 11.4 Questions 4–7	Questions 1, 3, 7 and 9	Practical Notes 11.3c Worksheet 11.3c

Learning Objectives

- 7ESs.04: Explain how solar and lunar eclipses happen
- 7TWSm.01: Describe the strengths and limitations of a model

Links to other topics

- Stage 8 Chapter 9 Light

Using models

- There is an opportunity here to address learning objective 7TWSm.01 where the students are asked to discuss the strengths and limitations of the models
- Remind students that the arrangements of 'Sun', 'Earth' and 'Moon' in Activity 11.4 are models. Use this as an opportunity to discuss which aspects of these models are representing different 'real life' objects (e.g. Sun is modelled by a torch).
- Looking at images or timelapse videos that show solar and lunar eclipses can be a good way to encourage students to appreciate the importance of time as an aspect of making models.

Common misunderstandings

- Students may have read or heard that some people say it is OK to look at the Sun, particularly during eclipses, for short periods of time. Explain that it is dangerous because damage to the eyes can occur almost immediately.
- Students may think that an eclipse, of Moon or Sun, must happen every 28 days because that is how long the Moon takes to orbit the Earth. Explain how the Moon's orbit is tilted slightly compared to the orbit of the Earth around the Sun, and that the distance from Earth to Moon is large. Then demonstrate how this means that the Moon only very occasionally passes between the Sun and Earth, using the same resources as in 11.3a below.

11.3a Starting point

Resource preparation

Bright torch (ideally narrow beam), large piece of white card (A4 will do), tennis ball or other solid/opaque ball, darkened room

Teaching and learning ideas

- Remind the students of their prior learning concerning light. Demonstrate light and shadows by setting up a bright torch shining on a piece of white card held at right angles to the torch beam. Darken the room if necessary to show the circle of reflected light on the white card.
- Hold the ball so that it slowly moves across and then blocks the light beam. Ask students to describe what they see on the white card (they should see a shadow forming and a decreasing amount of light being reflected from the card).
- Ask students to explain what is happening (light travels in straight lines and is reflected off the card; where light is blocked, a dark shadow forms).

11.3b Solar eclipses

Students will learn:

- To explain how a solar eclipse occurs
- To choose equipment needed to carry out an investigation and use it appropriately
- To carry out practical work safely

Glossary words

partial solar eclipse, penumbra, solar eclipse, total solar eclipse, umbra

Resource preparation

For Activity 11.3 (see Practical Notes 11.3b and Worksheet 11.3b, which shows the apparatus set up): two squares or A4-sized rectangles of thin, white cardboard, sticky tape, cooking foil, drawing pin or poster pin, scissors, plus time outdoors when weather is sunny, to test the observing devices.

Optional, for demonstration or discussion: Look for images or timelapse videos that show solar eclipses (the NASA website is a good starting point). This can be a good way to encourage students to appreciate the importance of time as an aspect of making models.

Teaching and learning ideas

- Explain to students how the Sun produces so much light, it is dangerous to look at it directly with our eyes. It is possible to be blinded or have other serious and permanent damage to our eyes.
- Explain to students that they are going to make a basic device for observing the Sun more carefully.
- Students should complete Activity 11.3. Worksheet 11.3b shows a larger scale diagram of the apparatus set up. Check that the students form a reasonably sharp image, by only making a small hole in the foil and by adjusting the distance from hole to screen.
- Watch very carefully for any students who decide to look up at the Sun – stop this immediately.
- Encourage students to explain how their device works; ensure they realise that their device only works because light travels in straight lines.

Differentiation

- Some students will need guidance to produce a safe device in Activity 11.3. Either form small groups with a mix of less confident and more confident students, or produce a model device that students can copy.
- More confident students could look more closely at the image produced on the screen. They may be able to pick out surface features like sunspots. Explain to them that sunspots look dark only because they are cooler than the bright areas of the Sun.

Extension ideas

- Ask students to find out what effect the size of the hole in their device has on the image (smaller holes generally produce sharper (better focused) images, larger holes make the image blurry). They could also investigate the effect of changing the distance between the hole and the screen. Students do not need to explore or know the reasons why at this stage.

Homework suggestions

Students answer questions 6, 8 and 10 in Topic 11.3 in the Workbook.

11.3c Lunar eclipses

Students will learn:

- To explain how a lunar eclipse occurs
- To describe the strengths and limitations of a model

Glossary words

lunar eclipse, partial lunar eclipse, total lunar eclipse

Resource preparation

Optional, for demonstration or discussion: Look for images or timelapse videos that show lunar eclipses (again, the NASA website is a good source). This can be a good way to encourage students to appreciate the importance of time as an aspect of making models.

For Activity 11.4 (see Practical Notes 11.3c, Worksheet 11.3c): bright torch (ideally narrow beam), large piece of white card (A4 will do), soccer/football, tennis ball or other smaller solid/opaque ball, darkened room with space to arrange the equipment

Teaching and learning ideas

- In small groups, ask the students to carry out Activity 11.4 to demonstrate the two different types of eclipse. Start with a solar eclipse (light beam (Sun) from one side of the room, football (Earth) at the other side, tennis ball (Moon) close to the Earth but on line from Sun to Earth). Ensure students form a shadow on the surface of the 'Earth'.
- Students should draw a diagram of how they arranged the apparatus to demonstrate a solar eclipse on the first half of Worksheet 11.3c.
- Then challenge students to demonstrate a lunar eclipse. Where should they position the 'Earth' and 'Moon' relative to the Sun? (Earth on a line between Sun and Moon). Ensure students understand how the Earth blocks light from the Sun from reaching the Moon.
- Students should draw a diagram of how they arranged the apparatus to demonstrate a lunar eclipse on the second half of Worksheet 11.3c.
- Discuss partial and total lunar eclipses.
- Explain how some of the light that falls on the Earth is 'bent' by the atmosphere, which then falls on the Moon even during an eclipse, and turns the light a red colour.
- Encourage students to think about the strengths and limitations of their eclipse model, and explain their reasoning. Questions might include: 'Is it possible to show the Moon as reflecting reddish orange light?', 'Are the relative sizes of the objects and the distances between them modelled accurately? If not, why not?'

Differentiation

- Some students will need help setting up the equipment at the right distances. If some groups struggle to do this, pick one more confident group and guide them if necessary, but have the rest of the class watch this as a demonstration.
- More confident students could be asked to explain why it is safe to look at the Moon, but not the Sun.

Extension ideas

- Ask students to find out when the next lunar eclipse is due to be seen from their area.

Homework suggestions

Students answer questions 7 and 9 in Topic 11.3 in the Workbook.

End of chapter reflection

- To review the learning points of the chapter
- To test understanding through answering questions

Resources

- Student's Book Chapter 11 [End of chapter review questions]
- Workbook Chapter 11 [Self-assessment grid, Test-style questions]
- Worksheets 11.1b, 11.1c, 11.1d, 11.2d, 11.3b, 11.3c [all of which may have already been used]

Approach

Use the 'Key facts' and 'Check your skills progress' boxes in the Student Book for each topic in this chapter, and the end of chapter review questions as a way of recapping on the main learning points.

Ask students to complete the self-assessment checklist at the end of Chapter 11 in the Workbook. Encourage students to work together in small groups to discuss which aspects of the material are the most difficult to understand, and then have a class vote. You may wish to revisit some Learning Objectives again if students find any areas particularly challenging. Use the Student Book text and questions to revisit these aspects. Go through the answers orally in class. Take note of whether giving the answer appears to resolve students' uncertainty or not, and work through further examples.

The Teacher's comments section in the Workbook can be completed to give students personalised feedback on next steps. Students could be asked to answer specific end of chapter review questions in their books. Alternatively go through some or all of the end of chapter review questions in the Student Book orally in class.

Use the Context worksheet (Worksheet 11.4) as a framework for students to conduct their own research enquiries about eclipses. For example, students could focus on how some ancient cultures were afraid of solar eclipses and thought they were a warning of bad things about to happen. They could also investigate when astronomers knew enough about the orbits of Earth and the Moon to be able to predict future eclipses so accurately. This activity provides the opportunity to cover Learning Objectives 7SIC.01, 7SIC.02 and 7SIC.04.

Finish by asking students to complete the test-style questions at the end of Chapter 11 in the Workbook. Provide feedback on students' answers, and work with students individually to identify areas that still need more work.

Planning guide

Number of 40-minute periods	Student's Book topic number	Learning episode	Learning and thinking and working scientifically focus	Downloadable lesson resources
Biology				
3	1.1 Characteristics of living things	1.1a Starting point		
		1.1b Working as a scientist	• Be able to talk about the importance of asking questions, inventing hypotheses, designing experiments to test hypotheses, making predictions, using data as evidence to draw conclusions • Make careful observations • Present results in the form of tables, bar charts and line graphs	Worksheets 1.1b(1), 1.1b(2)
		1.1c Life processes	• Describe the seven characteristics of living organisms • Make predictions and review them against evidence • Use hypotheses to make predictions, referring to previous scientific knowledge and understanding • Make careful observations • Make conclusions from collected data	Practical notes 1.1c(1), 1.1c(2), 1.1c(3) Worksheets 1.1c(1), 1.1c(2), 1.1c(3)
1	1.2 Cells, tissues, organs and organ systems	1.2a Starting point		
		1.2b Human organs	• Identify a range of human organs • Describe the functions of the main human organs • Research the work of scientists studying the human body • Use information from secondary sources	Worksheet 1.2b
		1.2c Human organ systems	• Describe how organs work together in different organ systems	
		1.2d Plant organs	• Identify the main organs of a flowering plant • Describe the functions of the main plant organs	Worksheet 1.2d Practical notes 1.2d
		1.2e Organs and tissues	• Understand that cells can be grouped together to form tissues, organs and organ systems	Practical notes 1.2e
3	1.3 Comparing plant and animal cells	1.3a Starting point		
		1.3b Cells, tissues, organs and systems	• Describe how organs are made up of tissues • Describe how tissues are made up of cells • Describe organisms in terms of cells, tissues, organs and organ systems	
		1.3c Plant and animal cells	• Identify the main parts of cells • Compare and contrast animal and plant cells	Practical notes 1.3c Worksheet 1.3c

Number of 40-minute periods	Student's Book topic number	Learning episode	Learning and thinking and working scientifically focus	Downloadable lesson resources
		1.3d Using a microscope	• Identify the main parts of cells • Describe how to use a microscope correctly • Make careful observations including measurements • Choose appropriate apparatus and use it correctly	Practical notes 1.3d(1), 1.3d(2) Worksheet 1.3d
		1.3e Unicellular and multicellular organisms	• Describe the difference between unicellular and multicellular organisms • Make careful observations	
2	1.4 Specialised cells	1.4a Starting point		
		1.4b Specialised plant cells	• Identify some specialised cells • Explain how some cells are adapted for certain functions • Make careful observations including measurements • Make conclusions from collected data	Practical notes 1.4b Worksheet 1.4b
		1.4c Specialised animal cells	• Identify some specialised cells • Explain how some cells are adapted for certain functions	Worksheet 1.4c
1	End of chapter questions			
2	2.1 Types of microorganisms	2.1a Starting point		
		2.1b Fungi	• Describe what microorganisms are like • Describe different types of microorganism • Outline plans to carry out investigations • Choose appropriate apparatus and use it correctly • Make careful observations • Carry out practical work safely	Practical notes 2.1b(1), 2.1b(2) Worksheet 2.1b
		2.1c Bacteria	• Describe what microorganisms are like • Describe different types of microorganism • Make careful observations	Practical notes 2.1c
		2.1d Viruses	• Describe what microorganisms are like • Describe different types of microorganism	

Number of 40-minute periods	Student's Book topic number	Learning episode	Learning and thinking and working scientifically focus	Downloadable lesson resources
2	2.2 Microorganisms and decay	2.2a Starting point		

		2.2b Pasteur and the scientific method	• Describe how microorganisms spoil food, including the work of Louis Pasteur and Joseph Lister
			• Describe stages of a scientific investigation, including:
			  o asking scientific questions
			  o making and explaining predictions
			  o using evidence to make conclusions
			• Be able to talk about the importance of questions, evidence and explanations
			• Make predictions and review them against evidence
			• Suggest hypotheses that may be tested
			• Predict likely outcomes for a scientific enquiry
			• Identify appropriate evidence to collect and suitable methods of collection
			• Make conclusions from collected data
			• Consider explanations for predictions using scientific knowledge and understanding and communicate these
				Worksheets 2.2b(1), 2.2b(2)
				Practical notes 2.2b

		2.2c Decay	• Describe some uses of microorganisms	
1	End of chapter questions			
1	3.1 Classifying organisms	3.1a Starting point		
		3.1b Variation of characteristics	• Identify variation in the characteristics of different species • Make careful observations • Use information from secondary sources	Practical notes 3.1b Worksheet 3.1b
		3.1c Kingdoms	• Classify organisms as plants and animals • Classify plants and animals into smaller groups • Make careful observations • Use information from secondary sources	Practical notes 3.1c Worksheet 3.1c
		3.1d Vertebrates and invertebrates	• Classify plants and animals into smaller groups • Make careful observations	Practical notes 3.1d Worksheets 3.1d(1), 3.1d(2)
		3.1e Plant groups	• Classify plants into smaller groups • Make careful observations	
		3.1f Carl Linnaeus	• Research the work of scientists studying the natural world • Make observations and measurements	

Number of 40-minute periods	Student's Book topic number	Learning episode	Learning and thinking and working scientifically focus	Downloadable lesson resources
		3.1g What is a species?	• Recall what a species is • Make careful observations • Use information from secondary sources	Worksheet 3.1g
		3.1h Viruses	• Describe the seven characteristics of living organisms • Explain why there is no virus kingdom • Use sources of information Classify organisms based on their characteristics	
1	3.2 Biological keys	3.2a Starting point		
		3.2b Dichotomous keys	• Use and construct keys Identify plants and animals • Make observations and measurements	Worksheet 3.2b
		3.2c Using keys Classify plants	• Use and construct keys Identify plants • Make observations and measurements • Choose the best way to present results	Practical notes 3.2c Worksheet 3.2c
1	End of chapter questions			

Number of 40-minute periods	Student's Book topic number	Learning episode	Learning and thinking and working scientifically focus	Downloadable lesson resources
Chemistry				
1–2	4.1 Physical and chemical properties	4.1a Starting point		
		4.1b Different properties	• Understand that all substances have chemical properties and physical properties • Collect and record sufficient observations in an appropriate form	
5–6	4.2 Acidity and indicators	4.2a Starting point		
		4.2b Hazard symbols	• Recall common laboratory hazard symbols and their meanings • Describe the advantages of using hazard symbols • Know the meaning of hazard symbols	Practical notes 4.2b Worksheet 4.2b
		4.2c Indicators	• Understand that the acidity or alkalinity of a substance is a chemical property • Describe how to use an indicator to find out whether a substance is acidic, alkaline or neutral • Classify materials through testing and observation • Collect and record sufficient observations in an appropriate form	
		4.2d The pH scale	• Understand that the acidity or alkalinity of a substance is measured by pH • Determine the pH of a solution using universal indicator • Describe how strongly or weakly acidic or alkaline a solution is using its pH • Classify materials through testing and observation • Collect and record sufficient observations in an appropriate form	Worksheet 4.2d
		4.2e Investigating indicators	• Make and use an indicator to distinguish between acidic, alkaline and neutral solutions • Know the meaning of hazard symbols, and consider them when planning practical work	Practical notes 4.2e Worksheet 4.2e, 4.2e(2)
3–4	4.3 The particle model	4.3a Starting point		Worksheet 4.3a
		4.3b Particle theory	• Describe the three states of matter using the particle model • Make careful observations • Use a scientific model to construct explanations	Practical notes 4.3b Worksheet 4.3b
		4.3c Using the particle theory model Explain the properties of solids, liquids and gases	• Use particle theory Explain the properties of solids, liquids and gases • Describe what a vacuum is • Describe the strengths and limitations of a model	

Number of 40-minute periods	Student's Book topic number	Learning episode	Learning and thinking and working scientifically focus	Downloadable lesson resources
2	4.4 Elements and the Periodic Table	4.4a Starting point		
		4.4b Atoms and elements	• Understand that elements are made of atoms • Make careful observations • Interpret data from secondary sources	Practical notes 4.4b Worksheet 4.4b
		4.4c Symbols and the Periodic Table	• Use symbols to represent different elements in the Periodic Table • Interpret data from secondary sources • Use symbols and formulae to represent scientific ideas	Worksheet 4.4c
3–4	4.5 Elements, compounds and mixtures	4.5a Starting point		
		4.5b Compounds and formulae	• Describe the differences between elements and compounds • Use the particle model to represent elements and compounds Use symbols and formulae to represent scientific ideas	Practical notes 4.5b Worksheet 4.5b
		4.5c Making mixtures	• Describe the differences between elements, compounds and mixtures • Describe alloys as an example of a mixture • Use the particle model to represent mixtures • Sort, group and classify materials through careful observation	
4–5	4.6 Properties of metals, non-metals and alloys	4.6a Starting point		
		4.6b The properties of metals and non-metals	• Describe the differences in physical properties between metals and non-metals • Explain why alloys have different properties to the metals they are made from • Sort, group and classify materials through careful observation • Make conclusions from results using scientific understanding	
		4.6c Conduction of heat	• Describe the differences in physical properties between metals and non-metals • Make predictions of likely outcomes for a scientific enquiry based on scientific knowledge and understanding • Make conclusions by interpreting results	Practical notes 4.6c Worksheet 4.6c

Number of 40-minute periods	Student's Book topic number	Learning episode	Learning and thinking and working scientifically focus	Downloadable lesson resources
		4.6d Conduction of electricity	<ul><li>Describe the differences in physical properties between metals and non-metals</li><li>Make predictions of likely outcomes for a scientific enquiry based on scientific knowledge and understanding</li><li>Make careful observations including measurements</li><li>Make conclusions by interpreting results</li></ul>	Worksheet 4.6d
		4.6e Alloys	<ul><li>Understand that alloys have different chemical and physical properties from the constituent substances</li><li>Interpret data from secondary sources</li><li>Use a model in an explanation</li></ul>	
1	End of chapter questions			
3	5.1 Making compounds	5.1a Starting point		
		5.1b Modelling reactions	<ul><li>Represent chemical reactions using the particle model</li><li>Describe the strengths and limitations of a model</li><li>Carry out practical work safely</li><li>Collect and record sufficient observations in an appropriate form</li></ul>	
		5.1c Evidence for reactions	<ul><li>Describe changes that happen in chemical reactions</li><li>Describe the chemical test for hydrogen</li><li>Describe the strengths and limitations of a model</li><li>Carry out practical work safely</li><li>Collect and record sufficient observations in an appropriate form</li></ul>	Practical notes 5.1c Worksheets 5.1c
		5.1d Testing for gases	<ul><li>Describe the chemical tests for oxygen and carbon dioxide</li><li>Identify hazards and risks in practical work</li><li>Carry out practical work safely</li><li>Collect and record sufficient observations in an appropriate form</li><li>Know the meaning of hazard symbols, and consider them when planning practical work</li></ul>	
1–2	5.2 Forming precipitates	5.2a Starting point		
		5.2b Precipitation reactions	<ul><li>Explain why a precipitate forms</li><li>Describe the strengths and limitations of a model</li><li>Carry out practical work safely</li><li>Collect and record sufficient observations in an appropriate form</li></ul>	Practical notes 5.2b Worksheet 5.2b

Number of 40-minute periods	Student's Book topic number	Learning episode	Learning and thinking and working scientifically focus	Downloadable lesson resources
2–3	5.3 Neutralisation reactions	5.3a Starting point		
		5.3b What is neutralisation?	• Understand what neutralisation means • Describe neutralisation in terms of change of pH • Carry out practical work safely • Collect and record sufficient observations in an appropriate form	
		5.3c Investigating neutralisation	• Plan an investigation into neutralisation • Choose and use a range of equipment correctly • Evaluate whether measurements and observations have been repeated sufficiently to be reliable • Carry out practical work safely • Collect and record sufficient observations in an appropriate form • Identify variables within an investigation • Plan fair test investigations	Practical notes 5.3a Worksheet 5.3a
1	End of chapter questions			

Number of 40-minute periods	Student's Book topic number	Learning episode	Learning and thinking and working scientifically focus	Downloadable lesson resources
Physics				
3–4	6.1 Energy at work	6.1a Starting point		Practical notes 6.1a
		6.1b Energy sources and energy changes	• Recognise the sources of energy involved in different activities, including food and fuels, and that when we use energy to make things happen there are changes in energy • Make conclusions from collected data	
		6.1c Energy stored due to motion or temperature	• Identify situations where there is a change in energy • Describe energy changes happening in a process or event – identifying how energy becomes stored in new ways • Explain how energy is stored in particles (atoms or molecules) due to their thermal motion • Use the particle Model Explain the link between energy and temperature	Worksheet 6.1c
		6.1d Energy transfers	• Describe energy changes happening in a process or event – identifying how energy is transferred • Recognise situations where work is done by a force moving something • Distinguish situations where work done moving something against a force results in more energy being stored • Recognise heating, light, sound and electric current as means of transferring energy • Use flow diagrams to represent the idea of energy changes in a process or event	
3–4	6.2 Energy dissipation	6.2a Starting point		
		6.2b Wasted and useful energy transfers	• Recognise that not all energy transfers are useful • Identify examples of useful and wasted energy transfers • Describe that the energy that is transferred wastefully is almost always transferred to the environment by heating • Present observations using tables • Analyse observations to draw a conclusion	Practical notes 6.2b
		6.2c Energy dissipates	• Recall that whenever energy is transferred some of it is wasted and that this is called dissipation of energy • Recognise that the kinetic energy of a moving car is dissipated by friction as the car is brought to a halt • Recognise that dissipated energy becomes widely spread in the environment and difficult to collect or control • Conclude that when energy is dissipated it becomes less useful	Practical notes 6.2c Worksheet 6.2c

Number of 40-minute periods	Student's Book topic number	Learning episode	Learning and thinking and working scientifically focus	Downloadable lesson resources
			• Write a plan for an investigation and choose which variables to change, control and measure • Make a prediction using scientific knowledge and understanding • Decide what equipment is needed to carry out an investigation • Carry out practical work safely • Present data using tables with column headings • Analyse data to draw a conclusion and evaluate the accuracy of predictions made	
		6.2d Using diagrams Describe how energy dissipates	• Use Sankey energy transfer diagrams Describe how energy is dissipated because of energy transfers that are not useful • Comment on the strengths and weaknesses of Sankey diagrams as a model for energy changes	Worksheet 6.2d
1	End of chapter questions			
2–3	7.1 Gravity	7.1a starting point		Worksheet 7.1a
		7.1b Gravity, mass and weight	• Describe that gravity is a force that attracts objects towards each other • Explain the difference between mass and weight • Apply the concept that the weight of an object is proportional to its mass • Recall the unit of gravitational field strength • Calculate weight given the mass and gravitational field strength • Recall that two masses exert the same sized gravitational force on each other, even though the masses may be of different sizes • Use arrows on force diagrams to show the direction of gravitational forces between two masses • Apply the concept that there are equal gravitational forces acting between two masses Describe the effect on their motion • Make accurate measurements of mass and force • Carry out practical work safely • Take accurate readings of mass and force • Describe trends and patterns in results and draw conclusions • Identify anomalous results • Use symbols and formulae	Practical notes 7.1b Worksheets 7.1b(1), 7.1b(2)

Number of 40-minute periods	Student's Book topic number	Learning episode	Learning and thinking and working scientifically focus	Downloadable lesson resources
2–3	7.2 Air resistance	7.2a Starting point		
		7.2b Slowing down	• State that friction and air resistance are forces • Describe the effects of friction and air resistance on the speed of moving objects • State that large surfaces cause larger air resistance than small surfaces • Use scientific knowledge to predict the performance, and hence design of, a parachute • Write a plan for an investigation and choose which variables to change, control and measure • Identify appropriate evidence to collect and suitable methods of collection • Choose appropriate apparatus and use it correctly • Make accurate measurements of time and distance	Practical notes 7.2b Worksheet 7.2b
		7.2c Moving through particles	• Describe the effects of air resistance on moving objects • Describe some factors that affect how large air resistance is • Describe trends and patterns in results, including identifying any anomalous results • Make conclusions by interpreting results	Practical notes 7.2c
1	End of chapter questions			
2–3	8.1 How sound travels	8.1a Starting point		Worksheet 8.1a
		8.1b How sounds travel	• Describe how sounds require a medium through which to travel • Explain that sound travels through the air by making the air particles vibrate • State that sound cannot travel through a vacuum • Explain that sound cannot travel in a vacuum because there are no particles of air to vibrate • Describe how a hypothesis can be supported or confirmed as wrong by interpreting the evidence obtained from an enquiry • Make conclusions by interpreting results • Carry out practical work safely	Practical notes 8.1b(1), 8.1b(2), 8.1b(3)
		8.1c Modelling sound waves	• Describe how sounds require a medium through which to travel • Explain that sound travels through the air by making the air particles vibrate • Use a model Explain how sound waves travel • Identify the strengths and limitations of that model	Practical notes 8.1c

Number of 40-minute periods	Student's Book topic number	Learning episode	Learning and thinking and working scientifically focus	Downloadable lesson resources
		8.1d The speed of sound in air	• Make measurements to calculate the speed of sound in air • Identify anomalous results that do not fit the pattern • Explain why repeating measurements is useful • Explain why measuring accurately and precisely is important	Practical notes 8.1d Worksheet 8.1d
		8.1e Applying ideas	• Use knowledge about the vibration of particles in a sound wave Describe how the ear detects sound • Use a physical model of an eardrum, and a scientific model of sound waves Explain how we detect sound	Practical notes 8.1e
1–2	8.2 Echoes	8.2a Starting point		Worksheet 8.2a
		8.2b What is an echo?	• Recognise that echoes are formed when sound reflects off a surface • Describe what happens when a sound echoes • Be able to calculate speed of sound from data about echoes • Use a physical model to show how reflection occurs at a boundary • Describe the strengths and weaknesses of a model	Practical notes 8.2b
		8.2c Measuring the speed of sound using echoes	• Make measurements to calculate the speed of sound in air using the idea of echoes • Design an experiment to measure the speed of sound in air using echoes • Decide what equipment is needed to carry out an investigation or experiment and use it appropriately • Carry out practical work safely • Collect and record sufficient measurements in an appropriate form • Evaluate whether measurement and observations have been repeated sufficiently to be reliable • Make conclusions by interpreting results and explain the limitations of the conclusion	Practical notes 8.2c Worksheet 8.2c
		8.2d Applying ideas	• Describe situations where echoes are useful and where they can cause problems • Describe how problems with echoes can be reduced when a material absorbs energy instead of reflecting it • Use a scientific model (energy transfer by a wave) to help describe the idea of sound absorption	
1	End of chapter questions			

Number of 40-minute periods	Student's Book topic number	Learning episode	Learning and thinking and working scientifically focus	Downloadable lesson resources
2	9.1 Charge flow in circuits	9.1a Starting point		
		9.1b Simple circuits	• Use a simple model to describe electricity as a flow of electrons around a circuit • Make predictions of likely outcomes for a scientific enquiry based on scientific knowledge and understanding	Practical notes 9.1b
		9.1c Conductors and insulators	• Describe electrical conductors as substances that allow electron flow and electrical insulators as substances that inhibit electron flow • Make predictions of likely outcomes for a scientific enquiry based on scientific knowledge and understanding	Practical notes 9.1c
2	9.2 Circuit diagrams	9.2a Starting point		
		9.2b Circuit symbols	• Use diagrams and conventional symbols to represent, make and compare circuits that include cells, switches, lamps, buzzers and ammeters • Decide what equipment is required to carry out an investigation or experiment and use it appropriately	Worksheets 9.2b(1), 9.2b(2)
		9.2c Comparing circuits	• Describe how adding components into a series circuit can affect the current (limited to addition of cells and lamps) • Make predictions of likely outcomes for a scientific enquiry based on scientific knowledge and understanding	Practical notes 9.2c Worksheet 9.2c
2	9.3 Currents in series circuits	9.3a Starting point		
		9.3b Measuring current	• Know how to measure the current in series circuits • Carry out practical work safely • Collect and record sufficient observations and/or measurements in an appropriate form	Practical notes 9.3b Worksheet 9.3b
		9.3c Comparing current in circuits	• Know how to measure the current in series circuits • Describe how adding components into a series circuit can affect the current (limited to addition of cells • and lamps) • Collect and record sufficient observations and/or measurements in an appropriate form • Describe trends and patterns in results, including identifying any anomalous results	Practical notes 9.3c(1), 9.3c(2)
1	End of chapter questions			

Number of 40-minute periods	Student's Book topic number	Learning episode	Learning and thinking and working scientifically focus	Downloadable lesson resources
Earth and Space				
3	10.1 The Earth's crust	10.1a Starting point		
		10.1b Inside the Earth	• Describe how Earth has a structure comprising outer rocky crust, molten mantle and metal core • Identify what parts of the model of the Earth's structure are testable	
		10.1c The movement of the crust	• Describe Wegener's hypothesis of continental drift and evidence that supported it • Describe how Wegener's hypothesis was supported or contradicted by evidence	Worksheet 10.1c
		10.1d Tectonic plates	• Understand the model of plate tectonics • Describe how the model of plate tectonics took time to be accepted by most scientists • Describe how scientific ideas can be supported or contradicted by evidence from an enquiry	
5	10.2 Earthquakes, volcanoes and mountains	10.2a Starting point		
		10.2b Plate boundaries	• Describe plate boundaries as the areas where two tectonic plates meet, and the different types of plate boundary • Describe the strengths and limitations of the plate tectonics model	
		10.2c Earthquakes	• Explain how the forces between two tectonic plates can produce earthquakes • Describe the effects of earthquakes and how people can protect themselves when an earthquake takes place • Describe how scientists are developing ways to predict earthquakes and their effects • Describe the strengths and limitations of the plate tectonics model • Understand how scientists make predictions of likely outcomes of events	Worksheet 10.2c (1) Worksheet 10.2c (2)
		10.2d Volcanoes	• Explain how the forces between two tectonic plates can produce volcanoes • Describe the effects of volcanoes and how vulcanologists investigate volcanoes to try and predict eruptions and their effects • Describe the strengths and limitations of the plate tectonics model • Understand how scientists make predictions of likely outcomes of events	Practical Notes 10.2d Worksheet 10.2d (1) Worksheet 10.2d (2)
		10.2e Mountains	• Explain how two tectonic plates moving towards each other can produce fold mountains • Describe strengths and limitations of a physical model of fold mountains	

Number of 40-minute periods	Student's Book topic number	Learning episode	Learning and thinking and working scientifically focus	Downloadable lesson resources
2	10.3 The Earth's atmosphere	10.3a Starting point		
		10.3b Earth's atmosphere	• Describe the percentages of the different gases in the Earth's atmosphere • Present data using a pie chart • Explain why accuracy and precision are important in measuring quantities of gases	Worksheet 10.3b (1) Worksheet 10.3b (2)
		10.3c Changes in the atmosphere over time	• Describe how the mixture of gases in the Earth's atmosphere can change because of natural processes and human activities • Describe how scientific investigations of the ozone layer in the Earth's atmosphere led to a worldwide ban on certain chemicals used in refrigerators • Describe how the hypothesis that certain chemicals (CFCs) damage the ozone layer has been supported by evidence	Worksheet 10.3c
2	10.4 The water cycle	10.4a Starting point		Worksheet 10.4a
		10.4b Evaporation, condensation and precipitation	• Describe the physical processes of evaporation, condensation and precipitation • Make conclusions by interpreting results	
		10.4c Water that falls on the surface of Earth	• Describe water run-off, open water and groundwater • Explain how evaporation, condensation, precipitation, water run-off, open water and groundwater together form the water cycle • Describe the strengths and limitations of the model used to demonstrate evaporation, condensation and precipitation • Choose equipment needed to carry out an investigation and use it appropriately • Carry out practical work safely	Worksheet 10.4c Practical Notes 10.4c
1	End of chapter questions			
4	11.1 The planets and the Solar System	11.1a Starting point		
		11.1b Our Solar System	• Describe how planets are held in orbits around the Sun by the force of gravity • Describe patterns in data about the planets • Describe patterns in data about the planets and identify anomalous results	Worksheet 11.1b Practical notes 11.1b
		11.1c Discovering planets	• Describe how understanding gravity allowed scientists to predict where new planets could be found • Describe how predictions of new planets were tested against evidence	Worksheet 11.1c
		11.1d The formation of planets	• Understand how planets form • Describe how scientific ideas can be supported or contradicted by evidence	Worksheet 11.1d

Number of 40-minute periods	Student's Book topic number	Learning episode	Learning and thinking and working scientifically focus	Downloadable lesson resources
2	11.2 Tides	11.2a Starting point		
		11.2b Water in the Earth's oceans	• Describe high and low tides • Present and interpret observations and measurements appropriately	
		11.2c The effects of the Moon	• Explain how the forces of gravity due to the Moon cause the oceans to bulge out • Describe how the effects of the forces of gravity and the spinning of the Earth cause high and low tides • Present measurements on a line graph • Make a conclusion by interpreting results	
		11.2d The effects of the Sun	• Explain how the forces of gravity due to the Moon and the Sun combined cause spring tides and neap tides • Describe the strengths and limitations of a model	Worksheet 11.2d
3	11.3 Eclipses	11.3a Starting point		
		11.3b Solar eclipses	• Describe how a solar eclipse occurs • Choose equipment needed to carry out an investigation and use it appropriately • Carry out practical work safely	Practical notes 11.3b Worksheet 11.3b
		11.3c Lunar eclipses	• Describe how a lunar eclipse occurs • Describe the strengths and limitations of a model	Practical notes 11.3c Worksheet 11.3c
1	End of chapter questions			

Below are some examples of lessons in *Collins Cambridge Lower Secondary Science Stage 7* which could be used to develop the Global Perspectives skills. The notes in *italics* suggest how the Science activity can be made more relevant to Global Perspectives.

Please note that the examples below link specifically to the learning objectives in the Global Perspectives curriculum framework for Stage 7. However, skills development in a wider sense is embedded throughout this course and teachers are encouraged to promote research, analysis, evaluation, reflection, collaboration and communication as general best practice. For example, there are numerous investigations and experiments in which learners work in groups which give the opportunity for them to collaborate positively and engage in teamwork.

Cambridge Global Perspectives	Learning Objectives for Stage 7	Collins Cambridge Lower Secondary Science Stage 7
RESEARCH	Information skills • Identify and begin to reference a range of print and multimedia sources and use them to locate relevant information and answer research questions	*There are a number of activities which give students experience of scientific research. In each case, support and guide learners to find a range of suitable sources. Some examples are:* • Chapter 2.2, Activity 2.3: SB p39, TG p49 • Chapter 3.1, Activity 3.1: SB pp54–55, TG p57 • Chapter 3.1: Worksheet 3.1f Species, TG p58 • Chapter 10.3c Changes in the Earth's atmosphere over time: Worksheet 10.3c
	Conducting research • Select an appropriate method and conduct research to test predictions and begin to answer a research question	• Chapter 5.3, Activity 5.3: SB pp119–120, Worksheet 5.3a, TG p104 *Introduce the investigation and then elicit an appropriate research question to focus the research. Students should include this in their plan before they conduct the investigation.* • Chapter 6.2, Activity 6.3: SB pp135–136, Worksheet 6.2c, TG p116–117 *After students have planned and conducted their experiments, discuss answers to the initial research question and whether their predictions were right or wrong.*
	Recording findings • Select, organise and record relevant information from a range of sources and findings from research, using appropriate methods	• Chapter 2.2, Activity 2.4: SB pp44–45 *Elicit which type of graph or chart students used to record their findings, and which they consider to have been the most successful (Results A3).*
ANALYSIS	Interpreting data • Explain how graphical or numerical data supports an argument	• Chapter 11.2c, Activity 11.2: SB pp227–228, TG p180 *Elicit and ask students to justify their conclusions using the data recorded in their graphs.*

Cambridge Global Perspectives	Learning Objectives for Stage 7	Collins Cambridge Lower Secondary Science Stage 7
EVALUATION	Evaluating sources • Evaluate sources, considering the author and purpose, recognising that some sources may be biased	• Chapter 2.1, Activity 2.1: SB pp32–33, TG p43 *Supply a range of sources (print and multimedia) of varying relevance and reliability. Monitor students as they work and, at the end, elicit and discuss the sources that students rejected (A3).* • Chapter 2.2, Activity 2.3: SB p39, TG p49 *When students have finished, elicit and discuss the sources they rejected (A3).* • Chapter 10.3c: Worksheet 10.3c *When students have finished, elicit what they have recorded in the Sources section of the worksheet and discuss.*
REFLECTION	Personal learning • Identify skills learned or improved during an activity and relate to personal strengths and areas for improvement	*The Self-assessment sections at the end of each Chapter encourage reflection. Focus on the skills section of the tables (You should be able to:) and encourage discussion of what skills learners still want to improve.* • WB pp18, 29, 39, 67, 82, 94, 104, 116, 129, 149, 166
COMMUNICATION	Communicating information • Present information and arguments clearly with some reasoning, referencing sources where appropriate	• Chapter 3.1: Worksheet 3.1f, TG p58 *Students should use the organisation of the Worksheet to give the structure for their presentation. As they prepare their presentations, discuss with groups to ensure they cover the key points and reference their sources.*